Lawlessness

Lawlessness

A BOOK OF REMEMBRANCE

William G Lord

Scripture quotations are from The Holy Bible, English Standard Version®
(ESV®), copyright © 2001 by Crossway, a publishing ministry of Good
News Publishers. Used by permission. All rights reserved.

ISBN: 1516945980
ISBN 13: 9781516945986

Endorsement

David L. Allen, Ph.D.
Dean School of Theology
Southwestern Baptist Theological Seminary
Fort Worth, Texas

Lawlessness is something of a unique book. I've never seen anything that traces the biblical history of what the Scripture says about lawlessness as humanity's rebellion against God. In addition, this book's historical and philosophical orientation tracks the subject very well. Lord demonstrates that God's answer to man's lawlessness is the cross of Christ. This work will be an interesting read for just about anyone.

Abstract

§

I FIND MOST PEOPLE VIEW the world at its surface. In order to understand what I mean, think of riding on a boat over a calm sea. What do you see? You may see a beautiful surface reflection with water ripples reflecting the sun's light like diamonds. The sun is so bright that it fills one's very soul with light. The scent of the sea breeze fills the intellect with surreal visions of universal harmony with nature. It is an invigorating experience, and I have found the worldview of most who call themselves Christian to reflect the seaward view.

The contemporary Christian surface view is defined in books on the Christian bookshelf. The books normally consist of devotional, self-help books for Christians. They answer the question: "How do I get the most out of life on earth?" They are books for the surface dweller. They are books for life in the shallows.

Lawlessness is different. It presents an organized approach to Judeo-Christian doctrine and the historical salvation story of the Bible. Doctrine of God is identified through the biblical historical events which created the need for salvation of mankind. The frame of salvation is restored and displayed as the reestablished ethical relationship with God. The journey is complete with exposure to the opposition to God's ethic. The comparison brings about awareness of a choice to follow God's ethic or mankind's developed ethic. *Lawlessness* provides clarity for mankind's choice between the ethic of God and the ethic of mankind.

Come with me into the deep and I will show you what is beneath the water's surface.

Introduction

§

THIS WORK IS THE PRODUCT of a simple prayer for understanding. In 1972 I sat on a pew at the back of a chapel on Parris Island, South Carolina. It was the first week we were allowed to attend chapel as Marine recruits. Actually, I went to escape the rigors of the barracks for a while. While I sat on the back pew, my mood became solemn. I missed my parents and family. I was homesick for what I had left. I was confused as to why I was homesick because the reason I joined the service was to leave behind the pain of isolation caused by poverty. I am a product of the impoverished southern United States.

There was nothing at home for me. I had tried working in several places, but it just did not ever seem to work out. I had gotten involved with my local church and thought God was calling me to the ministry. However, that did not work out for me either.

It appeared as though I was doomed to live in poverty forever. I did not have an understanding of the outside world. I wanted to enjoy my life, and I did not want to live in poverty. I especially did not want to raise children in the impoverished conditions that I had experienced. I wanted more for my future family than to live in a used mobile home on swamp land no one else would have.

I prayed for those things that I had reasoned were important to my future. I prayed that neither my future family nor I would ever again know poverty. I prayed for an understanding of what my life was to be. I knew nothing of the world, and I did not want to live in isolation any longer.

The Marine Corps was a culture shock for me, and I struggled with the harshness of it. I prayed God would see me through my commitment to the Corps. I ended this simple prayer with: "If You grant me this, when You call, I will come."

I completed boot camp in March of 1972. I was sent to Millington, Tennessee, for aircraft maintenance training. Following Millington, I was sent to New River Marine Air Base in Jacksonville, North Carolina, for my first assignment. I was not a particularly good Marine. For example, I spent thirty days restricted to base because I went home to see my girlfriend and future wife without a weekend pass. The Marines did not have a sense of humor about such things. They thought I should ask permission to leave. Okay, I chose to disobey, and I suffered the consequences. Lesson learned.

My girlfriend Peggy was my high school sweetheart. I married Peggy in 1973, and she came to live with me in Jacksonville, NC. I became we, and in 1974 we made a decision to re-enlist for four more years.

The Marine Corps was good for me. I learned honor, integrity and discipline. Those things of which poverty robs people, the Marines demanded from its members. Honor in commitment. Commitment to your brothers. Commitment to country. Commitment to truth. Integrity founded in responsible behavior and completed in trust of others. To be disciplined in commitment to one's responsibilities to others even at the cost of life itself. These Corps values became my own, and I applied the values to every aspect of my life. I found purpose in being counted and counted on.

In 1975, three years and eleven months after my initial enlistment, I was meritoriously promoted to staff sergeant and assigned to Okinawa, Japan. After a month of separation, my wife joined me in Okinawa. Peggy is Japanese-American, and the time in Okinawa, Japan, was a very special time for us. We lived in the village of Futenma at the bottom of the hill where the airbase was situated.

We rotated back to the States, and in 1978 my enlistment expired. This ended the first chapter of God's provisional answer to my prayer in the chapel on Parris Island. God had provided more than I had asked for.

In 1980 I took a job with American Airlines Training Corporation. By 1981, I was in Amman, Jordan, teaching aircraft maintenance to the Jordanian and Iraqi Royal Air Force maintenance technicians. Sikorsky Aircraft Company sold thirteen S-76 helicopters to Jordan, and Jordon's king gave several of the helicopters to Saddam Hussein of Iraq. Training was a part of the sale.

While there, I was exposed to Middle Eastern society. I learned to accept the culture as it was, and I learned to love my neighbor for his heart, not his culture or appearance. During my tenure at American Airlines Training Corporation, I also traveled to Brazil and taught aircraft maintenance to Brazilian government employees. I stayed in a hotel overlooking Copa Cabana Beach. What a culture shock! My senses were on overload. The visit to the seventh century theocratic world of the Middle East was a stark contrast to Brazil. It was another lesson learned. By the time I left American Airlines, I had lived and worked with Jordanians, Iraqis, Australians, Brazilians, Canadians, Chinese, Mexicans, Americans, and students from the UK.

After a while, however, I became restless and took a job with Sikorsky Aircraft as an inspector. I worked on the assembly line for the S-76 helicopter and later transferred to "Skunk Works" (experimental aircraft) in the Everglades outside West Palm Beach, Florida. Sikorsky was my first exposure to the union world. Florida is a right-to-work state, and I was not required to join the Teamsters Union at Sikorsky—so I didn't. However, I quickly learned that law has nothing to do with social coercion on the job with respect to unions. While the law may protect one in a court of law, the union convicts in social discourse. Isolation and harassment is the punishment for opting out of the union. It is more powerful than any state law. The lesson was learned and never forgotten.

I was laid off by Sikorsky and took a position as Director of Maintenance for National Helicopters in Dallas, Texas. A year later, I began a career in the airline industry. It was the 1980s, and airline jobs came and went due to deregulation of the industry. I worked for Continental, Airborne Express, local fixed-based operations, UPS, and the Duval County

Sheriff's aviation unit. During the course of those assignments, I worked as supervisor and employee, union and non-union. I have been a member of Teamsters and the American Federation of State and Municipal Employees union (AFSME). My longest tenure at a job was with UPS.

UPS treated me well, and I have a great admiration for the people with whom I worked. In the beginning, I was in the union. The previous assignments involving unions taught me to wear the union hat, and I did. When promoted to supervisor, I changed hats. It is here I learned friendships leave with the change of hats. Some will tell you it is not the case. However, all one has to do is watch the unions on the news, and hostility between union and employer/management is apparent.

During my tenure as a major maintenance representative for UPS, I worked in Hong Kong, Singapore, and Israel. The most coveted for me was the trip to Israel. The company leased a passenger aircraft (747-200), and Israeli Aircraft Industries won the contract from UPS to modify the passenger aircraft into a freighter. I got the call just a few days before I was needed in Israel. I was to relieve another maintenance representative who had personal issues to attend in the United States.

The Israel trip proved to be God's working to bring the Parris Island prayer to its conclusion. God had answered every request I had made in the pew at Parris Island. I had been very successful in my Marine years. God had blessed me beyond what I had earned. The meritorious promotion was not my doing; I was not a particularly good Marine. I have not only seen the world, but have lived and worked in it as part of its cultural diversity. My family has never experienced the pain of poverty. I am a pilot and have owned and operated several aircraft. I have lived in gated communities, and in my adulthood I have owned new rather than used goods.

God answered the entire list for which I prayed, and the time came to lay it down and go to God. I retired at age fifty-five from what I loved in order to fulfill the obligation I had made to God as a young man: "If You will do this, I will come when You call." This work is an answer to prayer.

My undergraduate degree is in occupational education, and I knew I would need an education in theology to complete God's task. After acquiring a Master of Divinity from Southwestern Baptist Theological Seminary, I served as a pastor for three years in northern New Mexico. God had other plans, and I have re-entered the aviation industry.

My experience with contemporary orthodox Christian existence is that it often misses the point. For example, while many Sunday sermons and Christian culture seek to use the Bible to fit into culture on earth, the true biblical theme speaks of setting one's self apart from the earthly culture. Christ is the example. Christ sacrificed himself so others could live. Mankind is different. Mankind, even those who call themselves followers of Christ, calls for the sacrifice of others so they may live. Well, that is not a revelation since it was people of God who demanded the Romans crucify Christ to save their religion. It is a stark reminder that the religion of the Pharisees and Sadducees was foreign to God.

I find myself asking questions about Christianity. When did Christianity become militarized? Why is the world's culture offended by Christians and the ethic of God? Why do Christians call the culture lawless, even though the ethic and laws of society support the law of the culture outside Christianity? Weren't Christian ethics here before contemporary culture? Should the culture be called lawless for rebelling against the laws of God? If Christians are correct in labeling the culture "lawless" for disobeying God's biblical law, should the cultural movement be called a rebellion against God's given ethic?

I was frustrated and needed to answer the questions for myself and others who ask. So I study and write in hopes God will use my work to inform and comfort the true follower of Christ. I am driven to expose the salvation story of the Bible from its roots to its end, to expose the tumultuous cyclic stories in the Bible which chronicle mankind's estranged relationship with God, and to expose the rebellion against God.

Table of Contents

List of Tables

SECTION I

In the Beginning

WHAT IS PHILOSOPHY? PHILOSOPHY IS the love of wisdom. The Bible encourages Christians to love wisdom and reveals God's love of wisdom in the books of the Bible called the "Wisdom Books" (Job, Psalms, Proverbs, Ecclesiastes, and Song of Songs). God loves wisdom and is Himself Divine Wisdom. Other cultures also have an appreciation of wisdom. For example in the Grecian culture, Plato, Aristotle, Epicurus and Democritus are among many Grecian men who loved wisdom and therefore philosophy.

Philosophy, being the love of wisdom, seeks to state wisdom. Philosophical documents such as the "Wisdom Books" in the Bible and *Plato's Republic* seek to state a way of life which is based in wisdom (moral philosophy). Moral philosophy may also be called *ethics*. Ethics is the discipline which promotes, defends, and recommends what is right and what is wrong for a particular group, society, or country to follow. God's people follow the ethic of God, and it is different from the ethic of mankind.

In the late first century and early second century, Quintus Septimius Florens Tertullianus (Tertullian), an early church father (approximately 160-225 AD), is credited with the quote: "What has Athens to do with Jerusalem?" Tertullian made this comment in a defense of Christian ethics. Tertullian's defense of Christianity was necessary because Greek mythology and philosophy were being injected into the Christian philosophic foundation (God's ethic). Tertullian realized Grecian philosophical approach to life was a threat to the philosophy and revelation of Christ and the mission of Christians to evangelize the world.

It was not the first time God's ethic had been challenged. In fact, the Bible is a history of God's ethic among mankind. As the stories go in the Bible, God introduces and reintroduces His ethic into communities of mankind. Mankind embraces God's ethic for a while until they begin to follow an experience-driven ethic (lawlessness) of mankind. The cyclic nature of God's ethic among mankind is the Bible story.

Lawlessness is the source of the grievance God has with mankind. Over time, mankind has meandered between lawlessness and the true ethic of God. The meandering path of mankind has left historical tracks.

The tracks reveal a historically cyclic and turbulent relationship between God and mankind.

The tracks are like tracks in the snow. One may follow the tracks to current events. The Bible is only one source of tracks in the snow. It chronicles the cycles from God's perspective. The end of the Bible is also the end of the cycles.

Mankind has also left tracks of lawlessness which may be followed. The tracks left by lawless mankind lead to the same end of cycles. Lawless perspective may be found in historical lawless books.

At the track's end is knowledge and understanding of the estranged relationship between mankind and God. Follow the tracks here to Christ and heaven.

CHAPTER 1

Adam and Eve

IN THE BEGINNING OF THE biblical story, God created the heavens and the earth (Genesis 1:1-3). It could have been an explosion of lifeless minerals, moisture and rocks forming globes drawn together by gravity and warmed by a distant star. The earth, like the other rocks in this created solar system in the vacuum of space, was a lifeless planet. However, God had a special plan for this particular rock called earth, and God's Spirit was projected in a supernatural act over the earth: the *Spirit of God was hovering over the face of the waters (Genesis 1:2)*.

The earth in its barren state was like a gardener's field in the spring. It was ready to explode with life. In the biblical account of the creation of life, God's supernatural abilities are projected through His Word, and when God spoke things happened.

He said, "Let the earth bring forth living creatures according to their kinds (Genesis 1:24)."

God, His Spirit, and His Word took a particular interest in forming a dominant presence in their newly formed aquarium called earth. They sought to create a living creature to imitate and represent God on earth.

God said, "Let us make man in our image, after our likeness. And let them have dominion over the fish of the sea and over the birds of the heavens and over the livestock and over the earth and over everything that creeps on the earth . . . male and female he created them (Genesis 1:26, 27)."

God named His masterpiece Adam and Eve and placed them in a special place He set aside for them called the Garden of Eden. In this place they would be comfortable, and God could provide for all their needs.

The Bible indicates the Garden of Eden was at a place where the Tigris and Euphrates Rivers converge in the country now known as Iraq.

Adam and Eve did have certain rules they had to follow. God wanted the couple to worship Him, and in an effort to bring consciousness of the Creator into the fresh minds of this new creation of mankind, God gave the first "way of life" (ethic) to Adam and Eve.

And the Lord God commanded the man, "You are free to eat from any tree in the garden; but you must not eat from the tree of the knowledge of good and evil, for when you eat from it you will certainly die (Genesis 2:16-17)."

God's nature would not allow Him to design an intelligent being which was required to serve and worship God compulsively. God desired that Adam and Eve would choose Him over all things, including themselves. In addition, God's desire to create and care for His creation displayed a neighborly core in God's ethic structure. God's ethic for Adam and Eve may be stated as:

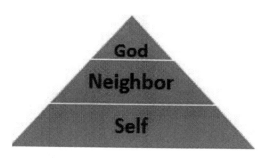

The rules set up a test for the couple. Would they choose to obey God's rule and enjoy the benefits of the Garden of Eden? Or would they choose disobedience and a life apart from God?

The Garden of Eden was not only a place where all things would be provided for God's prize creation, but it would serve to keep the couple from being harmed by God's other creations. There were, of course, the animals. However, God had created other intelligent beings which had rebelled against Him.

A few of these beings wished to frustrate God's planned relationship with Adam and Eve. A spoiler named Satan was allowed in the Garden of Eden with Adam and Eve. Obviously, God planned an evaluation of His creation, and it was not long before the evaluation began.

One day Satan appeared in the garden with Adam and Eve. He could not have been a stranger since there is no sign from Adam or Eve that they did not know him. As the story goes, Satan convinced Adam and Eve to disobey God and eat the forbidden fruit. Adam and Eve failed the evaluation.

Adam and Eve had known "good", which was an eternal relationship with God. As a result of their failure to live as God had instructed, they would now know "evil", an existence apart from God and eventually death.

God became angry and pronounced judgment on the couple:

"I will surely multiply your pain in childbearing; in pain you shall bring forth children. Your desire shall be for your husband, and he shall rule over you (Genesis 3:16)."

"Because you have listened to the voice of your wife and have eaten of the tree of which I commanded you, 'You shall not eat of it, 'cursed is the ground because of you; in pain you shall eat of it all the days of your life; thorns and thistles it shall bring forth for you; and you shall eat the plants of the field. By the sweat of your face you shall eat bread, till you return to the ground, for out of it you were taken; for you are dust, and to dust you shall return (Genesis 3:17-19)."

"Then the Lord God said, "Behold, the man has become like one of us in knowing good and evil. Now, lest he reach out his hand and take also of the tree of life and eat, and live forever—" therefore the Lord God sent him out from the garden of Eden to work the ground from which he was taken. He drove out the man, and at the east of the Garden of Eden he placed the cherubim and a flaming sword that turned every way to guard the way to the tree of life (Genesis 3:22-24)."

God banished His beloved creation from the special place He had built for them. He also took immortality from them and direct access to Him. Without access to God, mankind was lost and would suffer the consequences of disobeying God.

After Adam and Eve left the Garden of Eden, they multiplied on the earth. Numbers of mankind increased, and a social structure set in. Knowledge of God's ethic (way of life) faded into the past.

Mankind's social structure began to depend on what a particular group developed as habit. Habitual actions carried out by each particular individual or group would have required the children born to a particular individual or group to imitate the habits of others in the group. Group habits develop into a way of life (ethic) for the group.

A new ethic was developed apart from God. The new way of life (*ethic of mankind*) was a representation of the knowledge gained from the experiences of mankind. It would have been a social structure which developed solely among mankind.

God was not pleased with mankind's new ethic. God understood that an ethic built on the experience of knowledge developed by mankind was incurable and that mankind who followed such an ethic was lost to Him. God found the situation unbearable and made plans to destroy the society of experience (mankind's ethic) by destroying all mankind who followed it. He would reintroduce the ethic of God to those who would still follow His ethic.

Noah

§

GOD LOVED HIS CREATION OF mankind, and He wanted to save it. He longed to reestablish an ethical relationship with those men of whom He approved. God first sought to save mankind through a man named Noah (Genesis 10).

In this epic story, God recognized that all mankind except Noah and his family was hopelessly lost to the new society of experience ethic and not redeemable. God approached Noah and informed him of God's plans to destroy all men who had embraced an ethic offensive to God.

God's plan was to cover the earth with water and drown all men who followed ethics offensive to God's purposes. He instructed Noah to build a large ark which could survive the coming floods. The ark was to be large enough to carry wildlife. The floods came, and except for Noah and his family, all of mankind drowned in the floods.

The moral of the story is: those who did not follow God's way of life (ethic) were destroyed, and those who accepted God's ethic lived to enjoy God's blessings. A new start for the ethical relationship between God and His creation was realized. However, the beginning of the renewed ethical relationship with God is the beginning of a new *cycle* of disobedience and subsequent salvation. After God's salvation, mankind drifted back into an ethic developed apart from God (*mankind's ethic*) which requires God to step in again to save mankind. The cyclic nature of the stories in the Bible reveals the plot of the Bible:

> *Salvation of mankind is the renewal of mankind's ethical relationship with God.*

There are those who would challenge the historical value of Noah's story. However, whether the story is allegoric in nature or historically true is not at issue here. The story depicts the beginning of the cyclic nature of the Hebrew God's attempts to reestablish an acceptable ethical relationship with the creature defined in the beginning of the Hebrew Bible as "man". The relationship hinges on mankind's ability or inability to live by God's ethic.

The ethical cycles may be seen as key to the history of Judaism and key to the development of Jewish culture. The cyclic nature of God's ethical relationship with His creation of mankind eventually spawned Christianity, and the ethical cycles are the key to the development of communities which currently follow, have been evangelized, or at some past point have followed the Hebrew God depicted in the Bible.

Cycles in Western Culture*

Adam and Eve
Noah
Judaism
Judges/Davidic Kingdom
Intertestamental Period

Christ's Birth
Early Church
Roman Nationalism
Reformation of Christ's initiative
Rebellion of Lawless
The Final Cycle-The END of the Bible's story

Since the audience for this text is from the western culture, the cycles that are depicted in this text refer to God's initiative as it grew westward from Jerusalem.

There are more cycles depicted in the Bible and in the history of Christianity. The cycles written about here are representative of the totality of the cyclic nature of the ethic of God among mankind.

The rules for identifying cycle characterizations in this text are:

* The ethical cycles are the story of salvation as chronicled by the Bible.
* The story of lawlessness is the story of mankind's rejection of God's ethic (way of life) for man's replacement ethic (experience of society).
* A particular rejection of God's commandments may be viewed as a sin. Particular sins may be viewed as a mistaken act by the follower of God and redeemable by God.
* Practicing sin as a way of life in opposition to God's ethic (commandments) is called lawlessness, and those doing so are marked for destruction according to the Bible.
* In these ethical cyclic stories, God's intervention and initiatives are intended to revive and thus save the original ethical relationship He had with mankind chronicled in the Genesis story about Adam and Eve.

* Mankind resists God's controlling ethic and attempts to live by events and habits learned apart from God (experience of society). Mankind struggles to free himself of the obligatory God of the Garden of Eden.
* The priority in God's ethic is:

The ethical cycles may be followed through history in the writings of the Hebrew and Christian people. Opposition to God's ethic may also be followed through the cultural writings of those cultures which have opposed God's ethics (commandments) and wish to replace them with different ethics (experience of society) of mankind.

Those with a desire to follow the ethical cycles of disobedience (lawlessness — following an ethic other than God's ethic) and renewal, which have gripped the very soul of mankind for thousands of years, to their final end may not only find the end of those cycles and of the biblical story itself, but in doing so rekindle the ethical relationship that promises eternal life with God. Since Judaism is the Hebrew God's religion, from which Christianity is derived, and represents the ethical relationship God began with the nation of Israel, Judaism should be the first cycle explored.

Judaism: God's National Initiative

WHEN THE ORIGINAL SINNERS, ADAM and Eve, were cast out of the Garden of Eden for their sin, Adam and Eve and their offspring (mankind) learned a new ethic through experience apart from God.

The science of sociology uses the term "sociology of knowledge" to define the experienced-based ethics of mankind. The sociological ethic requires one to view mankind's ethic as one which is learned through one's daily experience. If a written ethic comes from the daily experience, the written guide simply states mankind's experience as authority.[i] In this philosophy, God is not a part of mankind's ethical development through sociology of knowledge. Karl Marx, one the founders of Communism in Europe, was the first to espouse daily experience as forming ethical models for mankind.[ii] It is important to understand Karl Marx discovered a human trait which already existed. He did not invent it. Something must already exist in order to be discovered.

After the Garden of Eden events, ethics learned through mankind's experience multiplied the sin of the original couple. Mankind became sinners. Consequently, if God was going to have an ethical relationship with mankind, mankind must now learn to live God's ethic instead of mankind's developed ethic.

The plan of salvation in the Bible revolves around restoring God's original ethical relationship with mankind. In the biblical account of mankind's ethical history, obeying God's given ethic or rejecting God's given ethic is the primary concern. Disobedience of God's ethic is called "lawlessness".

For this study the definition of lawlessness is taken from 1 John 3: 4:

Everyone who makes a practice of sinning also practices lawlessness; sin is lawlessness.

Specifically, John is referring to the law given to the Israelites by God during the formation of the nation of Israel and delivered by Moses. The willing departure of a particular law in the ethic of God is called a "sin". To practice sin as a way of life (ethic) is called "lawlessness".

SIN:

If a man/woman who lived according to God's ethic (commandment) gave in to temptation and stole an item from someone, that man/woman's act would be considered a sin.

LAWLESSNESS:

A man/woman who practices stealing as an ethic (way of life) is said to be lawless. Further, one who practices any ethic other than God's ethic practices lawlessness.

Since Judaism and Christ are at the center of God's plan to save His creation, the journey will concentrate on lawlessness among Jews and Christians alike.

Before continuing the journey into different Jewish cycles, a discussion on Judaism is in order. It is not practical to list all the individual rules and teachings regarding Judaism. However, the following are rules, passed down in the Torah (first five books of the Bible), which serve to differentiate Judaism from other religions in the world.

Rule one: There is only one God, and He is the Hebrew God.

The first book in the Bible called Genesis reveals that God created the heavens and the earth. The book further chronicles God's creative abilities in creating what is on earth and what lives on earth. In Exodus 19:5b, God tells the Jewish nation: *"for all the earth is mine."*

Rule two: God created the Jewish nation in order to have an influence on mankind, who had become lost to God when He expelled the first man and woman from the Garden of Eden for their sins (lawlessness).

The lawlessness of Adam and Eve in the Garden of Eden cost God His most precious creation, mankind. God was looking to reclaim His creation, but He was bound by His judgment of Adam and Eve. So God approached Abraham, a man without children, to be the beginning of His plan to reclaim mankind's obedience, which had been lost in the Garden of Eden, and therefore mankind was lost. God promised Abraham, a man without children, more descendants than he could count if He would follow and obey Him:

"Look toward heaven, and number the stars, if you are able to number them." Then he said to him, "So shall your offspring be (Genesis 15:5)."

Rule three: Abraham's second child Isaac is the patriarch of the Jewish nation.

Abraham first had a child with his wife's servant Hagar, and his name was Ishmael. However, Ishmael was not what God had intended for Abraham (Genesis 16). God had intended that Sarah, Abraham's wife, give birth to the promised offspring of Abraham.

Isaac was the son born to Sarah and is the patriarch who began the nation of Israel through his son Jacob. Isaac's son Jacob was given the name Israel by God:

And God said to him, "Your name is Jacob; no longer shall your name be called Jacob, but Israel shall be your name (Genesis 35:10)."

Israel had twelve sons: Rueben, Simeon, Levi, Judah, Issachar, Zebulun, Joseph, Benjamin, Dan, Naphtali, Gad, and Asher. From the sons of Israel sprang what we now call the nation of Israel.

Rule four: God delivered the nation of Israel from the bonds of Egyptian slavery in order that He might have a nation of people who would serve Him and through that nation reclaim mankind.

The delivery and subsequent departure of Israel from slavery is called the Exodus and is chronicled in the second book of the Old Testament, also called Exodus.

Through the trials and tribulation suffered in the wilderness area of the Sinai Desert, God brought the nation of Israel, under leadership of His prophet Moses, into Palestine, which to the current age remains their homeland.

The story chronicled in Exodus is sacred to the Jewish people. It tells the story of a people whose God intervened on their behalf by raining down ten plagues on the Egyptian ruler Ramses so as to convince Ramses of His power and thus force Ramses to release His people from slavery. The tenth plague is when God passed over the firstborn of all Israelite children while taking the firstborn of the Egyptians' children, including the child of Ramses. The event is celebrated even today among Jews:

This day shall be for you a memorial day and you shall keep it as a feast to the Lord (Exodus 12:14).

Over fifteen hundred years later, the Passover celebration was the meal Jesus and His disciples enjoyed before His crucifixion (Luke 22:14-22). Christians reference it as the Last Supper.

And when the hour came, he reclined at the table, and his apostles with him. And he said, "I have earnestly desired to eat this Passover with you before I suffer (Luke 22:14-15)."

Rule five: God established His ethic (way of life for the Israelites) for His people through the Ten Commandments and Levitical Law (Exodus and Leviticus).

On Mount Sinai, God gave Moses the Ten Commandments and the system of law laid out in the Old Testament books called the Torah (Genesis-Deuteronomy).

Ten Commandments:

1. You shall have no other gods before Me.
2. You shall not make for yourself a carved image, or any likeness of anything that is in heaven above, or that is in the earth beneath, or that is in the water under the earth.
3. You shall not take the Lord's name in vain.
4. Remember the Sabbath day to keep it holy.
5. Honor your mother and father.
6. You shall not murder.
7. You shall not commit adultery.
8. You shall not steal.
9. You shall not bear false witness against your neighbor.
10. You shall not covet your neighbor's house; you shall not covet your neighbor's wife, or his male servant, his female servant, or his ox, or his donkey, or anything that is your neighbor's.

The Old Testament books of Exodus and Leviticus contain laws which also state prohibitions against homosexuality, incest, eating blood, and child sacrifice. Jews are instructed to keep God's statutes and love one's neighbor through honest relationships. Jews are prohibited from oppressing neighbors or robbing them (Leviticus 19). The handicapped are to be treated with respect. Jews are further instructed: *"not be partial to the poor or defer to the great, but in righteousness shall you judge your neighbor . . . you shall love your neighbor as yourself."*

Rule six: God lived during the Exodus years among the Israelites and required recognition for the blessings and life given to the Israelites through the sacrificial observance of Him.

A tabernacle (temple) was built for God by the Israelites. The famous Ark of the Covenant was built at this time to reside in the tabernacle. The area where the Ark was placed in the tabernacle was cordoned off with curtains (veil). This special place inside the tabernacle is called the "Holy of Holies" and was the place where God received sacrifices from the Jewish priests. When the tabernacle was completed, God came to the Israelites.

Then the cloud covered the tent of meeting and the glory of the Lord filled the tabernacle (Exodus 40:34).

Rule seven: The Israelites must obey all the Ten Commandments and all the law in order to live with God.

This sets the stage for salvation. In the Old Testament book of Ezekiel, God reveals His position:

And I said to their children in the wilderness, "Do not walk in the statutes of your fathers, nor keep their rules, nor defile yourselves with their idols. I am the LORD your God; walk in my statutes, and be careful to obey my rules (Ezekiel 20:18, 19)."

All the Israelites had to do is obey God's law (ethic). In reality, all Adam and Eve had to do was obey God. The disobedience of God's statutes by mankind chronicled in the book called the Bible is God's grievance with His creation, mankind. Judaism was simply obedience of the laws (statutes) of God with a reward of living an eternity with God in heaven. Disobedience of the laws of God is *lawlessness* and punishable by death.

The world outside of the newly-formed Judaism (ethic of God) did not practice Judaism. Lawlessness competed with God's ethic through the existence of other gods and the ethics of mankind. The Old and New Testaments refer to the evils of following other gods and other ethics. In addition, the most important rule in God's commandments is that He is to come before all other gods or images and before your neighbor and before one's self.

Priority of the ethic of God:

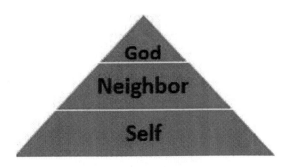

Even though the people of Israel had witnessed God's hand working miracles to free them, feed them and house them, they could not with consistency live out the ethic (way of life) God gave to them. The Israelites fell back again and again into lawlessness (sin, or following a different ethic). The cyclic stories in the book of Judges reveal the ethical predicament of the Jewish people.

The Jews failed to carry out God's instruction to rid the land of the lawless cultures and peoples which existed at the time in Palestine and thus rid the land of lawlessness. It was just too hard a task for them. God was not pleased with the Jews' lack of obedience. God explained His position to the Jewish people:

> *I said, "I will never break my covenant with you, and you shall make no covenant with the inhabitants of this land; you shall break down their altars." But you have not obeyed my voice. What is this you have done? So now I say, "I will not drive them out before you, but they will become thorns in your sides, and their gods shall be a snare for you (Judges 2: 1-3)."*

The Jews clearly identified with the predicament and lawlessness of mankind more than they identified with God or His way of life.

Period of Judges

§

IDENTIFYING WITH THE PLIGHT OF the surrounding cultures cost the Jews enormously. It was not long before the surrounding cultures imposed their will on the Jewish people, and lawlessness set in among the Jews. God challenged the lawlessness with judges He personally selected. The cycles of lawlessness are the major theme of the books of Judges, Samuel, and Kings.

Gideon was one of these judges (Judges 6-8). God recruited him to lead the Jews from the oppression of the surrounding cultures and lawlessness. When God first approached Gideon, he was hiding in a wine vat thrashing his wheat. The reason Gideon was hiding was that lawless people, who had come to dominate the Jews and their culture, would have taken his wheat and redistributed it among themselves.

Gideon eventually took up God's call to serve and was instrumental in leading the lawless Jews back into the way of life (ethic) of God which is called Judaism. The journey back to Judaism did not last long, and another judge was required to save the Jews from the oppressive lawlessness of the surrounding cultures. The Jewish people vacillated between Judaism and lawlessness repeatedly, which set the stage for the kings of Israel.

CHAPTER 2
Period of Kings

§

THE JEWISH KINGS ARE MEMORIALIZED in the Old Testament in the books of 1 & 2 Samuel, 1 & 2 Kings, and 1 & 2 Chronicles. These history books reveal the same cyclic philosophic and physical journeys to and from the lawlessness of the surrounding lawless cultures of mankind.

The peak of the era of kings was during the reign of King David, which is why the Jewish Kingdom is called the Davidic Kingdom.

King David was not a saint by any stretch of the imagination. He broke many of the Ten Commandments. He coveted his neighbor's wife, committing adultery with her and sending her husband to his death (2 Samuel 11). He unlawfully ate bread from the temple.

David broke several of the Ten Commandments regarding his neighbor. However he kept the commandments to love and cherish his God. For his love of God, he is immortalized. But his lawlessness against his neighbor led to the downfall of the Davidic Kingdom, beginning with his son Solomon, who was the product of the lawlessness committed by David.

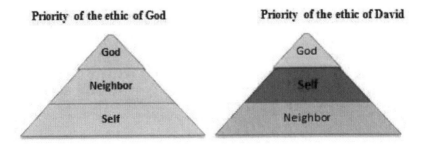

Solomon allowed and even invited lawless cultures and their gods into the Davidic Kingdom. The sacred temple of God was anything but sacred under Solomon's reign. The Jewish people slipped back into the cyclic journeys between Judaism and lawlessness.

Why would the insertion of cultural diversity cause the Jewish people to acquire an ethic of which God would disapprove? The answer may be found in the sociological studies in "sociology of knowledge." The sociological discipline requires one to view the experiences of everyday life as dominant when developing an ethical worldview.[iii] In other words, the Jewish people of Solomon's reign were introduced to and experienced polytheism (worshipping multiple gods), which included a wide range of ethical systems other than the system given to them by God at Mount Sinai. Experiences eventually became custom, and custom eventually became accepted ethic for the Jewish communities. The cycle into lawlessness from the established ethic of God occurs through generations. A plodding drift back into lawlessness is the nature of the cycles.

After Solomon's reign, the nation of Israel split into two kingdoms: the Northern Kingdom, which was called Israel, and the Southern Kingdom, which was called Judah. King Rehoboam of Judah was a son of Solomon and heir to the throne of Solomon. The city of Jerusalem in Judah was where the temple of God had been built by Solomon. Sacrificial worship was performed in the temple built for God in Jerusalem. There was only one temple of God as there were only one people of God. Another temple would serve to split the people and God into sects and would not be in accordance to God's ethic.

Jeroboam, one of Solomon's officials from the tribe of Ephraim, seized the opportunity of Solomon's death to rule in the Northern Kingdom, which was called Israel. In 1 Kings 12:25-33, Jeroboam sought to separate the people of the Northern Kingdom from the Southern Kingdom when he built Shechem to serve as the capital city for the people of the newly declared Northern Kingdom:

Then Jeroboam built Shechem in the hill country of Ephraim and lived there. And he went out from there and built Penuel.

Jeroboam's dilemma is revealed in the next verses:

If this people go up to offer sacrifices in the temple of the LORD at Jerusalem, then the heart of this people will turn again to their lord, to Rehoboam king of Judah, and they will kill me and return to Rehoboam king of Judah.

Jeroboam's focus was on him and what he envisioned in a kingdom called after his own name. He displaced God as first in priority.

He knew that unless he sold the people a new worldview of God and what he felt were God's ideas for Jewish society, the people would, if not immediately, eventually abandon him and return to God's ethical way of living and worship in Jerusalem. His answer to this dilemma was to lead the people of the Northern Kingdom into lawlessness through a clear contradiction of God's prohibitions on false idol worship.

So the king took counsel and made two calves of gold. And he said to the people, "You have gone up to Jerusalem long enough. Behold your gods, O Israel, who brought you up out of the land of Egypt (1 Kings 12:28)."

Jeroboam made the idols in order to take the people's minds back to a time in Egypt when they worshiped Egyptian gods. Exodus 32:1-6 chronicles the time in Jewish history that Jeroboam was seeking to recapture:

When the people saw that Moses delayed to come down from the mountain, the people gathered themselves together to Aaron and said to him, "Up, make us gods who shall go before us (Exodus 32:1)."

Their families and their priests had taught the Jewish people this historical passage, and because of this, they would have understood that the golden calves of Jeroboam were lawlessness. Jeroboam was asking the people of the Northern Kingdom to forget the God of their fathers and follow him into lawlessness.

As generations passed, the Jewish people of the Northern Kingdom learned a hybrid ethic, and the new hybrid ethic became their reality. Since the perspective of the people was polytheism, polytheism became the truth.

Jeroboam may be the first documented case of man-implemented pragmatic differences in society for the express purpose of changing the worldview of a nation by weaponization of what sociologists call in contemporary society *"sociology of knowledge"*. Jeroboam thought he could teach the people of the Northern Kingdom to follow his lead by introducing competing ethics of mankind. He could use new experience to drive an ethical wedge between the people of Judah and the Northern Kingdom. There would be no need to wage a physical war on Judah to keep his Northern Kingdom intact.

A contemporary example of weaponizing sociology of knowledge is in the West's attempts to teach Muslims to be Westerners. Islam may be defeated through the classroom and daily European experience, sociologists would say. In other words, daily contact with European culture would teach the Muslim to be Western.

The current radicalism in Europe is from Muslims who live in European communities and reject the experience-based assimilation process of the Europeans. Experts may be heard on all news outlets touting the increased need to teach the Muslim communities to be European.

Jeroboam did not know the contemporary label for the systemic change he implemented, but he surely understood the concept.

Jeroboam's battle for the people of Israel was nothing new to God. God is the original author of the concept of "sociology of knowledge." He used the concept throughout the biblical stories and cycles. Noah, Abraham and the nation of Israel are examples of how God implemented His ethic. Consider the quote from Ezekiel:

And I said to their children in the wilderness, "Do not walk in the statutes of your fathers, nor keep their rules, nor defile yourselves with their *idols. I am the L*ORD *your God; walk in my statutes, and be careful to obey my rules (Ezekiel 20:18, 19)."*

God's purpose was to lead people to Himself through the building of a society that held Him to be the most High God. God offered life in return for practicing Judaism, which is obedience to the laws given in the Torah. God desires mankind love Him above all things, including mankind.

And how does mankind show its love for God? Obedience is the only way: *"I am the LORD your God; walk in my statutes, and be careful to obey my rules."* Jesus also reiterates the love of God:

If you love me, you will keep my commandments (John 14:15).

If you keep my commandments, you will abide in my love, just as I have kept my Father's commandments and abide in his love (John 15:10).

There is no other way for a man or woman to show their love for God except through obedience. Mankind is incapable of bringing anything to God that does not already belong to Him. For example, consider Exodus 19:5:

Now therefore, if you will indeed obey my voice and keep my covenant, you shall be my treasured possession among all peoples, for all the earth is mine.

Jeroboam's journey into lawlessness was complete, and the people in his kingdom who followed him practiced lawlessness. The Northern Kingdom was eventually assimilated into the surrounding cultures. The final event is called the Jewish diaspora. The Kingdom of Judah was left to stare down the surrounding lawless cultures on its own.

The kings who ruled over Judah vacillated between lawlessness and Judaism depending on the king and pressures felt from the surrounding cultures. Consequently in 586 BC, God allowed Judah to fall to Nebuchadnezzar, king of Babylon.

During the cycles of lawlessness versus following the ethic of God (Judaism), the various prophets sent by God sang out to the people of Israel, warning them of the consequences of practicing lawlessness. The prophets' goal was to penetrate the acquired reality of the people. The people of God had learned an ethic from the surrounding culture which was not acceptable to God. The prophets used persuasive rhetoric in attempts to warn the people of the danger of accepting lawlessness in the place of God's ethic.

At one point before the fall of Jerusalem, the prophet Ezekiel envisioned an event where the glory of God left the temple in Jerusalem. The people had taken their lawlessness so far as to alienate God, so God left. The Minor Prophets in particular are a record of an exhaustive warning to the Jewish people about their acceptance of lawlessness as a way of life.

SECTION III

Minor Prophets

THERE WERE TWELVE MINOR PROPHETS which made the Jewish canon now called the Old Testament. They may be separated by the era and the Jewish kingdom to which they spoke.

Jonah, Amos and Hosea spoke to the Northern Kingdom of Israel (780 BC to 715 BC). Obadiah, Joel, Micah, Nahum, Habakkuk, and Zephaniah spoke to the Southern Kingdom of Judah (840 BC to 625 BC). Haggai, Zechariah, and Malachi spoke to the Jewish people after the fall of Jerusalem (586 BC). The time after the fall of Jerusalem is called the exilic period since many Jews were carried off by Nebuchadnezzar to live in exile (520 BC to 430 BC).

All the prophets could be thought of as preachers, their messages as sermons intended to move the Jewish people and ethic back to the ethic God gave the Jews at Mount Sinai. For the purpose of this text, the sermons of three prophets to the people will be explored. Amos prophesied to the Northern Kingdom, Nahum prophesied to the Southern Kingdom, and Malachi to the exiled Jews in Babylon. Malachi is the last prophetic voice heard from God until the birth of Christ 400 years later.

CHAPTER 1

Amos

〗

THE BOOK OF AMOS IS listed among the twelve Minor Prophets. Contemporary theological studies have made Amos the object of major critical study. Sixty different commentaries were written on the subject in the second half of the twentieth century and eight hundred publications.[iv] Typically, Amos has been probed and dissected by academia.

Amos lived and prophesied during the reigns of King Jeroboam II (Northern Kingdom) and King Uzziah (Southern Kingdom). Amos (1:1) dated his prophesy by referring to a large earthquake that occurred two years after he spoke. King Jeroboam II reigned in the Northern Kingdom from 793-753 BC, and King Uzziah reigned in the Southern Kingdom from 781-740 BC. The time in which Amos lived and prophesied may generally be stated as being between 793 and 740 BC.

Amos' message was directed at the lawlessness of the Northern Kingdom. The Northern Kingdom had followed Jeroboam (founder of the Northern Kingdom of Israel) into multi-theism. Many gods were worshipped. The golden calf Jeroboam had introduced to the kingdom as an alternative to Judaism served to open the door for all the Near Eastern gods. Fertility gods were reintroduced as well as all other forms of paganism. Egyptian gods, Grecian gods and Latin gods were a steady force in the Northern Kingdom. The Hebrew God was worshipped; however, He was just one of many. The first of the Ten Commandments given to Jews was: *"Thou shall have no other gods before me."*

In addition to multi-theism, the Northern Kingdom had developed a rich upper class that ignored and even oppressed the poor (Amos 6:4-7). Levitical law (Leviticus 19) requires the Jews to treat the poor with respect: *"not be partial to the poor or defer to the great, but in righteousness shall you judge your neighbor."* Evidence is found of the rich upper class in Alfred S. Hoerth's book *Archaeology and the Old Testament*. The Northern Kingdom residents had a wealthy upper class which had summer and winter homes. The homes were decorated with expensive ivory and other exotic building materials. The houses were located in the most coveted areas of the Mediterranean coast and Sea of Galilee.

In contrast to the rich upper class of the era, Amos was from the town of Tekoa (1:1). The town is thought traditionally to be in Judah about five miles south of Bethlehem.[v] Amos' occupation was that of a shepherd or sheep breeder. Amos also worked tending sycamore fig trees. The image is one of a man who has two occupations in order to subsidize his total earnings. The picture of Amos is then one of a humble working man called into service as a prophet by God.

The literary structure of Amos is divided into three parts.[vi]

CHAPTER 2

Oracles Against the Nations (Chapters 1-2)[vii]

§

AMOS PROPHESIES AGAINST EIGHT NATIONS: Syria, Philistia, Tyre, Edom, Ammon, Moab, Judah, and Israel. Amos prophesies against the Gentile nations for their war crimes. It is noted that Amos' prophesies are like legal indictments against his prophetic targets. Amos indicts the Near Eastern nations and cultures surrounding the Northern Kingdom with failure to follow God's ethic. God requires all mankind to follow His ethic given to the Israelites in Exodus and Leviticus. No one will get a free ride. The indictment brings comparison to the days of Noah. Everyone not following the ethic of God will be destroyed. Amos' indictment of the nations is telling of God's view of mankind. Specifically speaking, God's worldview is that the appropriate way of life is the one He gave to Israel. Those who choose to reject His way of life cannot expect to be spared. God views all mankind as His, and all mankind is accountable for rejection of His ethic. The Jewish population must have been thrilled with the indictment of the nations around them. However, after building a case against the nations, Amos in turn indicted Israel for its lawlessness.

An indictment is typically followed by an appearance before a judge. In this case, the Northern Kingdom must stand before the judge, and that judge is God. The subsequent judgments are from God as judge.

CHAPTER 3

Judgment Speeches Against Israel (Chapters 3-6)[viii]

§

THE COVENANT BETWEEN GOD'S PEOPLE and God is like other agreements of its era, requiring obedience from the client. In this case, God sent Amos as a "lawsuit messenger" to bring a case against the disobedient people for failure to live by the agreement, the ethic of God given in Exodus and Leviticus.[ix] The indictment against Israel for embracing a lawless lifestyle was more severe than the indictment against the lawless nations. The nations had not made an agreement to follow the ethic of God.

The Israelites did have a standing agreement to follow the ethic of God. The ethic of God was supposed to represent God through His people Israel. Instead, God's people Israel had joined with the lawlessness of the nations. However, the visions of Amos display a God who is patient with the Northern Kingdom.

CHAPTER 4

The Vision Reports
(Chapters 7-9)ˣ

§

AMOS RECEIVED FIVE VISIONS FROM the Lord. The first is a vision of a locust plague (7:1). The second is a vision of fire (7:4). In both visions Amos was successful in interceding on behalf of Israel.

However, Amos was unable to intercede for Israel in the third and fourth visions. The third vision depicts a plumb line *"in the midst of My people Israel."* The image of a wall out of plumb and falling to the ground is compared to Israel's fall. The fourth vision is of a basket of summer fruit. Fruit that is ripe as the nation of Israel was ripe for judgment.

The fifth vision is a vision of salvation and restoration of God's people. This vision (also the book of Amos) ends with God speaking: *"says the Lord your God."*

As is the case with the prophets in the Bible, Amos' prophesies follow the theme of God's sovereignty and God's judgment.

There are three levels in the process regarding God's sovereignty and judgment:ˣⁱ

* Personal, divine: It is God Himself who initiates judgment.
* Creation: Even creation itself rises in judgments against evil.
* Political history: God rules all nations all the time.

The failure to follow God's ethic and the embracing of lawlessness in the Northern Kingdom brought judgment from God. Even the worship of Yahweh was corrupted, and the rich oppressed the poor while they bathed in luxury.

Some scholars view Amos as having a new message. On the contrary, Amos sought to bring insight to the people's covenant with God, the covenant of Abraham and Isaac. He was a prosecutor indicting the guilty and warning of God's (the judge's) impending judgment.

Amos was not what Israel would have expected of its prophets. The people thought of the "Day of the Lord" as the day when God would set them above all nations. God would destroy all their enemies.[xii] Amos reversed this idea and prophesied of a day when the Divine Warrior would destroy Israel for her lawless ethic. God would then restore the people through His remnant.

The book of Amos reveals a genuine concern for the poor. The New Testament also requires good treatment of the poor (I Corinthians 11:22; James 2:1-10). Of the Gospels, Luke reveals Jesus' concern for the poor (Luke 11:18, 6:20; 7:22).[xiii] Paul cites Amos in Romans 12:9, and Stephen cites Amos in Acts 7:12. James argues for allowing the Gentiles into the church by pointing out that it fulfills God's promise to unite the Northern and Southern Kingdoms (Acts 15:16-17).[xiv]

Amos is a book for the ages. The Northern Kingdom exchanged the ethic of God with the ethic of the cultures around it in pursuit of prosperity and peace. It is a question people have faced since Adam and Eve and will face until the end of times. Who holds the key to salvation? Mankind and its ethic? Or God and His ethic? The prophet Nahum answered the question if one would only take note.

CHAPTER 5
Nahum

§

IN THE SOUTHERN KINGDOM (JUDAH), a king named Manasseh led his kingdom into multi-theism and the ethics of the surrounding cultures. Manasseh was so bad that God announced He would destroy the Southern Kingdom. God said:

> *Behold, I am bringing upon Jerusalem and Judah such disaster that the ears of everyone who hears of it will tingle. And I will stretch over Jerusalem the measuring line of Samaria, and the plumb line of the house of Ahab, and I will wipe Jerusalem as one wipes a dish, wiping it and turning it upside down (2 Kings 21: 12-13).*

God intended to destroy all and leave no one standing. The Noah story again compares to the destruction of the Southern Kingdom. However, Nahum prophesizes of God's relenting and why.

The book of Nahum informs the reader that the script is an oracle regarding Nineveh and a vision received from God by Nahum of Elkosh.

The date of the book of Nahum is stated in Nahum 3:8 where Nahum refers to the destruction of Thebes (No Amon/Egypt). The fall of Thebes occurred in 663 BC[xv]. The fall of Nineveh, Assyria, is placed by historians at 612 BC[xvi].

Nahum speaks of Nineveh's power in the present tense. The happenings, or at least components of the happenings, are current events to Nahum. In that setting, the Assyrian empire (Nineveh was the capital of

Assyria, the country called Iraq today) was a very powerful force in the Near Eastern theater.

If a powerful Assyrian empire (663 BC) is contrasted with its future destruction (612 BC), a mid-to-early date for the book's writing is implied.

The king of Judah at the time was Manasseh. Manasseh was carried off to Babylon in 650 BC (2 Chronicles 33:10-17; 2 Kings 21:1-11).[xvii] Nahum reflects a vision of change for Judah (Nahum 1:12-14, 2:1-3). The vision revealed salvation where destruction once reigned. In view of the evidence, a date of 650-663 BC is the most probable timeframe for Nahum's vision.

The Assyrian empire had made many enemies among its Near Eastern neighbors in their brutal ascent to Near Eastern world dominance. Babylon was among the most powerful of these enemies that Esarhaddon (680-672 BC), King of Assyria, faced.[xviii] In order to preempt aggression from Babylon after his death, Esarhaddon appointed one son, Ashurbanipal, over Assyria and another son, Šamas-šum-ukin, over Babylon.[xix] The move set brother against brother and created an intense rivalry. Šamas-šum-ukin led a revolt against Assyria in 652 BC.[xx] Ashurbanipal repelled the revolt, but the Assyrian Empire was weakened and left vulnerable. Attacks from the Scythians and an extended conflict with the Chaldeans further weakened the Assyrian Empire.[xxi]

Assyria had ruled the Near Eastern world for over a century before Nahum's voice was heard. They had dispersed the ten tribes of the Northern Kingdom in 772 BC and brutalized the other Near Eastern nations. They were the equivalent of a modern day evil superpower.

Nahum's vision anticipates the eventual destruction of the evil Assyrian empire and its evil capital Nineveh. Nahum's words are like a divine war cry: "*God is jealous, and the Lord avenges* (1:2)." Nahum continues with what will be God's righteous attack on an evil empire for most of the book of Nahum. However, Nahum moves his attention from Nineveh to Judah in 1:12-2:1. The verses tell of how God will rescue His people from the tyranny of the evil empire. The salvation of Judah is at hand. After decades of God's affliction on Judah, why did God choose "now" to rescue Judah?

Thus says the Lord, "Though they are complete and they are many, they will be cut down and they will pass away. Though I have afflicted you I will afflict no more (Nahum 1:12-14, 2:1)."

Nahum uses the prophetic *"Thus says the Lord"* here to identify the verses that follow as the words of God. This is the only time in the entire book that the prophet uses this phrase.

The beginning of the quote from the Lord is a conditional phrase: *"though they are complete and they are many."* The Lord says that although the condition of the Assyrian army is complete and they are many, they will be cut off. The meaning transfers an image of an Assyrian army at its peak of power.

It should be noted that the conditional statement places the words of God at a time before Assyrian power was weakened by conflict. Assyrian power was complete with nothing more that could be added. The climax of Assyrian power was probably attained under Ashurbanipal.[xxii] The attack on and subsequent fall of Thebes (3:8) to the Assyrians under leadership of Ashurbanipal relates the best likely date for completeness of Assyrian power. Thebes was a great city in Egypt during this era. The significance of the fall of Thebes at the hands of Ashurbanipal could be compared to the fall of France at the hands of Hitler during WWII—i.e., an evil power extending its territory.

The Hebrew literal translation of *"they will be cut down and they will pass away* (see above quote)" is *"and thus they will be sheared and pass."* The Hebrew refers to shearing as in shearing sheep. The Assyrians will be sheared, cut down, or mowed down with no possibility for continued life. They will pass into history forever.

The Hebrew literal translation of the next phrase (Nahum 1:12) reads: *"And I have afflicted you. I will afflict you no more."* The Hebrew *"afflicted"* is used in 2 Kings 17:20 in regard to the Northern Kingdom (Israel): *"And the Lord rejected all the descendants of Israel, afflicted them, and delivering them into the hand of plunderers, until He had cast them from His sight."* The common usage refers to the nation of Israel as a nation under bondage (Deuteronomy 8:2, Psalms 90:15, 1 Kings 11:39, Lamentations 3:33). Nahum's vision reveals an image of a Judean community that was afflicted by God for the purpose of humbling them.

Nahum's vision here reflects knowledge of the historical lawlessness of the people of Israel. For example, Manasseh (697-643 BC) ruled over Judah for 54 years, leading them into a life of idolatry. In 2 Kings 21 the narrator says: *"And he did evil in the sight of the Lord, according to the abominations of the nations."* Manasseh built *"wooden images"*, restored altars to Baal, and even desecrated the temple of God with idols of foreign gods. God was so angry with the abominations committed by Manasseh that He says in 2 Kings 21:12: *"Behold, I am bringing such calamity upon Jerusalem and Judah, that whomever hears of it, both his ears will tingle."*

The declaration by God in 2 Kings appears to conflict here with Nahum's vision of a God rescuing a people suffering oppression. If a date of composition is assumed to be between 663-650 BC, Nahum's vision would coincide with Manasseh's reign 697- 643 BC.

And now I will break his yoke from upon you and will burst your bonds apart (Nahum 1:13).

The **"now"** is temporal and reflects the time that God will break Judah free of the oppressive Assyrians. The proclamation here is by God. How then is 2 Kings correct in light of Nahum's vision? If the same King Manasseh (697-643 BC) was ruling at the time of Nahum's vision, why has God decided that **"now"** was the time to break the Assyrian stranglehold on Judah? What could possibly have happened between 2 Kings 21:12 and Nahum 1:13?

The answer to this question may be found in 2 Chronicles 33:10-17. Here the chronicler tells the reader that Manasseh was taken away *"with hooks"* to Babylon. He was afflicted by his captors, causing him to be *"humbled"* before the Lord. Manasseh repented of his lawlessness, and the Lord sent him back to Jerusalem. Consequently, the last years of Manasseh's reign were spent restoring the ethic of God and tearing down the images he had built to other gods.

The book of Nahum is a sermon whose core theme is King Manasseh's and the Kingdom of Judah's ethical relationship with God. The ethical relationship with God was reestablished when Manasseh rejected the ethics of lawlessness and embraced God's ethic. God at first was going to destroy Judah:

> *And I will stretch over Jerusalem the measuring line of Samaria, and the plumb line of the house of Ahab, and I will wipe Jerusalem as one wipes a dish, wiping and turning it upside down. I will forsake the remnant of my heritage and give them into the hand of their enemies (2 Kings 21:13, 14).*

> *And when he was in distress, he entreated the favor of the Lord his God and humbled himself greatly before the God of his fathers. He prayed to him, and God was moved by his entreaty and heard his plea and brought him again to Jerusalem into his Kingdom. Then Manasseh knew that the Lord was God (2 Chronicles 33:12, 13).*

> *Thus says the Lord, "Though they are complete and they are many, they will be cut down and they will pass away. Though I have afflicted you, I will afflict no more (Nahum 1:12-14, 2:1)."*

he view that God would relent in regard to His decree in 2 Kings 21:12-15 is supported by Jeremiah 18:7, 8. The Lord says: *"The instant I speak concerning a nation and concerning a Kingdom, to pluck-up, to pull down, and to destroy it, if that nation against whom I have spoken turns from its evil, I will relent of the disaster that I thought to bring upon it."*

Jeremiah's ministry stretched from 626 BC (death of Ashurbanipal) to 586 BC. While Nahum's writing is a vision, Jeremiah spoke directly to the people about their current relationship with God and the nations.

Some scholars place **"now"** in Nahum as a result of the restoration efforts of King Josiah, who began his rule two years after Manasseh. The Manasseh reforms would have been gaining momentum under Josiah's leadership (640-609 BC). However, the Josiahan revival lasted much longer than Manasseh's revival. Therefore, the change from destruction to prosperity in regard to Judah and Jerusalem (2 Kings 21:12-15) could be tied to Josiah. After all, the Josiahan revival is viewed as being much more effective in regard to God's people returning to God. However, Josiah took the throne at 8 years of age in 640 BC. It is unlikely his revival was a result of his own research into the Torah. It is more likely they came from his advisors who had lived in the era of Manasseh.

During the Josiahan revival, the Assyrian dominance in the Near East Theater had already experienced a considerable blow. As previously mentioned, in 652 BC Šamas-šum-ukin led the Chaldeans in a revolt against Assyria. Although Assyria put down the revolt, she was weakened. She was "incomplete" as opposed to God's description of her in Nahum 1:12 as "complete". Therefore, God's declaration of a complete Assyria in vs. 12a and the recognition that Judah was at this point a vassal of Assyria (afflicted) lends against a Josiahan source for God's change of heart. Furthermore, in 2 Chronicles 34:2, the chronicler reports: "(Josiah) *walked in the ways of his father David; he did not turn to the right hand or to the left.*" In addition, it is unlikely change would occur within one generation of mankind; specifically the generation of Josiah.

The evidence appears to support Manasseh's lawlessness, God's decree to afflict, Manasseh's repentance, and God's relent of the decree as the source of the relent **"now"** in Nahum.

Whether as a result of Josiah's reforms or Manasseh's repentance, Nahum 1:13 clearly reveals that the Assyrian yoke would be broken. Furthermore, verse 12a describes Assyria as being cut off, utterly removed from the earth.

The Lord has made a commandment about you: "No more shall your name be sown; from the house of your gods. I will cut off the carved image and the metal image. I will make your grave, for you are vile (Nahum 1:14)."

Here the familiar *"thus saith the Lord"* is absent. However, it is clear that the Lord is still involved in the conversation. Nahum reports that *"God has a commandment concerning Assyria."*

The wicked nation will be utterly destroyed with no possibility of returning in any capacity. The destruction of the Assyrian temple was so utterly complete that excavations were cut short when archeologists found that *"further exploration of these sites would not pay."*[xxiii] The remains of Nineveh are today nothing more than a dirt hill in the land. The site is reported as being a grave that is fitting of tyrants.

> *Behold, upon the mountains, the feet from whom bring good news, who publishes feast. Keep your feast, O Judah, complete your vows. For never again shall worthlessness pass through you (Nahum 1:15).*

It was customary for the people of Israel to shout out good news from the mountain (Isaiah 40:9).

Keep your feasts, O Judah; complete your vows. Jerusalem was finally free of the stifling yoke of the Near Eastern superpower of Assyria. Even the Jews that were left in the area of the Northern Kingdom were now free to make a pilgrimage to the temple in Jerusalem. It is issued in the imperative as a command:

> *For never again shall worthlessness pass through you (1:15).*

God had allowed the worthless to afflict the Israelites in order to humble them (Deuteronomy 8:2, Psalms 90:15, 1 Kings 11:39, Lamentations 3:33). However, **now** the worthless would pass away. The Hebrew word which is interpreted as worthlessness was thought to be so reprehensible in the Jewish meaning that it was eventually used as a synonym for Satan (2 Corinthians 6:15).

A lot of negative thoughts have been written about the evil King Manasseh. This reflects the accounts of the acts of Manasseh in 2 Kings 21.

Certainly Manasseh deserves the negative attention from the Jewish and Christian communities for his departure from God's ethic. He turned his back on the ethic of God and led a whole nation astray. He set up carved images in the house of the Lord, sacrificed his son in fire, practiced sooth-saying and witchcraft (2 Kings 21).

The sacrifice of his son is particularly troubling. Worship of Near Eastern gods required burning one's child in the valley of Hinnom. The term "passing through the fire" was used to connote the experience. Christ spoke of the valley of Hinnom as Ge- Hinnom; it was a place of everlasting fire and has become synonymous with hell.

The report in 2 Kings regarding Manasseh's reign is even more troubling considering that he was the leader of God's people. Manasseh's actions were never in isolation. The country followed his example, turning experience of environment into reality. In fact, in 2 Kings 21:8a, the writer explains that Manasseh *"seduced"* the people into performing even greater offenses against God than the evil nations that came before them. As a result of the evil of Manasseh's kingdom, God said: *"So I will forsake the remnant of My inheritance and deliver them into the hand of their enemies* (2 Kings 21:14)." However, the attention that the evil King Manasseh gets in 2 Kings should be in contrast with the good King Manasseh in Chronicles 33:10-17.

It is probable that Manasseh's repentance in Babylon is the key to God's relenting regarding Judah in Nahum 1:12-2:1. Manasseh was carried off to Babylon with nose hooks around 650 BC. It was as a result of the humiliation suffered at the hands of the Babylonians that Manasseh repented (Chronicles 33).

The book of Nahum is a prophecy of destruction of the evil Assyrian superpower. However, Nahum is also a message of salvation for God's people. There is no conflict in God's Word, and He is not acting rashly in removing the affliction he has placed on Judah for their wickedness during Manasseh's reign (2 Kings 21). He is responding to the repentance of Manasseh, and salvation is *"now"* and is God's righteous act for a king and his kingdom who returned to live the ethic of God.

Josiah continued Manasseh's reforms, and Judah prospered under Josiah's reign as king. After Josiah's death, however, Judah could not maintain the ethic of God and drifted back into the ethic of mankind. As a result, Judah and the precious city of Jerusalem fell in 586 BC, and many Jews were carried away into exile.

Manasseh's ethic before being captured reflected an ethic developed through daily experiences and adaptation of the experiences of others as a way of life. The shocking humiliation of his capture and imprisonment got his attention, and a change within his very soul occurred.

The science of "sociology of knowledge" proposes that daily experiences acted out and internalized is the source of the real ethic of human behavior. If this science is correct, there is no reason Manasseh would not regain the old ethic once he reentered the environment which spawned the terrible ethic. However, sociologists who study the science of sociology of knowledge indicate there can be exceptions to the rule. The Islamic European radicals and the nation of Israel itself are evidence the science is not infallible. Further, Christians have reported similar turns from socially developed ethics since the time of Christ.

Fifteen generations after the fall of Judah and Jerusalem, Jesus would tap the source of the soul-change phenomena to turn His followers and the nations to the ethic of God. Christ counters the experience-based ethic through a soul conversion. The Holy Spirit is given to protect the change from the effects of sociology of knowledge in mankind's world.

The book of Nahum and his prophecy to the people of Judah is a foretelling and witness to the coming of Christ and the soul-change phenomena. Nahum was a powerful prophet with a powerful message. God would continue to speak to the Israelite nation through powerful prophets even in exile.

CHAPTER 6

Malachi

§

THE PROPHET MALACHI SPOKE DURING the time when the Jews were allowed to return from exile and prior to the *intertestamental period* (the time between the Old Testament and the New Testament). The exile period was the time between the Fall of Jerusalem (586 BC) and Persian King Cyrus' degree (approximately 70 years after the fall of Jerusalem) allowing the Jews to return to their homeland to rebuild the temple and the walls of Jerusalem. The biblical history of the event and the era may be found in the Old Testament books of Nehemiah and Ezra. Esther, Zachariah, Haggai, and Malachi are also of the same Jewish exile period.

> *Thus says Cyrus king of Persia: "The Lord, the God of heaven, has given me all the kingdoms of the earth, and He has charged me to build Him a house at Jerusalem, which is in Judah. Whoever is among you of all His people, may his God be with him, and let him go up to Jerusalem, which is in Judah, and rebuild the house of the Lord, the God of Israel—he is the God who is in Jerusalem. And let each survivor, in whatever place he sojourns, be assisted by the men of his place with silver and gold, with goods and with beasts, besides freewill offerings for the house of God that is in Jerusalem (Ezra 1:1-4)."*

Jeremiah and Ezra led a group of Jews back to Jerusalem in order to restore the temple and rebuild the walls to the old city of Jerusalem. The groups that went back were confronted by Jews who had not been captured and led away to Babylon by Nebuchadnezzar.

The Jews who had escaped captivity and exile had learned to survive without a Jewish political influence by blending into their surroundings. The Jewish ethic which was given to the Jews by God in the Torah was not followed. The way of life of the Jews who had been left behind had become an ethic which was obtained through the daily experience of the Jews and was influenced by the surrounding established cultural norms. They had learned a new ethic foreign to God. God was no longer a priority in their lives.

New Jewish Ethic – Foreign to God

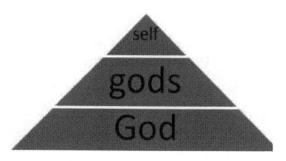

Ezra was a Jewish priest, and he tried to re-establish God's ethic among the Jewish groups.

He was concerned that the nation of Israel would become unrecognizable and eventually extinct if the existing cultural synchronization was allowed to continue. The nation of Israel was literally being assimilated into the surrounding cultures through the acceptance of a way of life foreign to God and Judaism.

Nehemiah was not a priest, but a manager. His role in the text was that of a leader who tried to rally the Jewish faithful around the cause of rebuilding the walls of the old city of Jerusalem. Nehemiah's concern was for the Jewish people as a nation. The walls of Jerusalem could be thought of as a border around the sacred people of God. Although the Jews were still subjects of the Persian empire of the era, the walls re-established identity with the nation of Israel. The re-established nation of Israel would eventually identify with God's ethic given to the nation of Israel after the exodus from Egypt.

However, the way of life which had been learned absent of God and through daily experience with other cultures was too strong. The book of Ezra ends with him on his knees crying out to God, fearing the end of the precious nation of God and the end of God's way of life.

In this setting Malachi spoke to the nation of Israel. Malachi opens with questions and answers:

> *The oracle of the word of the LORD to Israel through Malachi. "I have loved you," says the LORD. But you say, "How have You loved us?" "Was not Esau Jacob's brother?" declares the LORD. "Yet I have loved Jacob; but I have hated Esau, and I have made his mountains a desolation and appointed his inheritance for the jackals of the wilderness (Malachi 1: 1-3)."*

It appears the Jewish people were complaining and were lashing out at God for their predicament. Through Malachi, God answered the complaint. God had chosen Jacob and destroyed Esau whom he hated. The reference to Jacob is a reference to Israel (see Genesis 35:10: *"no longer shall your name be called Jacob, but Israel shall be your name."*), the son of Isaac, the grandson of Abraham. God is pointing out to Jews who were complaining that He chose to love them through Israel (Jacob) and destroy Esau.

Israel (Jacob) went on to give birth to the men who would become the twelve tribes of Israel, whom Moses led out of Egyptian slavery in the Exodus. They are the same twelve tribes to whom God gave the ethic (way of life) in the Torah (vv.1:2-3: *"Yet I have loved Jacob; but I have hated Esau."*). God chose Jacob to carry the seed of His ethic, and He discarded Esau. It is a stark reminder that the Hebrew God does not have to save all men to save mankind.

God, through Malachi, addressed the acquired ethic of the Jewish people:

A son honors his father and a servant his master. Then if I am father, where is My honor (Malachi 1:6)?

Then again from Malachi 2:10-12:

v. 10—Do we not all have one father? Has not one God created us? Why do we deal treacherously each against his brother so as to profane the covenant of our fathers?

v. 11—Judah (Southern Kingdom) has dealt treacherously, and an abomination has been committed in Israel (Northern Kingdom) and in Jerusalem (capital city); for Judah has profaned the sanctuary (temple) of the LORD which He loves and has married the daughter of a foreign god (broken the first commandment of the Ten Commandments: You shall have no other gods before me).

v. 12—As for the man who does this, may the LORD cut off from the tents of Jacob everyone who awakes and answers, or who presents an offering to the LORD of hosts.

Many have wrongly interpreted the above reference as indicating that marrying outside the Jewish family was sin or lawlessness of the people. However, Moses married an African woman in the desert outside of Egypt. If God's concern was interracial marriage, how could it be the most famous and heralded Hebrew prophet of all time married outside the Jewish family and was God's choice to lead Israel's exodus? God's concern is not interracial marriage, but the daily experience brought by the worship of other gods when men and women accept the way of life (mankind's ethic) of the spouse they marry. The books of Esther and Ruth chronicle God's blessings on interracial marriages which seed the ethic of God rather than tear it down. God is concerned with the learned ethic which mankind is prone to grasp when mankind is apart from God and His given ethic.

God promises to save those who follow His ethic. In Malachi chapter 3, He promises to destroy those who follow a different ethic.

Vs. 1—"Behold, I am going to send My messenger, and he will clear the way before Me. And the LORD, whom you seek, will suddenly come to His temple; and the messenger of the covenant, in whom you delight, behold, He is coming," says the LORD of hosts.

Vs. 2—But who can endure the day of His coming? And who can stand when He appears? For He is like a refiner's fire and like fullers' soap.

Vs. 5—"I will draw near to you for judgment; and I will be a swift witness against the sorcerers and against the adulterers and against those who swear falsely, and against those who oppress the wage earner in his wages, the widow and the orphan, and those who turn aside the alien and do not fear Me," says the LORD of hosts.

Vs. 6—For I, the LORD, do not change; therefore you, O sons of Jacob, are not consumed.

Vs. 7—"From the days of your fathers you have turned aside from My statutes and have not kept them. Return to Me, and I will return to you," says the LORD of hosts.

Malachi 3:1-7 is an apocalyptic saying and refers to the coming of the Lord and judgment of those who do not follow the ethic of God. In addition, it is both a warning and an invitation extended to the nation of Israel to return to God's ethic which He made a condition for a relationship between the nation of Israel and Himself.

Many Jews of the time ignored the call to return to the ethic of God. However, there were some who sought to do as God had asked.

Then those who feared the LORD spoke to one another, and the LORD gave attention and heard it, and a Book of Remembrance was written before Him for those who fear the LORD and who esteem His name (Malachi 3:16).

"They will be Mine," says the LORD of hosts, "on the day that I prepare My own possession, and I will spare them as a man spares his own son who serves him (Malachi 3:17)."

So you will again distinguish between the righteous and the wicked, between one who serves God and one who does not serve Him (Malachi 3:18).

The Book of Remembrance is a record concerning the ethic of God and the ethic learned apart from God by mankind. The Hebrew God is keeping records of those who follow His way of life. Those not in the Book of Remembrance will not be forgiven and will receive His judgment for not following His given ethic. Jesus indicates there will be accounting of names. He said in Matthew 7:21-23 of those He did not know:

Not everyone who says to me, "Lord, Lord," will enter the kingdom of heaven, but the one who does the will of my Father who is in heaven. On that day many will say to me, "Lord, Lord, did we not prophesy in your name, and cast out demons in your name, and do many mighty works in your name?" And then will I declare to them, "I never knew you; depart from me, you workers of lawlessness."

As typical in the writings of the Minor Prophets, Malachi ends with a promise of restoration of the Kingdom of God and His people. As stated earlier, Malachi and the Minor Prophets as a whole are a record of an exhaustive warning to the Jewish people about their acceptance of lawlessness as a way of life (ethic).

Eventually, this culminated into a prophetic silence:

> *"Behold, the days are coming," declares the Lord GOD, "when I will send a famine on the land—not a famine of bread, nor a thirst for water, but of hearing the words of the LORD. They shall wander from sea to sea, and from north to east; they shall run to and fro, to seek the word of the LORD, but they shall not find it (Amos 8:11-12)."*

From Malachi to Jesus, a period that stretched four hundred years, there was no word from God. The era of God's silence is called the ***intertestamental period***.

Intertestamental Period

THE JEWISH PEOPLE CRUCIFIED JESUS. This is an amazing contemplation considering the Jews were God's chosen people. If Jesus is the Son of God, how could it be that the Jews who loved God would be among those who crucified Him and stood at the cross mocking Him in His death? The answer lies in the cyclic ethical shifts into lawlessness of the imposing cultures which occurred during the time between the Old and New Testaments.

The Old Testament ends with the book of Malachi, and the New Testament begins with the book of Matthew. Scholars call the time span between the New and Old Testament the *intertestamental period*, and it spanned approximately four hundred years. While a case may be made for the Jewish people's lawlessness over the course of their history, during this four hundred year span of time, Jewish lawlessness took on a different character in the face of God's seeming absence. In addition, multiple kings and conquerors who ruled over the homeland of the Israelites pressed their agenda on the Jewish nation. Among the ruling kings were the Persians Artaxerxes II, Artaxerxes III and Darius III. The Persian reign was followed by the reign of Alexander the Great and his generals, the Jewish Hasmonean Dynasty, and finally the Romans who crucified Christ at the request of His own people.

The lawless cultures of Latins, Persians and Greeks bore down on the Jews like a sun drenched desert—ever present and no shade in sight. Cultural heat drained the Jewish spirit like sun draws and drains moisture from the earth's scorched desert sands. In the face of multiple occupations, it was understandable that the human spirit would become disheartened, resulting in many Jews forsaking the ethic of God as their faith in God became shaken. A natural human reaction would be to seek shade in the culture and lawlessness of conquerors in order to fit in with the new political environment and so quench a thirsty spirit.

Still, some Jews sought to hold on to Judaism despite these withering lawless assaults. Others sought shade by seeking the middle ground. The attempt to find acceptance by all included a pandering to:

1. Those holding to the new cultural order.
2. Those who were holding to new religious philosophies.
3. Those who were holding to old Jewish traditions.

The insurgence of the Persian, Greek and Roman lawless cultures on the Jews and the ethic of God served to divide the faithful into competing religious and sometime non-religious sects.

It should be noted that the area around Jerusalem did not merely consist of Jewish residents and the invading lawless culture. Descendants of old Jewish enemies also sought to salvage their own lawless culture among the invaders and the Jews. This placed the Jewish faith and faithful into a situation where they found themselves staring down a lawless multicultural insurgence which sought to impose change on Jews and Judaism alike.

This lawless cultural insurgence into the Jewish communities actually began before the fall of Jerusalem. If one looks back to the exilic period (approximately 597 BC) to count the generations exposed to the multicultural attack, fourteen Jewish generations were affected by lawless multicultural insurgence (Matthew 1:17). The Jewish faithful struggled mightily to maintain their faith and, in some cases, their very identity as a particular nation of people.

The pressure to defend their faith brought about change from within the ranks of even the most devout. From the influence of the lawless multiculturalism sprang the Pharisees, Sadducees, Essences, Hasidim, and Zealots.

In addition, Greek conquerors of the Jewish lands attempted to transform the Jewish culture into the lawless Greek cultural image in a process called the *Hellenization of the Jews*. As in the case of Hellenized Jews, there were Jews who went even further, choosing to cast aside Judaism altogether and actively join with lawlessness in an effort to conform all Jews to the lawless Greek culture.

Each of these Jewish sects was under tremendous pressure from competing Jewish sects. Lawlessness demanded conformity, and each Jewish sect came to view itself as the law. It was this lawless multicultural environment of the Pharisees, Sadducees, Essences, Zealots and Hellenized Jews that set the stage for the crucifixion of Christ.

CHAPTER 1
The Pharisees

§

THE PHARISEE SECT OF THE *intertestamental period* believed in and preached of the Messiah spoken of in the book of Daniel. They were the most popular sect among the Jewish people during this era. The Pharisees competed with the Sadducees and other Jewish sects over interpretation of scripture. Pharisaical interpretation of scripture established their worldview and their self-imposed authority. They were teachers and interpreters of what is now called the Old Testament, which is broken down by scholars into the following categories:

1. Torah (first five books of the Bible).
2. The books of Prophecy (Minor and Major Prophets).
3. The History books (biblical books dealing with history such as 1&2 Kings).
4. The Wisdom books such as Proverbs and Job.

Their students were called scribes and lawyers. The Pharisees resisted the cultural insurgents' attempts to incorporate them into new religions and/or the conquerors' lawless culture while trying to fit into the new society. Their position was similar to the exilic Jews of the Old Testament living in Babylon:

Thus says the Lord of host . . . "Build houses and live in them; plant gardens and eat their produce. But seek the welfare of the city where I have sent you into exile, and pray to the Lord on its behalf, for in its welfare you will find your welfare (Jeremiah 29:5, 7)."

The Pharisees sought to find religious and political distance from other Jewish sects through an acted-out Old Testament righteousness. The righteousness was a reach for religious identity. If one acts religious, one must be religious. The Pharisees' formula was transferred to the common Jew through Pharisaical demands. The strategy employed to encourage fellow Jews to follow their sect was to shame and ridicule the less studious Jews into following them. Shame and ridicule is a formative strategy to promote and adjudicate cultural change even in cultural battles of today.

The idea is to strategically shame someone in public for their stated view or belief. The concept of using shame and ridicule as a weapon to further one's cause over another is especially formidable when acted out by perceived authority.

One example is the contemporary name-calling in America. The "in vogue" metaphor of cultural adjudicators is to attach the symbol *"phobia"* to any perceived cultural crime: homophobia, Islamophobia and so on. Anyone not carrying the culturally correct flag gets a public beating through the humiliation attached to metaphorical intimidation.

Pharisees believed in the resurrection and afterlife. They believed man's destiny was controlled by God. In the Old Testament book of Jeremiah, God told Jeremiah that He knew Jeremiah before he was born and knew he was the right choice for God's prophetic mission to the Jews. The Pharisees understood God's knowledge of man as: "God knows all, even one's destiny, and one is predestined according to the will of God."

For the Pharisees, their interpretation of the text became tradition among their sect, and tradition in turn became God's Word. A Pharisee's life consisted of studying the details of biblical writings and commenting on those details discovered for the purpose of retaining Jewish identity among the lawlessness of the day. Jesus confronted the Pharisees in the Gospels and challenged their interpretation many times. In fact, Jesus' arguments came out of more than twenty of the Old Testament books which the Pharisees claimed were the foundation of their religion. A few of the passages Jesus quoted are:

You will indeed hear but never understand and you will indeed see but never perceive (Matthew 14:14; parallel passage Isaiah 6:9).

And if you had known what this means, "I desire mercy, and not sacrifice", you would not have condemned the guiltless. For the Son of Man is the Lord of the Sabbath (Matthew 12: 7; parallel passage Hosea 2:1, 3).

Then they will begin to say to the mountains, "Fall on us", and to the hills, "cover us" (Luke 23:30; parallel passage Hosea 10:8).

However, Pharisaical tradition did not fit into what Jesus was teaching. Jesus was teaching a different Gospel which was foreign to the Pharisaical palate.

This people honors me with their lips, but their heart is far from me; in vain do they worship me, teaching as doctrines the commandments of men (Matthew 15:8, 9).

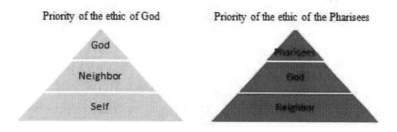

If Jesus is the messenger from God, then the Pharisees were the authors of a religion foreign to God's palate. The Pharisees not only put themselves before God, but made God their servant. Their ambition was to dominate the Jewish politic through a calculated self-gratifying exposé of God's law.

The Pharisees and their interpretation became first in order of their commandments. God was whatever they sought to make Him, and God's commandments and ethic were bent into Pharisaical tradition. God and His Word became merely a support system for their lawlessness. The first commandment of the Ten Commandments requires God to be first in the order of importance. Christ recognized the lawlessness even through the mask of Judaism.

CHAPTER 2

The Sadducees

§

THE SADDUCEES ARE SPOKEN OF as descendants of the Jewish priesthood and the temple keepers of the tribe of Levi. They interpreted the Old Testament differently than the Pharisees. Sadducees did not hold to the messianic views in Daniel (Acts 23:6-9). They believed the soul died with the body and that there is no afterlife.

> *For the Sadducees say there is no resurrection, nor angel, nor spirit, but the Pharisees acknowledge them all (Acts 23:8).*

Jesus directly confronted the Sadducee position on the resurrection in Matthew 22:29, 32:

> *You are wrong because you know neither the Scriptures nor the power of God . . . Have you not read what was said to you by God: "I am the God of Abraham, and the God of Isaac, and the God of Jacob?" He is not God of the dead, but the living.*

The Sadducees also felt mankind had power over his own destiny, and they did not accept the doctrine of predestination. Sadducee destiny was a product of how an individual believer lived. Events occurred in an individual's life as a result of an individual's choices. Destiny of an individual was not preordained by God. It is an interesting view since the very existence of the Jewish nation was a destiny engineered by God. The worldview of the Sadducees wrongly left the Sadducees believing they held a position of total control over their environment and destiny. God is the author of the law (ethic) of the Jews, and the position of the Sadducees was one of lawlessness.

In addition, Sadducees only acknowledged what was written in the Torah and rejected any supposed authority developed from the rest of the Old Testament. The religion of tradition which the Pharisees followed would have been especially offensive to the Sadducees.

The Sadducees were not as close to the common people of the era as the Pharisees were. Evidence reveals the Sadducees were rich and well-connected politically with whatever powers ruled over the Jewish people at any given time. Their economic condition prospered through the sale of sacrificial animals at the temple. The lawless religion of the Sadducees had as its purpose control over the people as if they were God.

The New Testament book of Luke reveals that Jesus was infuriated by the Sadducees' commercialization of Judaism at the temple:

And when He entered the temple and began to drive out those who sold, saying to them, "It is written, My house shall be a house of prayer, but you have made it a den of robbers (Luke 19:45)."

Sadducees of the era sought to profit from the image of God. God became a commodity which was sold at the temple. The money derived from the sale of sacrifices at the temple and perhaps as well the sale of priestly mediation to God on behalf of the people would have made the Sadducees individually and collectively very rich. Money is power in any culture. Power drives the political machines in the world of mankind.

Power, politics, and wealth served to disconnect Sadducees from the common Jew and the ethic of God. They were the political and religious enemies of the Pharisees. The Sadducees disappeared after the temple was destroyed by the Romans in 70 BC, approximately 35 years after Christ was crucified. Their fading from the scene after the destruction of the temple provides more evidence they were priests and temple keepers.

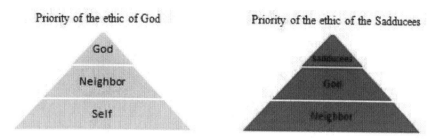

CHAPTER 3
The Essenes

THE ESSENES, ANOTHER JEWISH SECT of the time, responded to the hard times by fleeing conflicts created by the lawless multicultural insurgence. The Essenes have a possible connection with the Dead Sea scrolls of the now famous Qumran community. They lived a life similar to the European monks. Their life was spent studying biblical texts and possibly writing commentary derived from their study. Scholars believe the Essenes lived in celibacy. The community survived through an influx of men or youth wishing to join their way of life. According to scholars of the Qumran community, the Essenes were communal, sharing all they had equally among the group as any had need. The New Testament Christians mentioned in the book of Acts 4:32-5:11 may have copied their communal lifestyle from the Essenes.

If the lifestyle of the Essenes was copied by the Christian community in Acts, the source of the communal system described by Friedrich Engels in the Communist Manifesto may also be Essene. According to Eduard Bernstein, a prominent figure in the Communist movement of the 19th century, the Communist communal system's roots came from the Christian community described in Acts. In that regard, Essene culture may have influenced mankind to the very end of time.

The priorities of the Essenes may have been in line with God's ethic. However, there is not enough information on the Essenes to be sure. The absence of the Essenes at the cross and in the New Testament may be telling since the New Testament focuses on the adversarial relationship between the Pharisees, Sadducees, and Jesus. Further, there are some scholars who suggest John the Baptist's appearance from the desert indicates he may have been Essene.

Sadducees, Pharisees, and Essenes were not the only Jewish sects holding to a particular version of Judaism in the intertestamental period. There were the Hasidim, the pious (studious) ones, and the Zealots, who would fight anyone who challenged their religious beliefs as well as Hellenized Jews who freely joined with the opposing lawless Greek culture. Most, if not all, of the Jewish sects struggled with the ethic of God. It was much easier to blend in or surrender the Jewish faith to the invading cultures. The easier path led the Jewish faithful to lawlessness as an ethical priority.

CHAPTER 4
Gentiles

§

To make matters worse during the era before Christ, the conquerors brought their own gods with them. The lawless Greek cultural insurgence brought by Alexander the Great was particularly destabilizing. After Alexander's death, the territories he conquered were divided among his generals. Eventually a Greek emperor named Antiochus Epiphanies IV came to reign over the Jewish region. Antiochus portrayed himself as the Greek god Zeus. He sought to transform the Jewish culture into a Grecian one. The historical term used for this attempted transformation of Jewish culture is the *Hellenization of the Jews.*

Greek athletic events were staged for the purpose of aiding in this transformation. Stadiums were erected, and Jews were forced to attend Grecian events. Some of the athletic events had Greek athletes competing in the nude. For the lawless Greeks, nude athletic activity was normal, but it was shocking and obvious lawlessness to the Jewish crowds. The idea behind the events was that once the Jews experienced the superior lawless culture of the Greeks, they would readily convert and adopt the lawless ethic of the Greeks.

Antiochus understood that in order to replace Jewish culture, he had to replace the source of Jewish culture, which was the Hebrew God and God's ethic. However, his attempt to replace the Hebrew God and the ethic of God went badly. The plan was to challenge the Hebrew God and expose His inferiority to Zeus, thereby causing Zeus to reign as chief of the gods. The Greek god, of course, was actually Antiochus Epiphanies IV.

Antiochus sent some Greeks, along with Hellenized Jews, to force a Jewish priest named *Maccabeus* to sacrifice a pig on the sacred Jewish altar. In the Jewish faith a pig is considered to be an unclean animal and unsuitable for sacrifice to God. This sacrifice was to the Greek god Zeus (Antiochus Epiphanies IV had declared himself Zeus manifest on earth). The Jews called this act the *Abomination of Desolation*. It was the worst act the lawless Gentile community could possibly do to the Jewish community. In effect, this action involved asking the Jewish people to recant their faith in the Hebrew God in favor of worshipping a man by declaring him to be Zeus, a Greek god. It was an outrageous display of lawlessness.

Maccabeus refused to offer the sacrifice, killing both a Hellenized Jew standing with the Greeks and the Greek officer. The rest of the Greek contingent were rushed and killed by the Maccabean group. The event set off the *Maccabean revolt*, which eventually freed the Jews from their Greek conquerors. The celebration commemorating the successful revolution is called *Hanukkah* and is celebrated to this day in Jewish communities.

The Jewish Maccabean revolution produced sovereign rule over the Jewish homeland. The ruling body of the Jewish people following the era of the Greeks was called the *Hasmonean Dynasty*. However, the Jewish sects were set regarding their lawless perspectives, and Judaism as God intended it was now barely recognizable among the competing Jewish factions in the Hasmonean era.

Following the Hasmonean era was the lawless Roman era, which resulted in a further destabilization of the Jewish ethical norms. By the time Christ was born and His subsequent ministry occurred, an overabundance of lawless Jewish religious perspectives dominated the Jewish people. One question comes to mind: did Judaism in its original state even exist among the Jews during the time Christ walked the earth? Could the lawless ethical worldviews have changed the Jews' religious experience to the point Judaism mutated into lawlessness rather than Judaism? In Matthew

13:14-15, Christ embraced the Isaiah prophecy which told of a time when the people would not hear or see their God even though they had ears to hear and eyes to see (Isaiah 6:9-10).

Jesus declared that He was from the Jewish God. If Jesus is from God, the Jews did not recognize Him as such, and they crucified Him for His declaration. Jesus was crucified by the people of God, but what god?

Christians believe Jesus Christ came from the Jewish God, who is affectionately called Father by Jew and Christian alike. From a Christian perspective, how could the Jews not recognize that Jesus came from the Father? Why could the Jewish priests and sects who studied their particular version of Judaism not recognize the manifestation of their God?

The answers to those questions are found in the cycles of Christianity.

Christ's Birth: The International Initiative of God

WHEN CHRIST CAME TO EARTH, His goal was more than reestablishing Judaism among the Jewish people. Christ opened the door to an international society which would be called by His name. He sought to organize and launch God's version of international Judaism, i.e., God's ethic without the system of animal sacrifices. The new way (cycle) offered salvation through the sacrifice and resurrection of Christ. While there would be smaller cycles within the scope of this new way through ongoing history, the new way (Christianity) is representative of the beginning of the last cycle. The end of Christianity is the end of the Bible and the end of the salvation story.

The gospel (good news/truth) is that Christ died for all the lawlessness (sin) of all men; in consequence, all men are invited to accept Christ as their sacrifice before God and live and obey the statutes of God.

The righteousness of God through faith in Jesus Christ for all who believe for there is no distinction: For all have sinned (committed lawlessness) and fall short of the glory of God (Romans 3:21-25).

After Christ's resurrection, Christ went to be with the Father in heaven, leaving His followers with the promise that He would return and end the cyclic nature of God's relationship with mankind, thus also ending the biblical story.

The apostles preached and took the message of Christ to the Jews. On their missionary trips, they first preached the gospel in synagogues. When the Jews rejected Christ's message, the apostles then took the message to the Gentile communities in what is now called Turkey, Greece, Italy, Asia and North Africa.

In Jerusalem, the apostles focused on the Jewish community (Acts 1-8) in an attempt to include the Jews and Judaism. These followers of Christ believed that the new way introduced through Jesus' sacrifice was a necessary evolution of Judaism.

In the writings contained within the four Gospels, the apostles connected Christ with the elimination of the sacrificial system of Judaism.

The epistles from the apostles, which make up the balance of the New Testament, taught from the well of God's ethic, which included the Ten Commandments and Levitical law. The major difference in their teaching from Old Testament writings was that Christ's sacrifice had now eliminated forever the sacrificial system of Judaism. That is why Christ is called the Lamb of God and why Christianity was eventually considered to be the child of Judaism.

The Great Commission is the stated mission of Christ's initiative to expand the ethic of God to the international community. It was given to His disciples/apostles to organize and launch the initiative to save those who would accept the message of Christ and thus God's ethic (way of life).

And Jesus came and said to them, "All authority in heaven and on earth has been given to me. Go therefore and make disciples of all nations, baptizing them in the name of the Father, and of the Son and of the Holy Spirit. ___Teaching them to observe all that I have commanded you___*. And behold I am with you always, to the end of the age (Matthew 28:18-20)."*

In order to help launch the initiative to offer salvation to the international community, Christ granted powers to the apostles that humans do not normally have. Power of healing, power to speak in languages of the international community (speaking in tongues), power to harness the power of demons and demonic activity, and power of the knowledge of heaven was given to all the apostles of Christ at the Pentecost, except Paul (Acts 2). Paul acquired his powers individually as a result of meeting with Christ on the Damascus road (Acts 9).

The new way of worshipping God was introduced through Jesus' apostles. It was eventually called Christianity after its founder, Christ. The ethic of Christ spread to the international community, defeating lawlessness (ruling ethic of the specific Gentile societies) in communities where people and communities accepted Christ.

It is not practical to list all the individual rules and teachings regarding the Christian church. However, the following are rules, passed down by Jesus' apostles, which serve to establish God's ethic among international communities and differentiate original Christianity from man's ethic imposed by lawlessness.

In order to define the Christian church, one must turn to Jesus and His Apostles for the rules of an apostolic church.

First Rule

§

FIRST, JESUS IS GOD MANIFEST on earth. The Apostle Paul stated in Philippians 2:6 that Jesus existed in the very form of God. However, Jesus did not lean on His divine nature when He was among mankind. He came as a man in order to offer life to mankind and instruct those who chose Him in the study of God. The original students of Jesus are the men we now call the Apostles of Christ. In the Gospel of John, Jesus revealed how close His relationship was with His students (apostles) when He said in John 13:34:

> *A new commandment I give to you, that you love one another: just as I have loved you, you also are to love one another. By this all people will know that you are my disciples, if you have love for one another.*

In John 14 Jesus answers a question from Philip when he requested to see the Father (God). Jesus explains to Philip that he has seen God (the Father) because Philip has seen Jesus. In the conversation with Philip, Jesus encourages him to believe, if not the image of Jesus (God), then the works He has performed as God.

> *Philip said to him, "Lord, show us the Father, and it is enough for us." Jesus said to him, "Have I been with you so long, and you still do not know me, Philip? Whoever has seen me has seen the Father . . . The words that I say to you I do not speak on my own authority, but the Father*

who dwells in me does his works. Believe me that I am in the Father and the Father is in me, or else believe on account of the works themselves (John 14:8-11)."

So, the first rule of the Christian Church is: **Jesus Christ was in the form of God and came to earth in the form of man** (Philippians 2:6-7). If the first rule includes the Hebrew God as the source of Jesus Christ's divine nature, all things which follow in Christ must also agree with God the Father (Old Testament) since their source/nature is the same. In the Gospel of John, Jesus repeats over and over again that He must carry out the will of the Father, which is of course His own nature/will in this first rule of the Christian Church. God and Christ are of the same divine form.

CHAPTER 2

Second Rule

§

THE APOSTLES WERE FIRST OF all students of Jesus. Of course, if the apostles were students of Jesus, they were students of God. One might say the apostles went to the University of God (UG) with God as their professor during the three years of Jesus' ministry on earth. It was a personalized study of God for twelve of them, and three of the twelve received one-on-one tutoring. While the twelve students called apostles were closest to Jesus during His ministry on earth, there were at least seventy more students who are known to have been studying under Christ at UG (Luke 10). After Jesus was crucified on the cross and resurrected, He left His ministry and witness to be carried out by the apostles. Jesus specifically informs the apostles:

You shall be witness to Me in Jerusalem, and in all Judea and Samaria, and to the end of the earth (Acts 1:8).

So, the second rule of the Christian Church is: the apostles, who are the students of Jesus, are the witnesses Jesus charged with the ministry of Christ. All things Christian come from the witness of the apostles in the New Testament.

CHAPTER 3

Third Rule

THE THIRD RULE IS: THE **apostles are the only authority for rulemaking in the Christian Church.**

Where did the name Christ come from? Messiah is a word from the Old Testament reflecting the Jewish religious prophecy and hopes of a king appointed by God in order to bring about a destruction of lawlessness and so preserve a selection of mankind for Himself.

In the Jewish point of view, the emergence of the Messiah would result in peace on earth. The word Christ is a translation of the word "messiah" from the early Hebrew language into "Christ" in early Koine Greek. It was first translated into Koine Greek in a text called the Greek Septuagint (Greek translation of the Old Testament). The Septuagint translation occurred in the second century before Jesus' birth. The apostles referred to Jesus in the context of the Old Testament prophets' prediction of the coming of the Messiah (Hebrew) or Christ (Koine Greek). Since the apostles were students of Christ, bearing witness to Christ's divine nature with God and His mission of salvation, people outside the apostolic church began calling the apostles of Christ and their converts *Christians.* The first documented source of the followers of Christ being called Christian is in Acts 11:26:

And in Antioch the disciples were first called Christian.

The students of Christ are responsible for writing the New Testament (rules for the Christian church). One might say the books of the New

Testament are the papers written by the students of God. Authority for rulemaking concerning the Christian church comes from the papers written by these students of God (apostles). Now that these papers have been written and the apostles who wrote them are gone, any change in the rules of the Christian church cannot be validated and therefore must be categorized as another religion. The Apostle Paul makes this point in Galatians 1:6, 11:

> *I (Apostle Paul) am astonished that you are so quickly deserting him who called you in the grace of Christ and are turning to a different gospel— not that there is another one . . . For I would have you know, brothers, that the gospel that was preached by me is not man's gospel.*

The reference to the gospel in Galatians is the gospel Paul was given by the twelve apostles. In 1 Corinthians 15:3, Paul reveals a source that could have only came from the apostles of Christ.

> *For I delivered to you first of all that which I also received: that Christ died for our sins according to the Scriptures.*

The apostles left the rules for the Christian church in their papers, which are called the New Testament. If a church practices a religion under different rules, they cannot realistically be called Christian. A comparable analogy would be if a player walked onto a basketball court with a nine iron and chipped a golf ball into the basketball net. The game the player was attempting to play could not be called basketball. Although the playing area might look the same, the change in rules concerning how the game is played would require the game to be categorized as another game.

It is acceptable in mankind's society to create new games, and it is acceptable to create new religions. With respect to religions, it is unlawful in the United States to interfere with a person engaging in any type of religious worship they desire. However, as has been discussed, changing the rules changes the religious category. In fact, the crucifixion of Christ under Christian rules eliminated the required sacrifices under Judaism, and the rule change required the new way of worship to be called something besides Judaism. The new name was initially simply "the Way." Later in Antioch the new religious experience was called Christian after Christ.

CHAPTER 4
Fourth Rule

§

THE FOURTH RULE IS: CHRISTIANS **and Christian churches are about**
God and Christ's mission to save those who believe salvation is
through Jesus.

The papers of the apostles are centered on Christ as God and His mission to earth. The mission was to take from God's creation of mankind
a selection of mankind to live with Him in heaven. In other words, Jesus
is a vessel like Noah's Ark (Genesis 6-9) which exists to save species by
individual selection. One may choose or one may be chosen to board the
Ark of Jesus. Those who believe Jesus is God (the Ark builder) and board
the Ark will be saved. The mission is to save all men with whom God is
pleased. God tells mankind that He is pleased with those who obey His
laws and He is displeased with those who practice lawlessness.

In order to understand Jesus' attempt to save all mankind, the Ark of
Jesus might be compared to secular desires and hopes to save mankind by
finding a distant planet which is inhabitable by mankind. In this salvation
story, mankind's mission to save all mankind involves moving a representative few members of mankind to a friendly planet. In that way mankind
as an entire species would be saved by the salvation of the few. Likewise,
Jesus only has to move a representative from each race of mankind in
order to save all of mankind. An invitation to save every man or woman
is in place; however, salvation of everyone who has existed on earth is not
necessary to save the species (creation). Those with whom God is pleased

will board the Ark built by Jesus' life, death, and resurrection. That is why when Christ was born the text in the gospel of Luke states:

> *Glory to God in the highest, and on earth peace among those with whom He is pleased (Luke 2:14).*

The text is often misquoted to read: *"And on earth peace goodwill toward all men."* Men have intentionally left out the part in the original text which states: *"with whom He is pleased."* The idea behind the lawless interpretation was to include an "equality of man" component in order to convince all men to be Christian. However, the apostles' papers reflect God's initiative to save mankind through obedience of mankind; mankind will be selected according to God's pleasure.

The papers of the apostles quote Jesus when He gave the rule for the Christian church:

> *He said, "You shall love the Lord your God with all your heart and with all your soul and with all your mind. This is the great and first commandment (Matthew 22:37)."*

In other words, the Christian church is not about equality of man. It is about God and His mission to save a representative number among His creation of mankind for a society in a place where He has provided.

CHAPTER 5
Fifth Rule

§

THE FIFTH RULE OF THE **Christian church is that from God's nature three persons exist: Father, Son and Holy Spirit. Christians call the three the Trinity.**

Christians believe that upon their acceptance of Christ as the Savior of mankind, God sends His Holy Spirit to be with them during the Christian's life on earth. In fact, Jesus promised that those who came to Him would receive the Holy Spirit to help them keep His ethic along life's journey during their time on earth. God, Christ, and the Holy Spirit are three persons in one form and share the same nature. Christians call this formation of God, Son, and the Holy Spirit the Trinity.

The word Trinity was first used to describe the Father, Son, and Holy Spirit in the second century by an early church father named Theophilus of Antioch. Of course, the word "Trinity" is not itself found in the Bible. However the doctrine of the three—Father, Son and Holy Spirit—is found in the beginning of the Old Testament (Genesis 1:1-4) and throughout Scripture.

*In the beginning, **God created** the heavens and the earth. The earth was without form and void, and darkness was over the face of the deep. And the **Spirit of God** was hovering over the face of the waters (Genesis 1:1-2).*

And God said, "Let there be light (Genesis 1:3)."

And God said, "Let there be an expanse in the midst of the waters, and let it separate the waters from the waters (Genesis 1:6)."

The Gospel of John echoes the Genesis scripture. God and the Word (defined in chapter 1 as Jesus) were present from the beginning.

In the beginning was the Word, and the Word was with God, and the Word was God (John 1:1).

In addition, the Holy Spirit was present with God and the Word (Jesus), both "in the beginning" according to Genesis 1:1 and with Jesus during His temptation by Satan (Luke 4).

And Jesus, full of the Holy Spirit, returned from Jordan and was led by the Spirit in the wilderness for forty days, being tempted by the devil (Luke 4:14).

However, the final word regarding the Trinity should rest at the feet of Jesus. Jesus believed in the three and declared to the apostles in the Great Commission:

All authority in heaven and on earth has been given to me. Go therefore and make disciples of all nations, baptizing them in the name of the Father and the Son and of the Holy Spirit (Matthew 28:18-19).

CHAPTER 6
Sixth Rule

§

THE SIXTH RULE IS: GENTILE churches following Jesus may be called Christian churches if they renounce "(eating) sacrificed idols, blood, (and) what has been strangled (and) sexual immorality (Acts 15:20, 29)."

In order to start the process, the apostles of Christ first had to convince at least a few people that Christ was from the God of the Israelites. Peter, one of the three closest students to Christ at UG, gave a sermon which chronicled the miraculous demonstrations meant to bear witness to Christ's divinity (Acts 2:14-39). Furthermore, three of the Gospels, Matthew, Mark, and John, are papers written by these students of God as witnesses to Christ's divinity. The miracles recorded in the Gospels are evidence from eyewitness (apostles/students at UG) accounts of divine intervention by God in the world of mankind. The letters to individual churches (epistles) seek to set the rules of the church which follows Christ as God.

There arose a concern among the early Christian church and the original apostles around ethnicity. All the apostles were religious converts from Judaism, and, of course Jesus was a Jew. All of the apostles had originally been indoctrinated into Judaism through family and rabbis within the Jewish community. As mentioned before, the new way of church Christ introduced was also based in the Old Testament which, of course, is where Judaism is found. Furthermore, the Jews believed they were the children of God. For Jews the only religion was Judaism.

However, the Apostle Paul had taken Christianity to the Gentile communities in Turkey in a city called Antioch (see Acts). The Gentile community in Antioch which converted to Christianity had no background in Judaism as the Christians in Jerusalem did. The Levitical law and religious requirements of Judaism were not practiced among the group in Antioch. The Gentile Christians of the era ate foods like pork, which was prohibited by Judaism. They worshipped the same God in heaven, but different rules applied. Ceremonies involving ritual cleansing were also observed by Jews, but not participated in by the Gentile Christians. Some Jewish Christians called into question the practice of the Gentile Christians in Antioch and even demanded that if they wished to follow Christ, they would have to go through the process established in the Old Testament in order to become Jews. These Jews thought the Gentile Christians must follow the laws of Judaism.

In addition, it should be noted that for the Jew at this point in history, ethnicity was a very simple issue. If you were not a Jew, you were a Gentile (ethnic). For the Jewish Christian in the days of the early church, ethnicity was a national separation rather than a racial one—the Jewish nation against the lawless nations in the world. Ethnicity was not as much about genetic makeup, but more a national and a religious presence.

The issue was whether Christianity was a national or international initiative. This was a serious question for the apostles, who were raised in a nationalistic political and religious environment. Was the law of God, and consequently the love of God, through salvation to be extended to the lawless nations of the world? In other words, are Christians nationalists or internationalists?

The division between the apostles concerning the Christians in Antioch caused a crisis for the early church, resulting in their calling a meeting to deal with the crisis. The meeting is called the Jerusalem Council and is memorialized in Acts 15. A debate ensued among the students of God as to whether God intended to include people from groups outside of Judaism in the way of worship introduced by Christ. The meeting resulted in the apostles agreeing that Christ had always intended to offer salvation to all nations and people through the way of worship Christ had introduced to the students of God during His ministry, death, and resurrection.

A letter was drafted to the church of Antioch which set up the rules under which Gentile communities might be counted among the Christian church left by Jesus to the oversight of the apostles. The following, found in Acts 15:23-29, is the text of that letter:

Greetings

Since we have heard that some <u>persons</u> *have gone out from us and troubled you with words, unsettling your minds, although we gave them no instructions, it has seemed good to us, having come to one accord, to choose men and send them to you with our beloved Barnabas and Paul, men who have risked their lives for the name of our Lord* <u>Jesus Christ</u>. *We have therefore sent Judas and Silas, who themselves will tell you the same things by word of mouth. For it has seemed good to the Holy Spirit and to us to lay on you no greater burden than these requirements: **<u>that you abstain from what has been sacrificed to idols, and from blood, and from what has been strangled, and from sexual immorality. If you keep yourselves from these, you will do well. Farewell.</u>***

Seventh Rule

§

THE SEVENTH RULE IS: HEAVEN **is not on earth; heaven is the place Jesus has gone to prepare for those who choose to believe in Him as Savior of mankind.**

As can be found in the papers of the apostles, Jesus told them, and consequently His other followers, that He was going to prepare a place for them and that He would one day return to gather the ones with whom He is pleased (John 14:1-3). In other words, He will be back to gather those who have been chosen or have chosen to board the Ark built by Jesus as their God. Since the lawless will have their utopian society here on earth, they feel no need of Jesus, God, or gods. Modern lawless society has replaced God's law with an envisioned lawless utopian society. Feigned approval of religion is a diversion intended to mask their actual motives to destroy any competitive utopian societies such as was promised by Christ.

With respect to lawlessness, it strives to promote heaven on earth. Consider Moses Hess, an early lawless leader, who stated that the goal of the lawless was to have the equality Christians were looking for in heaven become a reality in this current life. In other words, lawless individuals desire to have their heaven here on earth.

How could Christ participate in a political movement which outlawed His participation? The utopia Christ has promised is not the same utopia promised by mankind.

CHAPTER 8
Eighth Rule

§

THE EIGHTH RULE IS THAT **the nation of Israel is the Bride of God (*Isaiah, Hosea*) and the Christian church as seen in the New Testament is the Bride of Christ *(Ephesians)*.** The Old Testament metaphor describing Israel as the Bride of God uses a marriage relationship in order to compare the worship of other gods and/or mixing worship of other gods to that of a spouse having sexual relationships with others during the marriage. In other words, the people of God, the nation of Israel, sought to try out other forms of worship and even mix those forms of worship with the worship of God. The biblical text reveals that this betrayal was particularly traumatic to God's nature.

Can two walk together, unless they agree (Amos 3:3)?

"If a man divorces his wife and she goes from him and becomes another man's wife, will he return to her? Would not that land be greatly polluted? You have played the whore with many lovers; and would you return to me?" declares the LORD. "Lift up your eyes to the bare heights, and see! Where have you not been ravished? By the waysides you have sat awaiting lovers like an Arab in the wilderness. You have polluted the land with your vile whoredom. Therefore the showers have been withheld, and the spring rain has not come; yet you have the forehead of a whore; you refuse to be ashamed. Have you not just now called to me, 'My father, you are the friend of my youth—will he be angry forever, will he be

indignant to the end?' Behold, you have spoken, but you have done all the evil that you could (Jeremiah 3:1-5)."

It was as if a spouse brought her new lovers home to live and share the marriage bed with her husband. The Old Testament prophets tell the story of God's pain.

Amos and Jeremiah are only two of the Old Testament prophets who tell of Israel's betrayal of God and how God feels about being betrayed. Amos 5 further explains God's reaction to His bride expecting Him to accept the bride's adultery with her new lovers in the house God built for Himself and His bride.

"I hate, I despise your feasts, and I take no delight in your solemn assemblies. Even though you offer me your burnt offerings and grain offerings, I will not accept them; and the peace offerings of your fattened animals, I will not look upon them. Take away from me the noise of your songs; to the melody of your harps I will not listen. But let justice roll down like waters, and righteousness like an ever-flowing stream. Did you bring to me sacrifices and offerings during the forty years in the wilderness, O house of Israel? You shall take up Sikkuth your king, and Kiyyun your star-god—your images that you made for yourselves, and I will send you into exile beyond Damascus," says the LORD, *whose name is the God of hosts.*

God had called the nation of Israel to an exclusive relationship. The relationship mirrored the marriage commitment between a man and woman on earth. The people broke from the exclusive relationship and sought after other gods, other relationships. The bride sought to impose her will on her husband and demanded God enter into a relationship with the bride and her new lovers. The bride was dictating the terms by which God would have to submit if He wished to continue His relationship with her. The people became sovereigns over their own destiny, and as a result, God opted out.

"You shall take up Sikkuth your king, and Kiyyun your star-god—your images that you made for yourselves, and I will send you into exile beyond Damascus," says the LORD, whose name is the God of hosts."

The relationship between God and the nation of Israel became strained. In Isaiah 50:1, God compares the state of the relationship to a divorce:

Thus says the Lord: "Where is your mother's certificate of divorce, with which I sent her away?"

The Israelite religion is Judaism; i.e., worshipping the God of Abraham through God's ethic in the Old Testament. Jesus sprang from the very womb of God's bride Israel and its religion Judaism (ethic). Jesus is a Jew, and His bride is the Christian nation of believers (Gentiles/mixed marriage), just as the bride of the Father is the Israelite nation. The husband/wife relationship of Christ and the Christian Church is beautifully explained in Ephesians 5:22-32:

Wives, submit to your own husbands, as to the Lord. For the husband is the head of the wife even as Christ is the head of the church, his body, and is himself its Savior. Now as the church submits to Christ, so also wives should submit fin everything to their husbands.

*Husbands love your wives, as Christ loved the church and gave himself up for her, that he might sanctify her, having cleansed her by the washing of water with the word, so that he might present the church to himself in splendor, without spot or wrinkle or any such thing, that she might be holy and without blemish. In the same way husbands should love their wives as their own bodies. He who loves his wife loves himself. For no one ever hated his own flesh, but nourishes and cherishes it, just as Christ does the church, because we are members of his body. Therefore a man shall leave his father and mother and hold fast to his wife, and the two shall become one flesh. **This mystery is profound, and I am saying that it refers to Christ and the church.***

It must be noted that the lawless community does not accept this metaphor for it requires submission of the Christian wife to the Christian husband. However, with respect to the Christian church, the church must submit to Christ's authority. To do otherwise is to invite comparison with the Jewish worship services in Amos.

The early Christian church and its rules evolved from the writings of Christ's students (gospels and epistles/New Testament) and subsequent mentoring by the students of Jesus. The early church held on to the writings and tradition handed down from the students of Christ and formed the doctrine of the early Christian church accordingly.

CHAPTER 9

Cultural Setting at the Time of Christ

§

THE WORLD AT THE TIME of Christ practiced lawlessness and worship of the gods. Fertility gods in the Near East were old enemies of Judaism. An example of the gods of the Near Eastern area may be found in the image of "Baal," the Canaanite god. Cultic practices required sacrifice of the firstborn of the Baal follower. The sacrifice of the first child born was performed in order to ensure the individual follower's economic future. God hated child sacrifice for any reason. In Numbers 3:11, He gives an alternative for the Israelites:

> *And the Lord spoke to Moses, saying, "Behold, I have taken the Levites from among the people of Israel instead of every firstborn who opens the womb among the people of Israel."*

Asherah, the mistress god of Baal, required the practice of ritual sex. The followers of Baal and Asherah believed the sexual relationship of the two gods would bring better crops and consequently a better harvest. Their followers practiced immoral sex before their gods in order to entice the two gods into having sexual relations, which their followers believed would make them prosperous.

God hates sexual immorality (lawlessness) and spent significant attention on it in the Torah, making laws against it. In the ethic of God, sexual immorality is prohibited and is considered lawlessness. The book of Leviticus is particularly explicit on this ethical requirement.

During the Roman rule, the time of Christ, the gods who required that their followers practice lawlessness in worship were: Jupiter (Zeus to Greeks), Artemis (fertility goddess), Aphrodite, (goddess of love), Dionysus (Greek god of orgies), and Pan (a Greek god similar to Dionysus).

There were many other gods, perhaps thousands, in the Mediterranean theater of the era. Christians in their writings in the New Testament wrote of the struggles with the gods of the Mediterranean area. One example is in Acts 19:35:

> *And when the town clerk had quieted the crowd, he said, "Men of Ephesus, who is there who does not know that the city of the Ephesians is the temple keeper of the great Artemis, and of the sacred stone that fell from the sky."*

In Corinth the temple of the goddess Aphrodite is reported to have held over a thousand prostitutes during the time period of the Corinthian church as mentioned in the New Testament.

The Christian church was formed by apostles of Christ and those who followed Jesus in order to introduce to the world God's salvation through Christ and the ethical way of life of God.

CHAPTER 10
Gift of the Holy Spirit

AFTER JESUS' SACRIFICE ON THE Cross and His departure to the Father (Acts 1:1), the early church consisted of just a small group of Christ followers. These men and women were told to wait on the Holy Spirit, for the power of the movement would be in the coming gift of the Holy Spirit:

> *But you will receive power when the Holy Spirit has come upon you, and you will be my witness in Jerusalem and in all Judea and Samaria, and to the end of the earth (Acts 1:8).*

The apostles of Christ and fellow Jesus-followers huddled together in Jerusalem, awaiting the gift of the Holy Spirit which came to them on the day of Pentecost (Acts 2). The Holy Spirit transformed those who received it into powerful witnesses to Christ's life, death and resurrection.

This transformation of one's spirit by the Holy Spirit is the engine which drives God's international initiative to reach the world of lawlessness. The transformation of one's spirit into something which God may use to further His Kingdom is called by Christians **"the conversion experience."** One may compare the transformation to a quickening experience in pregnancy. New life felt in the mother's womb for the first time is called quickening. The concept carries the notion that a new life has stirred within the old life.

A parody of the above analogy would be the imagined concept of the vampire world. In the imaginary world of vampires, once a vampire bites a human, he/she is transformed into a new creature and becomes a citizen of a world apart from the natural world.

However, the Christian conversion experience is not imagination. Jesus spoke of the phenomenon in the book of John, chapter three when He was addressed by a rabbi named Nicodemus. Jesus' comments on being **"born again"** carry the meaning of the conversion experience or quickening one must receive to enter the Kingdom God.

This man came to Jesus by night and said to him, Rabbi, we know that you are a teacher come from God, for no one can do these signs that you do unless God is with him.

Jesus answered him, "Truly, truly, I say to you, unless one is born again he cannot see the kingdom of God."

Nicodemus said to him, "How can a man be born when he is old? Can he enter a second time into his mother's womb and be born?"

Jesus answered, "Truly, truly, I say to you, unless one is born of water and the Spirit, he cannot enter the kingdom of God.

That which is born of the flesh is flesh, and that which is born of the Spirit is spirit. Do not marvel that I said to you, 'You must be born again.'"

Jesus was speaking of the spirit of man passing through a spiritual amniotic immersion, a transforming baptism of the Holy Spirit. Jesus stated the issue contrasting the earthly birth against the heavenly birth in three ways:

Jesus' Comparison of Earthly and Heavenly Spirit

Born of water	*Born of Spirit*
Flesh is flesh	*Spirit is spirit*
I have told you earthly things and you do not believe	*How can you believe if I tell you heavenly things*

As the Holy Spirit penetrates the soul, transforming it, the spirit of the individual is reborn into a new existence which is called to live the ethic (way of life) of God.

While the Christian conversion accepts Jesus' sacrifice as a once-for-all sacrifice and replacement of the sacrificial system of Judaism, **Christians are not uncoupled from the ethic of God which was given in the Torah**. Consider Jesus' statement in Matthew 5: 17:

> *Do not think that I have come to abolish the Law and the Prophets; I have not come to abolish them but to fulfill them.*

One may see the tension of the requirement to fulfill the ethic of God with the new initiative of salvation offered to the world by Christ in the life and writing of the Apostle Paul.

> *If one is in Christ, he is a new creation (2 Corinthians 5:17).*

> *Do not be unequally yoked with unbelievers. For what partnership has righteousness with lawlessness? Or what fellowship has light with darkness (2 Corinthians 6:14)?*

The Holy Spirit's transformation not only changes the human spirit into a new creation, but also serves as a helper in resisting the converted body's desire to embrace the lawlessness of the converted human's previous life.

> *When the Spirit of truth comes, he will guide you into all the truth, for he will not speak on his own authority, but whatever he hears he will speak, and he will declare to you the things that are to come (John 16:12).*

So according to Christ, what is a Christian? **A Christian is an individual whose spirit has been transformed by the Holy Spirit into a new spirit.** The new spirit requires that the individual follow the ethic of God given in the Torah.

For Gentiles, exceptions are given in Acts 15 (the Jerusalem Council). Gentiles are not required to be Jews (ritual cleansing, circumcision, and prohibitions against eating wrong foods). However, the ethic of God is still required of the new convert. The Ten Commandments and laws given in Exodus and Leviticus concerning sexual immorality, God's sovereignty, and civic discourse are required to be followed. Further, recognition of a Christian is manifest in the daily exhibition of the obedience to the Ten Commandments and laws against sexual immorality and following the ethic of God in their daily experiences.

It was understood by Christ and the apostles that there would be those who claim the name of Christ but would not have experienced the conversion. Christ addressed the issue of identification of true Christians in Matthew 7:15-20:

> *Beware of false prophets, who come to you in sheep's clothing but inwardly are ravenous wolves. You will recognize them by their fruits. Are grapes gathered from thorn bushes, or figs from thistles? So, every healthy tree bears good fruit, but the diseased tree bears bad fruit. A healthy tree cannot bear bad fruit, nor can a diseased tree bear good fruit. Every tree that does not bear good fruit is cut down and thrown into the fire. Thus you will recognize them by their fruits.*

Those who call themselves Christian but do not act out God's ethic (bear Christian fruit) are not Christian. For example, if someone says he/she is Christian but acts in opposition to the ethic of God as given in the Christian Bible, they are Christian in name only. They identify with Christ's salvation, but reject His ethical way of life. Those leaders who work to displace God's ethic with the ethic of man or other gods are not Christian, even if they insist they are. How could a man or woman who has been transformed by God's Holy Spirit and has the Holy Spirit living inside his own spirit as a helper overcome God's influence and work to displace the ethic of God? Is man's spirit stronger than God's Spirit such that he may override the purposes of God?

If Christ introduced an international movement to change the ethical worldview of people on earth, what was the status quo with respect to the ethic of man? Why did God come to earth and plan a crucifixion experience so horrible for His Son? What was so bad with the ethic of mankind?

Judaism (God's ethic) was designed by God to introduce a way of life free of other gods and the lawless ethic people on earth had learned through their daily experiences absent of God. **The mission of the Christian church is to affect the peoples of the world through the witness that individual conversion experience brings when it occurs in an individual.**

> *And Jesus came and said to them, "All authority in heaven and on earth has been given to me. Go therefore and make disciples of all nations, baptizing them in the name of the Father and of the Son and of the Holy Spirit, teaching them to observe all that I have commanded you. And behold, I am with you always, to the end of the age (Matthew 28:18-20)."*

The conversion of individuals in the lawless communities of the world seeds the following of God's ethic. Those who are converted will board the Ark of Jesus for the last exodus and go with Jesus to the place Christians call heaven (return to the Garden of Eden).

The mission of the Christian church is to fill the ark of Jesus with men and women who receive the conversion and follow Him in the ethic of God while Jesus is away. When the ark is full, the churches work is complete.

Early Christian Church

THE EARLY CHURCH PERIOD BEGAN at the Pentecost in Jerusalem, which was the moment when the Holy Spirit joined with the souls of men for the purpose of reaching the international community with the message of Christ. One may view the early church as the beginning of mankind's push to the end of the last cycle.

The book of Acts may be used to follow the actions of the apostles in the early church period.

+ After the Pentecost and empowered by the Holy Spirit, the apostles began preaching to crowds in Jerusalem. The preaching was heard in many languages (spoken in tongues). Three thousand were converted in one sermon made by the apostle Peter. The three thousand increased the community of followers in Jerusalem greatly (Acts 2: 41).
+ The new way of Judaism (Christian community) organized and developed a social order. The social order is described in Acts 4:32-5:11. The social order was probably adopted from the Essenes, a Jewish sect, which lived in the Dead Sea area. The *Manual of Discipline* left behind by the Essenes of the Dead Sea community reveals the social construct of its ancient community.
+ Stephen (the first Christian martyr) was stoned to death in Jerusalem for professing Christ as the Messiah. Paul attended the stoning of Stephen. At the time Paul was not an apostle; he had not been converted and at the time of Stephen's stoning he approved of the murder of Christians (Acts 7: 58).
+ Paul directed Jewish attempts to stamp-out/destroy the new way of Judaism (Christianity). He was on his way to Damascus to apprehend followers of Christ and bring them to Jerusalem for punishment (Acts 9).

But Saul (Paul), still breathing threats and murder against the disciples of the Lord, went to the high priest and asked him for letters to the synagogues at Damascus, so that if he found any belonging to the Way, men or women, he might bring them bound to Jerusalem (Acts 9:1-2)

- Paul was converted by Christ on the road to Damascus. Paul began preaching the new way of Christ, and the Jewish leaders sought to kill him (Acts 9:23).
- Paul was accepted by the disciples of Christ as an apostle and was given the gospel

For I delivered to you as of first importance what I also received: that Christ died for our sins in accordance with the Scriptures, that He was buried, that He was raised on the third day in accordance with the Scriptures, and that He appeared to Cephas (Peter), then to the twelve (1 Corinthians 15:3-5).

- Peter preached to some Gentiles, and they were converted to Christ (Acts 10).
- The church at Antioch was formed and the new way was given a new name: Christian.
- Paul began his first mission trip (Acts 13).
- The international nature of the Christian message was challenged and confirmed by the apostles. The Jerusalem Council struck down ethnic barriers in the Christian community while maintaining the divine ethical discipline of the Torah (Acts 15).
- Paul's missionary work seeds churches across the Roman Empire.
- Paul and the apostles write to churches to encourage and defend the Christian ethic. The letters compliment the Acts of the Apostles and the Gospel of Christ and eventually become books in the New Testament.

The events detailed in the Acts of the Apostles were the foundation of the Christian church for three centuries after the crucifixion of Christ. Men and women who were converted to Christ and received the Holy Spirit were mentored in the ethic of God. The ethic was written down in order to pass it on to converts everywhere and to future generations of Christians. The *Didache, Teaching of the Twelve Apostles,* is an example of an instructional text used by early Christians to teach God's ethic to those who were converted to Christianity.

The Gospel books and letters written by the apostles as well as those who were mentored by the apostles were quoted by the men who became leaders in churches across the Roman Empire and beyond. An example of one of the post-apostolic leaders in the early church is Ignatius of Antioch, Syria. He lived between 35-107 AD and was martyred by being fed to lions in Rome. Ignatius was a student of John (Gospel of John). Ignatius wrote many letters to Christians similar to the apostles. His letters are available in early church archives and may be accessed by internet or book form in today's library systems. In his letters Ignatius quotes:

Matthew 5:2, 12:33, 23:35, Luke 23:34, Romans 2:4, 10:10, Acts 9:15, John 1:14, 8:29, 17:11-12, James 4:6, Philemon, 1 Tim, 2 Tim 2:24, 1 Peter 2:9, Ephesians 6:16, 6:12, Luke 10:27, 1 Corinthians 1:20, 4:20, 2 Corinthians 6:16, 8:18, 2 Thessalonians 3:10, Philippians 3:18, Hebrews 10:12-13, Galatians 2:20.

In fact, when the writings of early church fathers like Ignatius, Polycarp, Clement of Rome, and many others are reconstructed; nearly all of the writings of the apostles (New Testament) can be found quoted at some point. These quotes in the writings of early church fathers are the best defense against those who would attempt to minimize the New Testament by assertion of a post-apostolic date for the New Testament. How could the first century and early second century church leaders quote something which did not exist? However, the early church was not without challenge, and the second century of the new way of Judaism called Christianity struggled to maintain the apostolic identity of its doctrine.

Recorded second century doctrinal battles reveal ethical conflict between Christians and those who followed other gods or man as god. The Hebrew God from Jerusalem brought with Him through the Christian conversion an ethical war against the sexual immorality and worship practices of the so called gods.

It should not be surprising to learn of the conflicts in the cultures which Christianity had penetrated. Sociologists have revealed the obvious.

Mankind learns his ethic through a daily exposure of events. The sexual immorality practiced by the communities of the Mediterranean Sea was a result of experiential ethical development. The new Christian ethic required a change in ethical behavior. Christians had to instruct converts in the ethic of God.

In addition, Judeo-Christian ethics required all worship practices other than those prescribed by the Judeo-Christian ethic to be referred to as lawlessness. The very first commandment of the Ten Commandments requires total commitment to the Hebrew God.

As one can imagine, the people of the vast Roman Empire were drawn into a cultural war which promoted enmity between those who desired to follow the old ways of their communities rather than the new way brought by the Christian ethic. In addition, there were those in the second and third century who wanted to just get along, to find a common ground through a blend of old religious thought and the new Christian ethic. The ideologies of the competing groups may be split in to three components:

1. Judeo-Christian ethic
2. Ethics of mankind:
   a. Greek gods and culture
   b. Latin gods and culture
   c. North Africans gods
3. Those who desired to find a syncretistic blend between the competing cultural/ethical worldviews. This blended cultural worldview may be compared to the contemporary religious tolerance movement in Europe and North America.

Of the competing cultures, the culture of the gods could be dealt with clearly. Christians could present their belief in a clear alternative to the worship practices and lifestyles of the competing gods. Once a convert realized the distinct difference, he/she could freely choose to accept the sacrifice of Jesus and receive the Holy Spirit.

However, the blended approach of those who sought to find a common ground between the old and new cultures proved to be problematic to the early church fathers. For example, the controversy with the Gnostic movement during the second century required an early church father named Irenaeus to respond to the Gnostic version of Christianity. Gnosticism was regarded as a heretical form of Christianity by the early church fathers.

Gnostics played on the same playing field, but by a different set of rules. Second century Gnosticism was really a synchronized Platonic and Christian belief system. The "demiurge" spoke of in Platonic writings is an inferior creator god. He was a messenger sent by the higher god. Christ was viewed by Gnostic Christians as the demiurge of the higher god in second century Gnosticism.

In addition, second century Gnostics believed in a dual existence of humans. One part of an individual was in the form of a physical man/woman and the other in the form of that man/woman's spirit. Further, Gnostics believed any sin committed in the physical world did not matter because their real world was the spiritual world of the individual.

The word Gnostic comes from the Greek "*gnosos*" which means "to know." To claim to be Gnostic was to claim to have a superior knowledge of God than those who were not Gnostic (not knowledgeable about God).

As a result of this perspective of superiority, second century Gnosticism sought to interpret Christianity in terms of current events.[xxiv] The religious identity took on problems philosophically and even attempted to synchronize religion with daily experiential encounters with nature.

The Gnostic god was revealed in secret events/gatherings of the Gnostics. In these gatherings Gnostics claimed to find power and religious presence and even their individual deity in some cases. In addition, Jesus' death on the cross was treated as an allegory rather than truth. For the Gnostic, Jesus was not crucified. The synchronistic nature of the Gnostic religion attracted many Christians. After all, Gnosticism called itself and its believers "Christian".

Irenaeus viewed the secret meetings and the doctrine as a heretical form of Christianity. His response was to write what is now called the **"rule of faith."** The rule of faith became a major cornerstone of Christian society. The rule of faith was a declaration of apostolic teaching as the only true Christian religion. The rule of faith became a standard measure for Christian teaching. The rule of faith is stated in the **Apostle's Creed**:

- I believe in God the Father, Almighty, Maker of heaven and earth,
- And in Jesus Christ, His only begotten Son, our Lord,
- Who was conceived by the Holy Ghost, born of the Virgin Mary,
- Suffered under Pontius Pilate; was crucified, dead and buried; He descended into hell.
- The third day He rose again from the dead.
- He ascended into heaven and sits at the right hand of God the Father Almighty.
- From thence He shall come to judge the quick and the dead.
- I believe in the Holy Ghost.
- I believe in the holy (*universal*) catholic church: the communion of saints,

(The Roman Catholic Church as a denomination did not exist at this time in Christian history. Alexandria, Egypt, Carthage, Grecian, Syrian, Jerusalem and other churches were thought of as belonging to a universal (international) community of Christ followers. The word catholic is from Latin "catholicus" and Greek "katholikos" or kata-according and -holos meaning whole. Historically speaking the vernacular of the second century requires catholic/universal church to be in lower case. The second century vernacular "universal" included all those churches which followed Jesus and the apostolic teaching regardless of geographic location or national origin.)

* The forgiveness of sins,
* The resurrection of the body,
* And the life everlasting. Amen.

The Apostle's Creed was quoted in early Christian churches of the period and served to establish the ethic of God as doctrine for the early Church. It became a measure for all Christian churches which followed. Along with the Apostle's Creed, early churches quoted the Ten Commandments.

Rome had ruled that Christ was a Messianic pretender and King of the Jews in His trial in Jerusalem, and it is the ruling which led to His crucifixion. In that respect Rome and Christian communities and Christians themselves were judicious enemies. Further, Christian religious rules forbid worshipping, or kneeling, to another god. Add in the Roman emperor's self-appointed divine status, and one has the reason Christians were persecuted by the Roman Empire in the second and third centuries.

Christians were not such a threat to the Roman Empire that it launched military campaigns against the religion and those who followed it. Christians were convicted and prosecuted as they were called out by their enemies. For example, if a Jew wanted to cause trouble for a Christian, the Jew would simply accuse the person of being a Christian. The accused would be summoned before a Roman magistrate. The magistrate would simply ask if it were true the accused was a Christian. If the accused replied in the affirmative, they were punished even to the extent of death. If the accused denied he/she was Christian and kneeled before the magistrate to prove it so, the accused was released.

The Christian relationship with the Roman Empire required Christians to defend themselves and their religion. A plethora of written responses to judicial and cultural encroachment on Christianity evolved in the second and third century. The act of defense in the Greek vernacular of the era was called *"apologia"* and is referred to contemporarily as *"apologetics."* The men who defended Christianity from the government and cultural attacks are legendary in Christian history. A few of the greatest apologists of that era are Justin Martyr, Aristides, Tatian, Athenagoras, Theophilus, and Minucius.[xxv]

The literary works of these church fathers not only defended the Christian existence against its detractors, but provided encouragement to those living in an era of government and cultural persecution.

However as time went on, the Christians grew in number and influence, and the government and culture began to focus on other events. Political shifts within the Roman Empire were at crisis levels by the third century.

CHAPTER 1
Constantine the Great

§

THE ERA OF CONSTANTINE THE Great is the time in which the Christian battle against the pagan cultures and ethics turned toward the Christian cultural movement. Constantine's father was a Neoplatonist. Platonism of the era was a blended form of Platonic philosophy, Gnosticism, and Christianity. His mother was Christian. A blended family produced a tolerant child.

The Roman Empire was divided in the era of Constantine the Great (312 AD): the West (Rome) and the East (city of Byzantium [Istanbul, Turkey]). After Constantine's father died, the western section of the Roman Empire was contested by Constantine the Great and Maxentius. The two contestants were set to do battle and settle the issue. Prior to the battle, it is reported that Constantine had a vision which led him to place the Christian symbol on the banners of his armies. Constantine replaced the traditional Roman banners of his army with the banners of the Christian God. He was betting on the Christian God to give him victory over his opponents even though he had the smaller army.

The battle was won at the Milvian Bridge, and Constantine's subsequent reign favored Christians. In fact, Constantine issued orders (Edict of Milan) to the eastern section of the Roman Empire (city of Byzantium) to allow Christians freedom to worship openly. What was once illegal was now legal. What was once legal (old ethic and cultural norms) would eventually have to give way to the new ethic of Christ.

CHAPTER 2

Eastern Rome under Licinius

THE ROMAN RULER IN THE East was not so gracious when it came to Christians. His name was Licinius, and he was pagan in his religious affiliation. Licinius went in the opposite direction of the edict, once again persecuting Christians. In 324 Constantine defeated Licinius and became emperor over the entire Roman Empire.

CHAPTER 3
United Rome under Constantine

§

CONSTANTINE'S BATTLES TO THIS POINT might be referred to as physical since they were won on the battle field. However, the Christian church fathers were still battling the encroaching Greek mysticism and pagan religious efforts to blend the old ethic with the blossoming Christian ethic.

In 325 AD Constantine turned his attention to uniting the philosophical and religious sects of the Roman Empire. Since he was Christian, he became involved in the arguments the Christians were having. He called the church leaders together in Nicaea (Council of Nicaea, 325 AD). Constantine must have thought teaching two different ethics in the community is not good for communal harmony. The council was an attempt to bring the community together under one doctrine.

The council dealt with the Arian teaching, which held Christ was not divine but rather a created being as normal men. This perspective, taught by a heretical church leader named Arius, was derived from John 1:34:

And I have seen and have borne witness that this is the Son of God.

Arius concluded from the text that since Jesus was born (Son of God), he was created. If he was created, Jesus was not God, but God's messenger similar to the Gnostic's demiurge.

The result of the council was that the church fathers agreed that the writings and teaching of the apostles demanded a definition of Christ as

Jesus Christ is from the form of God and came to earth in the form of man.

The importance of the Council of Nicaea cannot be overstated. The Christian existence from the apostles to 325 AD involved risking their life to tell the lawless cultures of the Mediterranean about Christ in hopes of converting them. The apostles' teaching was protected by the life of the Christian. At the Council of Nicaea that all changed. Christian leaders openly debated heresy in full view of the government, pagans, and those who worked to blend the old Mediterranean ethics and culture with Christian ethics and culture. It marked the time in history when the Judeo-Christian ethic was legitimized through government sanctioned hearings. The hearings moved Christianity from national (Judaism/Jerusalem) to international (World/Christianity) existence. The impregnation was complete. The gestation period was beginning. The child called **Christendom** was growing in the womb of mankind.

A contemporary comparison may bring about a further understanding of the council's importance. In the United States the Supreme Court is a council which decides interpretation of law much like the early church decided interpretation of Christian doctrine. For example, in 1947 the Supreme Court heard a case for separation of church and state as it applies to the Republic of the United States and its Constitution. The court heard arguments from both sides. One piece of evidence given was a letter from Thomas Jefferson to a Danbury Baptist Association concerning favoritism of one church over another in the political climate of the era. Jefferson's letter addressed separation of church and state. Jefferson, a founding father of the republic and the Constitution, was the deciding factor in the ruling by the Supreme Court of the United States.[xxvi] While churches and religions had enjoyed freedom from government between 1802 and 1947, the decision by the Supreme Court legitimized the position of those who sought freedom from government intervention into churches. In addition, the ruling legitimized the position of those who wanted religion out of government. The decision of the Supreme Court is final, and the law of the land in America dictates a separation of church and state. One might seek to change the law through legislation, but if the current law were overturned, the new ruling would be something else and would be called by a new name. *Likewise, the definition of* **Christianity** *given out by the early church Fathers in the Council of Nicaea and following councils is the official definition of Christianity.* Any change in the ethic of God followed by Christian churches is something else and should be called by a new name in order to clarify its difference with the original decisions of the early church.

Early church councils (1st–7th century) stood watch over the encroachment of manmade ethics in the same manner the Supreme Court stands guard over constitutional law in the United States. The councils used the records of the apostles (writings of the apostles) to decide the cases brought before the councils, just as the records of the founding fathers of the United States Constitution are used to decide cases in the Supreme Court.

The western early church councils eventually narrowed the documents of the New Testament to 27 books by mid-300s AD. Syrian Christians continued to debate the 27 book canon of the New Testament until the sixth century. Debate on the New Testament canon (27 books used by the early church) was closed and the canon was accepted by a majority of Christians in the world by the seventh century.

The Old Testament is also a part of the Christian canon. The Old Testament according to the apostles and Christ relays the ethic of God given to the Jews and gives witness to the coming of Christ through the prophets. The New Testament is the apostles' witness of Christ as the manifestation of the Messiah which was predicted by the Old Testament prophecies. The combination of the Jewish canon (Old Testament) and the Christian canon (New Testament) is the Bible. The Bible is witness to the Hebrew God and His relationship with mankind.

While the Bible is the Scripture recognized by the early church leaders, the books contained in the Bible were not the only text recommended as good reading by the early church. The following is a list given by church fathers to read, although they are not included in the canon: *The Wisdom of Solomon, The Wisdom of Sirach, Judith, Tolbit, Didache, and the Shepherd.*

The early church cycle may be compared with the early years of the Davidic Kingdom. King David loved God and tried to set up a kingdom which worshipped God. He moved the Ark of the Covenant with God to Jerusalem and made sure his kingdom knew God's ethic was the ethic of the kingdom during his reign. However, as things went with the cycles of Israelite kings, lawlessness moved in on the kingdom. David's son Solomon disregarded the ethic of God, and as a result the sons of Solomon forged a life with lawlessness.

Roman intervention into Christian development must have seemed divine for the early Christian church leaders. It turned out to be anything but divine. The Romans would seize an opportunity to take possession of the ethic of God as if they were God. The cycle back into lawlessness would begin with the Roman acquisition.

Roman Nationalism and Christianity

THE EARLY CHURCH FATHERS AND Constantine officially defined Christianity, and Constantine even extended favor to the religion in his official position of Emperor of Rome. The legitimization of Christianity by the Roman government required that the pagan religions of the Roman Empire not only recognize Christianity but embrace it. One could say: "What was before Constantine unacceptable was now acceptable." The people who worshipped the old pagan gods and deities of the Mediterranean area were forced to learn to live by the new Christian ethic. Roman laws in support of the Christian ethic, which has its roots in Judaism, were put in place. Roman enforcement came through the legislative and judicial arms of the government.

1. Christian churches were permitted to receive death benefits left to them by wealthy Christians. Money is power, and the social implications of the move must have been immediate.[xxvii]

2. Government coins began to appear with Christian symbols. A contemporary comparison would be "In God We Trust" on US currency.[xxviii]

3. Christian symbols also began to appear on official government buildings. A contemporary comparison may be found at the US Supreme Court where the Ten Commandments hang on the wall behind the justices in the court.[xxix]

4. Pagan worship was strictly monitored and many components of paganism prohibited. Constantine's successors went further:

5. In 341 AD Constantius II abolished pagan sacrifice.

6. In 356 AD Constantius II closed all pagan temples.

7. The Roman emperor Gratian cut off government subsidies to paganism and removed pagan statues from the Roman Senate.[xxx]

8. Finally, the original move by Constantine reached a climatic end when Theodosius I issued the legislation which officially declared Christianity the religion of Rome.

CHAPTER 1

Christianity Became Law

§

THE CHRISTIAN ETHIC WAS NOW the accepted law of the land, and disobedience was prosecuted under the Roman judicial system. For example, those who left Christianity for Judaism were required to hand over all their property and holdings to the government.

Everyone desires acceptance, and Roman Christianity expanded exponentially. If one was not Christian, one was not accepted in Roman society. Loyalty to the nation of Rome (nationalism) was tied to Christianity through legislative and judicial discourse.

The conversion experience which built the early church was replaced with a government requirement to be Christian or at least profess to be even if one was not. Christianity was Roman nationalism.

CHAPTER 2

Capitalizing on Roman Nationalism

LEO I WAS BISHOP OF Rome 440-461 AD. He desired to unite the Christian leadership under one authority. In the Western Roman Empire, there was little resistance to the idea. However the Eastern Empire (Byzantine) was not convinced of the supremacy of the bishop's office in Rome. A political argument between East and West Christian leaders erupted.

Leo I offered his persuasive argument for the Roman bishop as the Pope of the world in a theory which compared the apostles Paul and Peter to the mythical Roman founders Romulus and Remus. The move tied Roman Nationalist enthusiasm to the Christian movement of the era.

It is extremely curious that Leo I used the comparison. The mythical brothers of Roman creation were the twin sons of the mythical *Rhea Silva* (earth dweller) and Hercules or the god Mars, depending on the story teller. As the story goes, the twins were left to die in the wilderness, but a wolf allowed the infants to feed with her litter. The twins were found in the wilderness and raised by a poor couple. Eventually the two became aware of their heritage and destroyed the king who attempted to dispose of them. They renamed the recaptured city, Rome.

The argument then was that Paul's and Peter's leadership in Rome was history repeating itself. According to Leo I, just as it was ordained by the gods that Romulus and Remus would rule the new city of Rome (world), so the bishops of Rome were ordained by God to rule the Christian world.

The papacy was born with support from the gods; its first Pope was Leo I (Leo the Great).

Leo I was a politician. His Christian intellectual footing was furnished in the writings of St Augustine, Bishop of Hippo, Carthage, North Africa. One may find the Christian doctrine of Leo I in the Christian writings of St Augustine. Further, one may find contemporary Roman Catholic doctrine in the writings of St Augustine. The most famously quoted St Augustine book is *The City of God (413-426 AD)*.

The *City of God* was written by St Augustine in defense of the Christian religion in Rome and is relevant to this conversation. It is a tale of two cities: the perishing city of mankind (pagan Rome) and the immerging eternal city of God. The Roman Catholic view during the era in which St. Augustine wrote this book viewed Rome as the emerging utopian City of God.

The book was written at a time when Rome and its empire were turning away from pagan religions (400s). The process of becoming a Christian empire did not happen overnight, nor did the people who followed the pagan religions disappear overnight. Pagans openly blamed Christianity for any evil which came to Romans. For example, the barbarians overran Rome around 410 AD, and the pagans blamed this disaster on Rome's departure from the pagan gods to Christianity.

St. Augustine was called to Rome and asked to mount a defense of Christianity. This included the writing of the *City of God*. The book compares the actual communities of pagans and all their lawlessness against an eternal City of God. In the book the City of God is a mythological utopian city which follows the ethic of God in every way. The eternal City of God has not come to pass as of yet. It is the city sought after by Christians everywhere. According to Jesus, the City of God (heaven) can only be realized through His second coming.

In the book *City of God*, St Augustine commented on Christian doctrine. He is known among theologians around the world as a theological genius with respect to biblical interpretation. It is the value of his scriptural interpretation and the promised utopian City of God which is seized on by theologians like Leo I (Leo the Great) and those who came after him. During the time of Leo I and the formation of the papacy, it was cutting-edge theology. In addition, Leo I could easily connect ordination of Rome as a great city under gods Romulus and Remus to the emerging City of God under the Hebrew God.

The following is one quote from St. Augustine's text Leo I missed:

This, in fact, is the difference between good men and bad men, that the former make use of the world to enjoy God, whereas the latter would like to make use of God to enjoy the world—if, of course, they believe in God and His providence over man, and are not so bad as those who deny even this (St Augustine, City of God).

It is under St Augustine's doctrinal genius and the manipulative Leo I's political genius that Christianity was converted from an international movement to a Roman national movement. One might ask: "What has Rome to do with Jerusalem?"

Not all the world agreed with the Roman political takeover of Christianity. The Eastern Orthodox Church at first submitted to the grand scheme of the Western Romans in Rome. However, there was tension. The tension eventually caused a rift between Eastern Orthodoxy and Western Catholicism.

Through the centuries, Christianity became entangled in government and even became the source of policy of the government. Charlemagne is the best example of the historical government entanglement. Anointing Western European monarchs by the Pope began before Charlemagne; however, it was under Charlemagne the Western papal interest became synonymous with government.

Charlemagne was a devoted Christian leader and viewed church and state as inseparable. His favorite book was St Augustine's *City of God*, and he strove to create the mythical City of God for his subjects. His military campaigns were also missionary campaigns. He took it as his mission to organize the clergy even with respect to how the clergy dressed. Under Charlemagne the clergy became uniformed and churches and their liturgy standardized.

It was Pope Leo III who crowned Charlemagne as Emperor of Rome in 800 AD. Charlemagne's coronation is probably the beginning of what is now called the "**Holy Roman Empire**.[xxxi] From Charlemagne forward, in order to obtain legitimacy as emperor in the Holy Roman Empire, one had to be anointed by the Pope. Papal authority engulfed even emperors.

One other thing of note concerning Charlemagne must be discussed. Charlemagne connected religious service with military service. Under Charlemagne and Pope Leo III, Christianity began sliding down the slippery slope called "holy war". It would move the Christian ethic from passive to violent.

It is curious that men and women so devoted to Christ could interpret His passive walk to the cross as a call for holy war. Christ calls His followers to *pick up their cross and follow Him* (Matthew 16:24). Christ did not gather forces to destroy His enemies. He did not lead a crusade to destroy heresy. He did not gather political consensus to destroy those who disagreed with Him. In His trial, torture, and crucifixion, Christ sacrificed Himself so others could be saved. To follow Him is to sacrifice one's self on one's individual cross. The model is clearly displayed in Christ and in His witnesses, the apostles. In addition, the early church fathers faced lions and the cross and in doing so lay claim to the footsteps of God in their own martyrdom. The Charlemagne/Papacy concept which militarized Christianity was itself heresy and lawlessness.

The result of obtaining power over emperors and the ability to make holy war on enemies eventually led to a dictatorial papal authority. The dictation from the papacy can be stated as:

* God founded the Roman Church in order to lead the universal church.
* The Bishop of Rome was the only bishop who could be called universal.

- Princes and rulers should kiss the Pope's feet.
- The Pope obtains his holiness from Peter.
- The Pope can make law.
- Literary works must be approved by the Pope.
- Only the Pope can object to his statements or revise them.
- The Pope may dispose emperors.
- The Pope can be judged by no one.[xxxii]

The papacy, for all intent and purposes, viewed itself as God in the City (Temple) of God. What was God's/Pope's position on war? No war was to be carried out for secular interest. Holy war approved by the Papacy was allowed, justified, and even ordained.

CHAPTER 3

Islam and the Crusades

$$\int$$

HERESY HAS ALWAYS BEEN AN issue for Christians (all Christians, not just Roman Catholic Christians). Protection of the apostles' teachings on Christ is the concern. In Africa a new heresy cropped up in the seventh century. A prophet named Mohammed received a vision from God (real or supposed is not at issue here), and Islam was born. This religious doctrine was developed on the foundation of the Jewish Pentateuch and the claim that followers of Islam were by birthright of Abraham's firstborn Ishmael the true children of God.

By 1000 AD, Islam had swept across North Africa, converting Christian communities with threats of death. Any who would not convert were killed. Those who chose to profess Islam and stay in their country were taught the new version of godly observance. The method is effective since the new Islamic theocracy teaches Islamic ethics to all subsequent generations. By the third generation from the conquest, the conquered territory is fully Islamic and taught to view all other civilized people as infidels and worthless.

Examples of this method of conversion can still be seen repeated by Islamic crusaders even today, as evidenced among Islamic groups like Al Qaeda and ISIS.

In the early days of Islam, the Christian response was to write in defense of Christian doctrine. However, Islam was not listening to reason.

The slaughter of Christians in territories once called Roman Catholic was troubling. Islamic conquest moved up through Jerusalem and into

Syria and Turkey. Islam stood on the door step of Rome and Roman Catholicism. Pope Urban II provided an answer to the Islamic threat.

Pope Urban II called for a holy war against the Islamic threat, and he tied salvation to war. If one wanted to buy relatives out of purgatory or forgiveness of one's own sin, one could join the crusades against the Islamic invasion in the south and east of the Holy Roman Empire. The pope would grant eternal salvation in return for military service. It is clear the decree from the pope required faith in the pope's ability to provide salvation. Faith in Christ was misdirected and used for the benefit of powerful men. Christ did not ask others to die for His Kingdom. He sacrificed His own life on the cross to save mankind. The acquisition of others to kill and die for the kingdom is not Christian; it is lawlessness.

The first crusades went badly. Their ranks were filled with peasants, ill-equipped to fight a war. They also lacked supplies. The peasant crusaders filled their need along the way; they raped, plundered, and burned their way to the battle field where they were defeated by the Islamic armies.

The subsequent crusades became more organized and backed by knights of the era. The Templar Knights are the most famous of knights leading crusades against Islam.

The vicious fighting of crusading knights of the era has been vilified, even demonized, by atheists and liberals for years in order to bolster their own war against Christianity in the West. However, the Islamic armies were just as vicious. Furthermore, the contemporary secular war on terrorism is a war on Islamic expansionism just as the crusades were a war on Islamic expansionism. The war against Al Qaeda and ISIS in Iraq, Afghanistan, Syria and the world is just as brutal. Decapitation by a bomb delivered by drones is no less gruesome as decapitation by the hand.

In the vacuum left by the absence of the warring Holy Roman Empire, the contemporary secular conquerors of Christian territories are sending crusades into Islamic territories to control the Islamic threat. Should the seculars lay down their weapons and allow their children to become Islamic?

In any event, to go to war in order to save philosophic or physical borders is not what Christ did. When confronted with the option to convert or die, He chose to die without lifting one finger in protection of Himself. His faith in the Father to deliver Him from beyond the grave saved His life. It is His act of faith which carved out the salvation vessel for the trip to Heaven. If one is to have a seat on the vessel, one must have the same faith in Jesus and His resurrection as Jesus had in the Father. The individual cross is a journey to death and resurrection for the Christian. Faith in war is not Christian.

The Holy Roman Empire is representative of the cycles of good and bad; God's ethic being replaced by mankind's learned ethic. God needed to establish order among the followers of Christ. He would do it through the sacrifice of His servants.

Reformation of Christ's Initiative

CHAPTER 1
John Hus

§

THE ROMAN EMPIRE BEGAN TO decline, and European monarchs took their kingdoms from what was once called Roman. Roman Catholicism also began to decline, and challenges to the primacy of the Roman pope evolved. The papal crisis known as the Great Schism is an example of historical deterioration of the Roman Catholic pope's authority. The Great Schism occurred between 1378 and 1417 AD.[xxxiii] It was a time when Europe experienced two elected popes who served at the same time. It was at the end of the dual pope schism when a Bohemian priest named Jon Hus challenged papal authority.

Roman Catholicism had seized control of the Bible and treated it as if it was the exclusive property of the papacy. The belief that others may mishandle the Scripture or misinterpret was the reason given for exclusive rights to the text. In addition, according to Roman Catholicism, the text could only be read in Latin.

Control of God's Word is control of God's people. Jon Hus challenged the exclusivity of access to Scripture when he read the Bible in its original Koine Greek script and found that the Latin Vulgate of Roman Catholicism was lacking critical Christian thought. In fact, he argued for allowing the Scripture to be freely read in the vernacular of the people.

The transparency proposed by Jon Hus threatened the very foundation of Roman Catholicism. If the people read the text and interpreted it for themselves, why would priests be required? Another issue was Roman Catholic traditions developed by the papacy after the time period of the early church and apostles. Those traditions reflected Roman nationalist traits and would be exposed as Roman Christian, not universal (catholic) Christian.

Jon Huss believed so fervently in the people's ability to read and interpret the Scripture that he translated the text into the local Bohemian language. Enraged, the papacy labeled Hus a heretic and all his work as heresy.

In an effort to reconcile Hus, the pope summoned Hus to a council in 1415 AD. The pope assured Hus safe passage if he would attend. Hus attended the council, which instead became a trial. Sentenced to death by papal authority, Hus was burned at the stake. As he burned, he worshipped God.

The martyrdom of Jon Hus is the historical marker which symbolizes the beginning of the Reformation period. Martin Luther, in turn, is the historical marker which initiated the battle for religious freedom and set in motion the eventual denominational structure of the church today.

CHAPTER 2

Martin Luther

§

SIMILAR TO JON HUS, MARTIN Luther (1517 AD) discovered that the Catholic Church was not exactly accurate about the way people were supposed to worship and pray to God. The major issue Luther had with the papacy was its creation of purgatory and indulgences.

Sheol (purgatory) is a place referenced in the Old Testament to which Jews were sent when they died. For example, when Jacob was told his son Joseph was dead, he exclaimed,

"No, I shall go down to Sheol to my son, mourning." (Gen 37:36)

Sheol in Jewish tradition and scripture is a place where the dead await judgement day. The dead according to Jewish tradition and scripture are captives and cannot escape until God frees them. Christians believe Jesus came to free the captives,

"He has sent me to proclaim liberty to the captives and recovering of sight to the blind, to set at liberty those who are oppressed, to proclaim the year of the Lord's favor (Luke 4:18-19)."

After Jesus' death on the cross, the tombs opened up.

> *The tombs also were opened. And many bodies of the saints who had fallen asleep were raised, and coming out of the tombs after His resurrection they went into the holy city and appeared to many (Matthew 27:52-53).*

In addition, the apostles and the early church fathers believed Jesus' return was eminent and had no reason to believe Sheol (purgatory) still existed. However, the concept of purgatory began to resurface when Christ did not immediately return. By the 11th century, Catholicism in the west had adopted purgatory as a physical place where Christians went after death. Eastern Christians did not buy into the concept, and the doctrine of purgatory became problematic during the "Great Schism" between eastern and western Christians.

According to Catholic doctrine established in the 11th century, purgatory is a place of purification of sin. Purification/punishment in purgatory was torturous and could be torturously long according to Catholic doctrine. Indulgences were payments to the papacy to intercede on behalf of the believer's relative in purgatory. The pope literally became the source of forgiveness in this scheme, and in the case of indulgencies, forgiveness of sin was for sale.

One may note if Christ is the Messiah of Jewish prophesy and apostolic witness, purgatory had to end when He was resurrected. **The absence of purgatory in the New Testament is telling. Martin Luther got it.**

One other thing Martin Luther got was the similarity between Luke 19:45-46 and the indulgence scheme of the papacy:

> *And He (Jesus) entered the temple and began to drive out those who sold, saying to them, "It is written, 'My house shall be a house of prayer,' but you have made it a den of robbers."*

Unlike Jon Hus's situation in 1415 AD, by Martin Luther's time period many in the Catholic Church were ready to reform the church. A polarization of combatants occurred, those who wanted to follow Luther's lead in reform against those who wanted things to remain the same. The result

CHAPTER 4

Arminianism

§

ALONG WITH FREEDOM FROM THE oppressive Catholics came a desire to worship God as one would see fit. With hundreds of people interpreting the Koine Greek script of the early church fathers and the apostles in the book of Acts, interpretations began to vary. For example, Joseph Armenian, a Dutch Theologian (1560-1609 AD) preached a different gospel than Calvin.

The differences caused a major problem for the Protestant community.

ARMINIANISM

Conditional Election: *God elected individuals based upon His foreknowledge of their choice to accept salvation.*

General Atonement: *God died for all, but only the elect have the benefits of the atonement applied to them.*

Prevenient Grace: *Man cannot do good or achieve saving faith without God's gracious empowering through the Holy Spirit.*

Resistible Grace: *Though God empowers us to overcome our depravity, He does not do so in a way that overrides human free will.*

Possible to Lose Salvation: *A believer can fall from grace.*

During the mid-17th century, a council was called to settle the issue. The council was called the Synod of Dort. This conference is significant in that it defined two different approaches to Protestant belief and worship. The five point definitions given above were developed at the Synod of Dort.

Contemporary theologians and Christians still argue the different points of these two Protestant theologians. They are presented here solely to outline John Calvin's theology of predestination and Joseph Armenian's alternative theology.

These different approaches to Protestant belief and worship would become problematic as Christ's initiative moved west.

CHAPTER 5
Church Structure

§

THE DIFFERENCES IN PROTESTANT CHURCHES did not end with doctrine. Church leadership and structure are major players with respect to how one worships God. Who is the leader in the church?

The hierarchal structure of the church has contributed greatly to the cyclic nature of the Christian church. The history of the papacy reveals a back and forth of good and bad papal leadership influencing the doctrine and faith according to who is in charge at the papacy. A contemporary example of the papal influence on doctrine and faith is the former conservative Pope Benedict compared to the current progressive Pope Francis. Pope Benedict appeared to lead the Catholic faithful using the Bible as his guide, which opposes the cultural movement outside the church. Pope Francis appears to lead the Catholic faithful according to cultural experiences happening outside the church. The good pope gives way to the bad pope much like the good king gave way to the bad king in the Old Testament books of Kings I and II.

The Reformation sought to break the cycle of power and influence imposed by the office of the Pope. Many Protestants viewed the centralized power of the papacy as detrimental to Christian doctrine and faith. To combat future power structures within the Protestant faith, many Protestant denominations sought to democratize membership through congregational influence in church policy and leadership.

It should be noted that the Catholics did not easily give up their power over the people. There were consequences for bucking the papacy. The early days of the Reformation were brutal. Protestants had to run for their lives. Ulrich Zwingli, a Catholic Priest who had joined with Protestants in Switzerland, is a good example of a Protestant leader who lost his life for the Reformation. He preached on the book of Matthew from the Greek text, and many in his congregation grasped the text as if they had heard the Gospel for the first time. Those Protestants who emerged from Zwingli's church in Switzerland found themselves running for their lives. From the movement in Switzerland came the Ana-Baptist (later just Baptist), Mennonites, Quakers, and even the Brethren church in Germany, to name a few. All of these denominations ran from the oppressive Catholics to the new world of America.

Protestants began to understand there was a difference between church organization and the personal relationship between Christ and the individual follower. The church is an organization formed by a group of individual followers. The purpose of a group affiliation is to provide fellowship/companionship among the faithful and an organized approach to informing the community around that particular group of Jesus' sacrifice and God's plan of salvation. The outreach of a particular church group may be international as in the case of missionary work around the globe.

In a congregational church, leaders are elected or assigned by the church members. The New Testament encourages individual Christians in the church group to follow their leaders. The Apostle Paul encouraged cooperation with church leadership:

We ask you brothers, to respect those who labor among you, and to esteem them very highly in love because of their work (2 Thessalonians 5:12, 13).

However, the individual follower of Christ has direct access to God through the high priest Jesus Christ:

Therefore, holy brothers, consider Jesus, the apostle and high priest of our confession (Hebrews 3:1).

The Roman Catholic Church sought to control access to Christ, the high priest, by inserting the hierarchal papal structure between the individual Catholic and Christ.

Protestants sought to follow the early church model. There are many different versions of the following models; however, the following are simplified illustrations depicting church structure since the time of Christ.

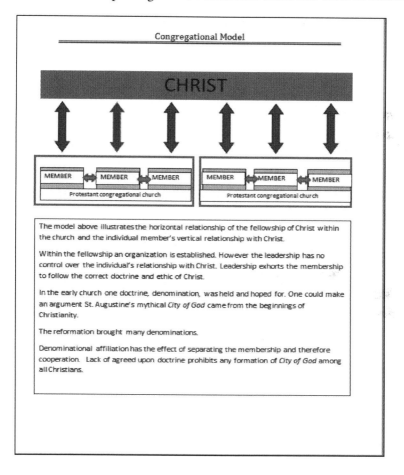

Roman Catholic/Protestant priest model

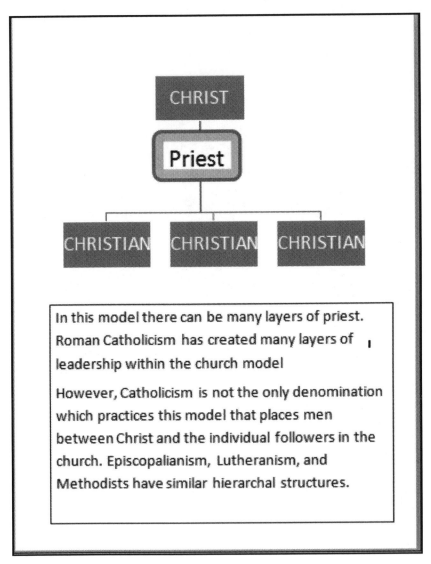

In this model there can be many layers of priest. Roman Catholicism has created many layers of leadership within the church model

However, Catholicism is not the only denomination which practices this model that places men between Christ and the individual followers in the church. Episcopalianism, Lutheranism, and Methodists have similar hierarchal structures.

The Roman Catholic model's slide from the ethic of God is a part of history and may be recounted in the history of priests who sought control of Christ's initiative of salvation. The most glaring example of the priestly model's departure from the ethic of God is in the Roman Catholic priest's sale of salvation through indulgences and the militarization of Christianity by Pope Urban II and Charlemagne during the Crusades era.

However, the congregational model has not fared any better. Each church is an autonomous organization controlled through a congregational process. In other words, local church members control all activities from within the local congregation. In addition, many Christians view each individual member as being a priest carrying out the will of God, with the member responsible only to Jesus. In these churches, pastors may be viewed by some members as merely subject matter experts guiding the membership's decisions—if the member would recognize even that!

An example of congregational church autonomy preventing outside influence is in the way pastors are hired. Hiring a pastor involves looking for a preacher who shares the views of the members of the local autonomous church. The term used by autonomous churches to hire a pastor is referred to as "calling a pastor" to serve. Frequently, a search committee is formed from within the members of the church. The search committee may have as many members on the committee as deemed necessary by the membership. The committee works together to find the right ideological fit for their membership.

The committee's mission ensures that throughout the interview process any pastor hired reflects the beliefs and traditions of their particular autonomous church. In this way the particular autonomous church holds on to traditional beliefs passed from one generation to the next. While this may have some positive benefits, wrongheaded tradition and poor biblical interpretation is also maintained during the process.

Autonomy of the local congregational church also serves to teach children from the well of divinity and tradition handed down in the particular church. The idea is to maintain control over doctrine through the media of local membership control.

The autonomous congregational Christian church is free to teach and follow any doctrine, Christian or otherwise, approved by the voting body of the congregation. The fact is that the congregational style church is an isolated democratic structure accountable to the voters of the congregation. The congregational church will follow God's ethic as long as God's ethic has the controlling democratic vote.

Members are free to challenge their pastors with homespun theology even if the pastor is formally trained in a seminary. If a member is unsatisfied with how their local church is conducting church activities, he/she is free to join another church or start a new church which fits into the traditional activities and traditions they desire. Members are also free to campaign for the removal of a pastor they do not like. If the pastor receives enough votes to maintain his status as pastor, he stays. If he does not have the votes, he is dismissed. In the same way, members are free to change Christian doctrine with a vote. In some cases congregational churches break with denominational affiliation over issues of doctrine because they cannot muster enough votes to affect change in denominational doctrine and policy.

The ethic of God cycle of the congregational style church is dependent on the individual's vertical relationship with Christ. If the individual's relationship with the world is greater than the vertical relationship with Christ, the ethic within the church membership will shift with the relationship. The ethic of mankind will at least begin to influence the ethic of God. Democracy reflects the will of the people not the will of God.

God willed through the Great Commission:

Go therefore and make disciples of all nations, baptizing them in the name of the Father, and of the Son, and the Holy Spirit (Matthew 28:19).

Congregational style churches are vulnerable when membership is not based on the conversion experience by which the converted believer receives the Holy Spirit. Membership whose foundation is other than the Holy Spirit working through individual relationships with Christ will reflect the democratic ethic of mankind. There are many congregational style churches, regardless of their denomination, which do not reflect the ethic of God.

The congregational style churches are democratic, and in a world which assigns democracy as the preeminent governing media of modern man, many church members feel empowered. One would think that democracy has the potential to bring about the famous *City of God*. All that is required is to control the government through the electorate the same way members control the church.

CHAPTER 6

Influences on Government

DIFFERENCES IN PROTESTANT DENOMINATIONS CAUSED problems in the early United States. For example, Protestant denominations were attacked by competing Protestant churches, in particular, the Episcopal Church which refused to accept other denominations as legitimate believers. The Episcopal Church is akin to the Church of England (Catholicism) regarding its liturgical view and beliefs. The Episcopal Church broke with the pope in Italy because King Henry VIII wanted a divorce from one of his wives. When the pope refused to grant the divorce, the Catholic Church in England broke with Catholicism and formed the Church of England. The Episcopal Church is essentially the American version of the Church of England.

The Episcopal Church saw no reason it should not be anointed the state religion of the new republic. Its members employed political influence in an attempt to make Episcopalianism the government religion and even tried to force members of other denominations into becoming Episcopalians through oppressive means such as jailing their leaders. As a result, the leadership of these denominations and their members became active in government matters. For example, when the founding fathers of the Republic were having trouble getting the Constitution passed in Congress, a Protestant preacher named John Leland met with James Madison and formed an agreement which resulted in likeminded Protestants' political influence being thrown behind the Constitutional document. In return Madison promised to put a provision in the Constitution guaranteeing religious liberty for all. The agreement worked out between the Protestants and Madison resulted in the *Bill of Rights* that Americans both cherish and hate. The first amendment was first in importance to Protestants:

Congress shall make no law respecting an establishment of religion, or prohibiting the free exercise thereof; or abridging the freedom of speech, or of the press; or the right of the people peaceably to assemble, and to petition the Government for a redress of grievances.

Protestants, it seemed, were on the right track, and they began to flourish in America, which was now a country they could love. A Protestant preacher even wrote the pledge of allegiance to the American flag in 1892. Protestants adored their new country.

With the Bill of Rights protecting the nation from a dominant Protestant or Catholic presence, Christians in America all united around the idea of each denomination worshipping in its own way.

While denominations would still compete among themselves in America, the law set the stage for Christians to unite politically on the issues they had in common. This freedom enabled America to become a Christian political electorate. Christians saw this Christian electorate as "one nation under God". The phrase brings up memories of the City of God. But as happened with Rome's reach for the eternal City of God, one nation under God would not be realized.

American culture was changing even as the denominations found peace. The lead-up to the civil war and its aftermath served to split Christians into different camps. Northern Christians saw an opportunity to join the movement to free slaves in America, while southern Christians were infected with a flood of southern nationalism. They allowed rising nationalist pride in the South to affect their allegiance to God. This nationalism caused them to ally themselves with rich slave owners, and in some cases these Christians were rich slave owners themselves.

After the civil war the southern Christians were left dealing with the pain of defeat, but all Christians in America were damaged spiritually and politically.

Churches who believed in the southern cause continued to teach and preach division. Their idea was to pick off the separatist models in the Old Testament that God used to maintain the Israelite nation's purity and use it to support their goals. Although the war ended slavery, those who lost the war were not about to let it go.

It appears Christians in America forgot that God's initiative through Christ was an international affair. New differences in society and doctrine rekindled old denominational battles. Christians became isolated from other Christians through denominational interpretive experience, geographic location and sectarian tradition. Each denomination followed its own set of rules (doctrine). The doctrines served to place boundaries around particular denominations. Examples are Catholic, Church of God, Southern Baptist, or Episcopal. The differing doctrines create doctrinal borders, just as a state or nation has physical borders.

The early cooperation with the framers of the constitution and Bill of Rights in reality only created a separation of church and state governance.

Differing Protestant denominational policies create confusion among the people of God. For example, is it a sin to drink a glass of wine with the evening meal? Some denominations say no and some say yes. The truth is that the prohibition on drinking of alcohol by some denominations is founded in the American prohibition movement of the 1920s and has little to do with biblical ethics. Denominations that agreed with prohibition kept the requirement as denominational policy. Through generations of denominational experience, the prohibition policy became denominational ethics.

In the end, Protestant denominations did influence western government. The Bill of Rights, especially in the United States, has helped men and women worship their God freely. However, it has also provided the path to lawlessness. One may worship any god or not worship God or gods at all. One may even worship Satan. Many Protestants mirror the actions of Pope Urban II and approve of a militarized Christian following. The idea is to destroy others before those others destroy Christians. Many Christians appear to have forgotten that the power of Christ is in His sacrifice. A Christian's power is in Christian sacrifice, not the sacrifice of others.

Protestant denominations have not acted very neighborly toward each other. The friction between them is reminiscent of the Pharisees and Sadducees and other Jewish sects during the intertestamental era. The sects of the intertestamental period acted more like enemies than neighbors. So do the Protestant denominations. God's ethical priority calls for a neighborly priority.

However, to treat neighbors as neighbors, one has to know who is the Christian neighbor.

CHAPTER 7

Neighbors

§

WHAT IS THE FULL JUDEO-CHRISTIAN doctrine of the neighbor relationship? The question of the neighbor and treatment of the poor and well-
off was a concern even among the Exodus Jews over four thousand years
ago. God's ethic is clear on the issue of balance being a critical part of the
Judeo-Christian neighbor relationship. In Leviticus 19:9-18, God said:

> *When you reap the harvest of your land you shall not reap your field right up
> to its edge, neither shall you gather the gleanings after your harvest. And you
> shall not strip your vineyard bare; neither shall you gather the fallen grapes of
> your vineyard. You shall leave them for the poor and for the sojourner:*

> *You shall not oppress your neighbor or rob him. The wages of a hired ser-
> vant shall not remain with you all night until the morning. You shall not
> curse the deaf or put a stumbling block before the blind.*

> *You shall not be partial to the poor or defer to the great, but in righteous-
> ness shall you judge your neighbor. You shall not go around as a slanderer
> among your people, and you shall not stand up against the life of your
> neighbor; I am the Lord.*

God's ethic requires dignity, respect and a helping hand be given to the
poor and unfortunate by those who have been blessed by God. God's ethic
further requires the poor and unfortunate to treat the well-off with the

same dignity they wish bestowed on themselves. One shall not in God's ethic ignore the poor and save the entire blessing of God for one's self-centered lifestyle. One shall not in God's ethic take up a movement to rob from the well-off and give to the poor. The modern doctrine which unfairly attacks the rich to gain favoritism from the poor is a lawless doctrine. The selfish "doctrine of enabling" used by some Christians to justify ignoring the poor and unfortunate is also lawlessness.

Jesus was quizzed regarding the Judeo ethic concerning ones neighbor in Luke 10:25-37:

And behold, a lawyer stood up to put Him [Jesus] to the test, saying, "Teacher, what shall I do to inherit eternal life?" He [Jesus] said to him, "What is written in the Law? How do you read it?" And he answered, "You shall love the Lord your God with all your heart and with all your soul and with all your strength and with all your mind, and your neighbor as yourself." And He [Jesus] said to him, "You have answered correctly; do this, and you will live."

But he, desiring to justify himself, said to Jesus, "And who is my neighbor?" Jesus replied, "A man was going down from Jerusalem to Jericho, and he fell among robbers, who stripped him and beat him and departed, leaving him half dead. Now by chance a priest was going down that road, and when he saw him he passed by on the other side. So likewise a Levite, when he came to the place and saw him, passed by on the other side. But a Samaritan, as he journeyed, came to where he was, and when he saw him, he had compassion. He went to him and bound up his wounds, pouring on oil and wine. Then he set him on his own animal and brought him to an inn and took care of him. And the next day he took out two denarii and gave them to the innkeeper, saying, 'Take care of him, and whatever more you spend, I will repay you when I come back.' Which of these three, do you think, proved to be a neighbor to the man who fell among the robbers?" He [lawyer] said, "The one who showed him mercy." And Jesus said to him, "You go, and do likewise."

In God's ethic (way of life), there is a priority of human effort. God is to come before all things in man's effort to live in God's ethic. The lawyer, who was a lawyer within the discipline of the law (Torah and Ten Commandments) of God, understood that God came first in priority, and his second question seeds the "God first" priority in God's ethic. He challenged Jesus on the priority of the neighbor. It is obvious the lawyer was thinking of "neighbor" as in a national relationship and was looking for Jesus to trip on the question: *"And who is my neighbor?"*

The answer reflects the international relationship of men. To understand the parable, one must analyze the characters who would be neighbor.

The man *"going down from Jerusalem"* was a Jew who was leaving Jerusalem and going to Jericho. Implied is that he had been in Jerusalem to make his sacrifice to God in the temple.

The robbers were those wishing to take from this man his wealth and redistribute it among themselves. One might guess they were poor. However, theft does not indicate the wealth of the robber. It only indicates his desire to live off of what belongs to someone else.

A priest *"was going down that road"*, which gives weight to the implication that the road from Jerusalem was filled with people *"going down"* from a religious function in Jerusalem. The priest crossed the road to avoid the stricken Jew. Since the stricken man was a Jew and of the same national origin, under the lawyer's definition of neighbor this would mean that the priest was required to give aid to the man in need.

The Levite in the parable was also *"going down"* from Jerusalem, most likely from the same religious function at the temple. Levites were temple keepers in Jewish society and lived through the gifts of the people of Israel. It is telling that the parable left him out of the help given the Jewish brother who was robbed.

The Samaritan was a calculated move on Jesus' part in the parable. Samaritans, as they were called by the nationally oriented Jews of Judea, were a people who populated the old Northern Kingdom area. They were Jewish people who had married into the different cultures which moved into the area after the northern Jews were dispersed among the Gentiles.

In the lawyer's nationalist Jewish view, Samaritans were not Jews at all, but belonged to the Gentile community outside Judaism.

The Samaritan was a rich man. He had resources to put the stricken man in an inn and pay for all the stricken man's needs while he carried out his business in Judea.

The lawyer was left with:

* If I object to the Samaritan as the neighbor, I leave open the question of survival of the stricken man.
* The Jewish priest and the (Jewish) Levite refuse to help their national neighbor, leaving the stricken Jew to die on the side of the road.
* The Samaritan followed the second commandment in the (ethic of God) law: "You shall love your neighbor as yourself."

Anyone who is robbed and beaten and left to die would wish that someone would help, that someone would act as if they were their neighbor.

The international twist to the story is the Good Samaritan parody. Luke was written for the Gentile (international community), and this parable from Jesus indicates an international neighbor relationship among men who would follow the ethic of God.

The answer to the parable is:

Neighbor = following the ethic of God.
Enemy = following the ethic of mankind.

Priority of the ethic of God

The discussion regarding the Good Samaritan in Luke foreshadows a time when Judaism would give way to Christianity. Christianity would, through Christ's sacrifice on the cross (the good neighbor), spread throughout the world. Missionaries from the original group would share the message of salvation to all who would listen.

Rome, the oppressive lawless master of Israel after Christ was crucified, was conquered. The Roman Empire was not conquered with weapons and armies killing each other on the battlefield of men. The Roman Empire was conquered by the ethic of God and those who follow the ethic of God. All the old enemies of the Near East and West fell like dominos.

Every time a split in the church occurred, a new initiative took ethical ground. One of the most glaring examples is the reformation of the church which produced the Protestant denominations and a westward initiative which reached the New World of America.

The initiative was so strong that the United States placed *"In God We Trust"* on their currency. Presidents in the beginning of the new republic were Christian men. For example Protestants who became president were George Washington, Ulysses S. Grant, Franklin D. Roosevelt, Theodore Roosevelt, William Taft, Gerald Ford and Lyndon Johnson. Denominations such as Presbyterian and Baptist contributed leaders who lead the new republic to God's ethical priority.

However, even as the international movement of God marched out from the simple missionary trips of the original apostles, a new thing formed in the wake of God's priority. A new movement sprang from the bowels of Europe. The enemy of God rose like a phoenix from the remnant of lawlessness in the Old World.

The Enemies of God

THE ENEMIES OF GOD ARE manifest in lawlessness. Lawlessness seeks to replace the ethic of God with the ethic of mankind. Further, lawlessness rebels against God and His ethic forming a new ethic around man. The process moves the cycle away from God.

The last rebellion seeks to expel God and gods from the dominion of man. It moves in the open, and like Christianity the rebellion of lawlessness seeks to remove one ethic and in its place introduce a replacement. The rebellion of lawlessness is happening now and has a historical connection with the Greek society Paul spoke to in 1 & 2 Thessalonians. The priority of the ethic of lawlessness may be recognized as:

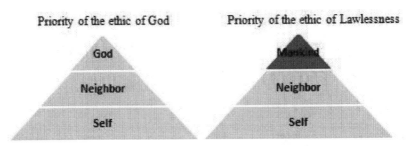

God is not found in the ethic of lawlessness. Mankind's ethical rules even in some churches and members who call themselves Christian follow the replacement ethic. The shallowness in which the ethic of God is being exposed probably has a lot to do with acceptance of the replacement ethic.

Examples of books giving the human existence priority include Lynn R. Davis' *Lord Deliver me From Negative Emotions*, a book which instructs the reader on how to make life on earth easier through positive talk to one's self, and Lilliet Garrison's *Getting Unstuck, Moving Beyond What's Holding You back*. Other books which instruct the reader how to have a successful life on earth are Joel Olsteen's *Every Day is Friday: How to Be Happier 7 Days a Week* and *Your Best Life Now: 7 Steps to Living at Your full Potential*. Osteen's books appeal to people looking for a way to tap into the power of God for a prosperous and happy life on earth.

The self-help Christian books pander to an audience seeking the riches of heaven on earth.

What is the problem with seeking a biblical formula for a rich life on earth? It is in the priority of God's ethic.

God requires He be thought of first in all things. Take, for example, the Lord's Prayer:

> *Our Father in heaven,*
> *Hallowed be your name;*
> *Your will be done*
> *On earth as it is in heaven.*

The second priority is the neighbor. Tertiary in priority is oneself.

The above-mentioned books may be well intended, but give the reader the false assertion that God's purpose is to deliver a prosperous and peaceful life to the individual Christian on earth. If that assertion is true, Christ's life, ministry and death were false. Christ said:

> *If anyone would come after me, let him deny himself and take up his cross and follow me (Matt. 16:24).*

Christ lived an impoverished lifestyle, and His life was in danger most of the time during His ministry. When He was crucified, He accepted the life and death God intended for Him. If the prosperity doctrines are correct, there are no impoverished Christians on earth or in heaven. If one knows God, one is prosperous on earth and in heaven.

How could God justify poverty among Christians on earth while giving riches to those with certain theological formulas? How could Christ ask Christians to follow Him to the Cross if God had not intended Christ's life, ministry and death to be an example to follow for all Christians, poor and rich alike?

The Christian self-help books are focused on the individual. The book reviews reveal the intended target audience (*quotes below taken from public book reviews*):

* *"The life you've yearned a lifetime for."*
* *"It's time to take back control of your life."*
* *"He shows readers how every day can hold the same promise and opportunities for pure joy that they experience at five o'clock on Friday."*
* *"He encourages readers to be people of faith, for if you can see the invisible, God will do the impossible."*

Self-help books probably have much to do with the growth of unorthodox churches. The books promise a positive result from God if only the reader follows the formula. What of Christians living in poverty in many places around the world where their Christian life is wrought with peril? Is it that these poor Christians cannot read the authorial theological formulas written in the books and therefore cannot escape poverty?

The poor can read and hear the rhetoric, and according to the formulas in these books, the poor have been left out. The message may be interpreted by the poor as:

* The prayers of the poor for a better life are not heard by God.
* God only hears the prayers of the affluent.

Christ's mission was to reach all people of the earth. His mission was inclusive of the poor and impoverished. The self-help books mean well, and they do sell a lot of books about God. However, Christ did not come as arbiter of wealth among men.

> *Someone in the crowd said to Him [Jesus], "Teacher, tell my brother to divide the inheritance with me." But He [Jesus] said to him, "Man, who made me a judge or arbitrator over you (Luke 12:13, 14)?"*

The doctrines in self-help books are shallow and do not reveal an in-depth ethic of God nor the ethical journey of mankind.

Not all self-help Christian books fall into the above category, but many do. Attempting to use biblical formulas to remove trial and tribulations and deliver prosperity on earth may be compared to a godless doctrine. Moses Hess, an early communist leader, revealed that the goal of communism and communist is to have the equality of wealth and prosperity, promised to Christians in heaven, here on earth. In Hess's view, the godless will have their best life now.

If a poor person reads and acts on the formulas of the self-help prosperity doctrines and still find they are in poverty or emotional distress, would not the promised economic equality of the godless be a tempting alternative? If that doctrine comes from a renowned pastor with supposed close ties to God, would the poor individual feel rejected by God?

Harmonizing the experience on earth with the ethic of God is not new, however. The book of Amos reveals an affluent class among the Northern Kingdom who thought God's admiration of them had made them wealthy. The promised *"Day of the Lord"* was interpreted as a time when God would make them ruler over all their enemies. Their interpretive focus was on themselves. The Northern Kingdom Jews were sure their harmonized existence with the world around them was the key to their wealth. The poor of the Northern Kingdom were left out and, according to the developed doctrine of prosperity, could count themselves rejected by God.

The use of God's Word to build competing theological movements is a source which fuels the cycles of lawlessness among mankind who may otherwise follow Christ. Many, if not all, of the movements intend to move mankind closer to God. However, the movements' doctrines in some cases may cause a wedge to form between God and mankind.

The use of God to vanquish the enemy was developed during the era of the crusades and Charlemagne. It is called Liberation Theology. In the late 1800s, a movement started to correct biblical errors among some who called themselves Christians. The result was to fill in the voids with mankind's own ethics. Eventually the name of the movement became the Liberal Church.

CHAPTER 1
Liberal Theology

§

This, in fact, is the difference between good men and bad men, that the for-
mer make use of the world to enjoy God, whereas the latter would like to
make use of God to enjoy the world—if, of course, they believe in God and
His providence over man, and are not so bad as those who deny even this.[xxxiv]

IN RECENT YEARS ATTEMPTS HAVE been made to harmonize Judeo-Christianity with the ethic of lawlessness through calls for religious tolerance. Many liberal churches believe all mankind has a place on the Ark Jesus built regardless of a belief in God or in the laws of the Christian church set up by the apostles. In other words, God and salvation must bend to the sacrosanct holy grail of liberalism's call for equality in the church on earth. Why would there be a need for Christ to come and be crucified if all men were acceptable to God regardless of their sins? Why would there even exist a need to be saved? Christ calls for equality, but before God rather than mankind.

Liberal theology came into existence in response to modern challenges to the Old and New Testaments. For example, in 1836, a book was written by David F. Strauss called *The Life of Jesus*. This book was highly critical of the synoptic gospels: Matthew, Mark and Luke. Strauss was unable to find the source used by the authors of the Gospels and thus viewed the New Testament as unreliable at best and at worst a book of fiction. For the first time Christians were faced with having to provide proof of God. It became popular for academia to look for inconsistencies, real or supposed, in the text of both the Old and New Testament. The Bible in the 19th century was under siege from the cultural enemies of God.

Along with academia's assault on the text came a new ethic for society. Those embracing criticism of the text found they no longer were able to live in a culture which, in their mind, had been worshipping a lie. The old orthodox religious order—ethic based in the moral laws given by God in the Torah—had to go. A new Christian initiative which supported or at least formed a partnership with the developing lawless cultural rebellion against God would be required.

It is in this setting that liberal theology was born. Liberal theology tracks a course common to the lawless (liberal) political ideology. This political ideology, which strives for a utopian society led by a governing force free of God or gods, is the world vision of lawlessness. In order to fit in the developing lawless order, liberal theology must, where biblical values conflict with lawless values, choose to conform to lawless values.

An example of liberal theology would be the writings of Julius Wellhausen. Julius Wellhausen wrote major commentary of the Old Testament (1883), challenging the timeline of the Hebrew text. He made a case for the Torah (first five books of the Old Testament) and the history books in the Old Testament as belonging to the same era. His work contradicted long standing Jewish and Christian interpretation of the scriptures.

Wellhausen's commentary relies heavily on interpreting internal evidence from mankind's perspective. A close look into the Wellhausen method of internal evidence reveals that his perspective is from socialist indoctrination. For example, in his work, *The Pharisees and Sadducees (1874)*, he uses socialist words to describe Jewish beliefs of the Maccabean period such as those listed below:

* Nationalist.
* Hated aristocracy.
* Antinationalistic tendencies.
* Hierocrats.
* Popular party.

* Party conflict.
* Maccabean liberation.
* Internationalists.

Wellhausen's choice of words in his work reveals internal evidence of a biblical scholar interpreting biblical text from a strictly socialist frame.

Wellhausen and other liberal-minded commentators commenting on the Bible during the era formed the liberal theological worldview and molded their theology into a religion that would be acceptable to the evolving lawless culture forming in Europe at the time.

Liberal theology seeks to harmonize mankind's lawless ethic and God's ethic. In doing so, liberal theology must base religion on tradition rather than text. For example, the battle over women as pastors in the church follows secular tradition established through the women's rights movements over the last 150 years. Modern culture dictates women must find equality in all things. In many denominations and churches, women have assumed pastoral positions, thus contradicting the biblical role of men as pastors in the Christian church.

The pastoral epistles, 1 & 2 Timothy and Titus, are clear on men being the pastors of the Christian church (Bride of Christ). This contradiction has its roots in the feminist movement that evolved alongside and fed off of the lawless movement in the West.

One might ask, "What is the problem with women as pastors?" While all can agree on the pastoral abilities of women being equal to men, the Bible and the Christian church organization as established by the apostles and the early church councils appoint men as pastors of the Christian church. Why do such a thing, since women are as capable as men? Men were appointed pastors because of the image of the Father in heaven. God constructed the Christian church in a manner that will point the way to the heavenly Father. Jesus continually stated that He was performing the will of the Father:

Not everyone who says to me, "Lord, Lord," will enter the kingdom of heaven, but the one who does the will of my Father who is in heaven (Matthew 7:21).

For whoever does the will of my Father in heaven is my brother and sister and mother (Matthew 12:50).

So it is not the will of my Father who is in heaven that one of these little ones should perish (Matthew 18:14).

For this is the will of my Father, that everyone who looks on the Son and believes in him should have eternal life, and I will raise him up on the last day (John 6:40).

Christians are instructed to pray to *"our Father who art in heaven."* The idea in all instructions given by God to both men and women is that men and women are to worship God the Father in heaven.

The instruction for male pastorate carries the same remembrance scenario as does the commemorative seven-day cycle of the Sabbath. Christians are to remember God the Father in heaven as the creator of all things and the giver of eternal life. They are to love Him above all else, including themselves and their gender. Catholics understand the connection between the earthly father and the heavenly father in the church organization. The priest is affectionately referred to as father. If the lawless movement is to replace Christianity with lawlessness successfully, the destruction of the biblical father figure image is and must be a primary goal.

The evolving liberal church found its leadership in the work of revolutionary groups like the ***Conspiracy of Equals.*** The Conspiracy of Equals was a product of the French Revolution, and the group is recognized as the first communist group in Europe. The group believed religion to be the cause of economic and class inequality among men and women. The group's constitution documented a plan for eradicating religion in France. The Judeo-Christian father figure had to be destroyed, they thought, in order to eradicate religion. Here is what they agreed had to happen to the father:

No more domestic education—no more parental sway, but, for the individual authority thus taken from fathers at home, the law would compensate them with authority a hundredfold greater in common.[xxxv]

George Lakoff, a liberal activist for the Democratic Party, in his work, *Moral Politics 2002*, makes the case for replacing the Christian father figure with a liberal father figure.[xxxvi]

The concept George Lakoff proposes, if accepted by the reader, replaces the ethic of God by replacing not only the biblical earthly father figure but God as the biblical father figure.

Liberal theology and many who are called conservatives have traded the biblical father figure in an attempt to obtain peace with the secular community in the arena of women's rights. In a secular frame of reference, women should have every right to pastor in non-Christian churches or any other organization. It would be wrong to do otherwise.

However, there is debate over biblical interpretation of women as pastors in the Christian church. The issue is whether to interpret the text from a sociological (knowledge of society) view or a contemporary cultural view. For example, Paul in his writings would have written as one who had been indoctrinated and educated into first century Jewish rabbinical culture. If one interprets Paul using the sociological science which dates his statements in the pastoral epistles as Jewish culture of the first century, his thoughts on men as pastor are as they appear in the pastoral epistles. If one interprets the epistles as isolated statements meant for a parochial audience, one may ignore the pastoral epistles and apply differing supporting argument from women's participations in Paul's missionary churches in the book of Acts.

The sociological science which states one's ethic is based in indoctrination and education of a given social group and era clearly limits any interpretation which is foreign to the era or sociological make-up of the Jewish rabbinical ethic. Paul was a Jewish rabbi before he was Christian. The Jewish rabbinical view of priest from Moses to Paul influenced, if not dictated, the pastoral epistles. It is not practical to reason otherwise.

The truth about the modern era inclusion of women as pastors is it reflects the will of the people which respond to modern era cultural movements of women's rights.

The interpretation which places modern era cultural ethics as a source for the first century writings of men is ridiculous at best, at worst it is simply a pandering of biblical scholars and leaders looking to fit God into a changing culture.

The situation has a comparison in Matthew:

> *And Pharisees came up to him and tested him by asking, "Is it lawful to divorce one's wife for any cause?" He answered, "Have you not read that he who created them from the beginning made them male and female, and said, 'Therefore a man shall leave his father and his mother and hold fast to his wife, and the two shall become one flesh'? So they are no longer two but one flesh. What therefore God has joined together let not man separate." They said to him,* **"Why then did Moses command one to give a certificate of divorce and to send her away?" He said to them, "Because of your hardness of heart Moses allowed you to divorce your wives, but from the beginning it was not so. And I say to you: whoever divorces his wife, except for sexual immorality, and marries another, commits adultery."**

One might rephrase the quote for the modern audience; Moses allowed them to divorce because they were going to do it anyway. However, the fact that the Jews divorced with Moses' approval did not change God's view of divorce. It simply reflected a culture of divorce among the Jews. Women as pastors may be viewed similarly. The phenomenon represents a departure from what was Judeo-Christian for 6000 years.

A similar cultural scenario has occurred with respect to liberal theology and homosexuality. In recent years, this issue has opened a rift that has further exposed the differences between liberal churches and conservative churches. Liberal theology has taken its idea of equality for all people to include accepting homosexuals as members, deacons, pastors or bishops in their churches.

It should be noted that lawless acceptance of homosexuals in any capacity of public or private life should be granted. It would be a travesty of secular justice if secularism were to refuse to accept them in any capacity public or private, including rights of marriage. There is no argument here with secular treatment of homosexuals. But with respect to Judeo-Christian law, homosexuality is lawlessness and unacceptable.

Since liberal theology does not follow biblical Christian doctrines, what specifically is followed in the liberal church? Liberal theology has a social structure that defines Christianity as being solely modeled on the biblical teaching regarding the love of one's neighbor. Consider the following quote *(Matthew 22:37–39)*:

> *You shall love the Lord your God with all your heart and with all your soul and with all your mind. This is the great and **first** commandment.*

> *And a **second** is like it: You shall love your neighbor as yourself. On these two commandments depend all the Law and the Prophets.*

If the second commandment becomes the first commandment, then God simply becomes a support structure for arguments that God will accept everyone regardless of their beliefs. For example, those who say "God is love" and "there is room at God's table for all neighbors." One would think from man's perspective that God would allow all at His table. The table in question is the marriage supper table of Christ and His bride, the Christian church (Revelation 19:9).

> *Blessed are those **<u>who are invited</u>** to the marriage supper of the Lamb.*

The ones invited are the ones who have boarded the Ark of Jesus and will be saved. The uninvited neighbors will not be at the table.

If the first commandment were to be to love one's neighbor, then logically, treating all neighbors fairly and equally is the primary goal and the foundation for Christianity. The second commandment, when acted out by liberal theology, implies that if you love God you must comply with the first commandment. While lawless culture is godless, the terms of religion for liberal theology agree with the sacred principles of equality held by the lawless, and through that a partnership is forged.

Liberal theology appears to view these two commandments of Jesus as being new commandments. However, when Jesus gave a new commandment, He announced it as a new commandment. Consider John 13:34:

A new commandment I give to you, that you love one another.

Also, liberal theology reverses the order of the two commandments given by Jesus in Matthew. Liberal theology does not view the Bible as being without error, which allows for a lawless interpretation of the text.

Upon further examination, it is clear that the two commandments given by Jesus in Matthew are actually a synopsis of the *Ten Commandments* found in Exodus.

Love your God	Love your neighbor
You shall love the Lord your God with all your heart and with all your soul and with all your mind. This is the great and first commandment.	And a second is like it: You shall love your neighbor as yourself. On these two commandments depend all the Law and the Prophets.
1. You shall have no other gods before me. 2. You shall not make for yourself a carved image, or any likeness of anything that is in heaven above, or that is in the earth beneath, or that is in the water under the earth. 3. You shall not take the name of the Lord your God in vain. 4. Remember the Sabbath day, to keep it holy.	5. Honor your father and your mother. 6. You shall not murder. 7. You shall not commit adultery. 8. You shall not steal. 9. You shall not bear false witness against your neighbor. 10. You shall not covet your neighbor's (wealth).

Equality and fairness are approached from a different perspective in the Bible. To follow the two commandments given by Jesus in Matthew and the Ten Commandments given by God in Exodus requires the

Christian to put God before all things, including the neighbor or himself/herself. The second requirement is to put the neighbor before yourself by honoring your mother and father, protecting life, honoring your chosen spouse, bearing witness to truth among your neighbors, and refraining from developing a desire for your neighbor's wealth.

Examples of Jesus' philosophy agreeing with God's given Ten Commandments on coveting and inequality are found in the New Testament text:

Someone in the crowd said to Him [Jesus], "Teacher, tell my brother to divide the inheritance with me." But He [Jesus] said to him, "Man, who made me a judge or arbitrator over you?" And He said to them, "Take care, and be on your guard against all covetousness, for one's life does not consist in the abundance of his possessions (Luke 12:13-15)."

The poor you will always have with you (Matthew 26:11).

A final example is the story of the Good Samaritan in Luke 10.

Although the commandments given by Jesus in Matthew or by God in Exodus (the Ten Commandments) do not support a doctrine of equality, the lawless and liberal theologians insist on a reinterpretation of the commandments in an attempt to force their own doctrine of equality onto the Christian church.

Christianity is a religion with specific criteria for being called Christian. The New Testament doctrine regarding sexual immorality and specifically homosexuality in the Christian church may be found in Romans 1:26-27, 1 Timothy 1:8-10, and 1 Corinthians 6:9-10, which defines homosexuality as unacceptable to the Christian Church.

In order to meet the doctrine of equality, homosexuals must be accepted as members, deacons or pastors in liberal churches. Once a religious organization accepts homosexuals in these areas, it ceases to be Christian. It can still be a religious entity, and perhaps liberal theology can rename their religion as Neo-Christianity or near-Christianity; however, it is not genuine Christianity.

One might argue that times have changed and since homosexuality is accepted in the lawless culture it should be accepted in the Christian church as well. However, homosexuality has always been a part of the culture outside Judaism and Christianity. The fact that homosexuality existed at the time of the formation of both Judaism and Christianity and was prohibited by God prohibits an argument for acceptance due to cultural changes of today. To include homosexuality as normal among Jews or Christians is to modify the rules which govern the religions. Modifying the rules changes the religion (game).

For example, Christianity changed the rules of Judaism at the time of Christ. The change in rules regarding Christianity required a different name for the new religion because Christianity marked a new way of worship which left Judaism behind. Similarly, liberal theology leaves Christianity behind. Liberal theology worships in a new way. The difference is that God ordained for Christianity to separate from Judaism, but liberal theology falsely builds their new religion as if it were Christian while functioning contrary to Christian doctrine.

In contemporary society when someone takes another's identity and uses it for their own purposes, it is called identity theft and fraud. This rule should apply to the liberal church, especially since they are driven by rules developed in opposition to God's law. One should not take what is not theirs.

Some might say that liberal theology is ignorantly unaware of the complications arising from using Christ's name to build their new religion.

The problem is that liberal theology prides itself on its academia. In fact, its very existence rests on a strict reliance on secular academic sources rather than faith. Because of this, it would be disingenuous for liberal theology to feign ignorance over whether it meets the plain criteria laid out in the New Testament to be called Christian. The situation is similar to one who has stolen a credit card and uses the stolen credit to provide legitimacy to his/her purposes.

Liberal theology seeks to seize the leadership of the people of God through lawless tradition and statutes rather than longstanding biblical truths. This was the tactic used by Jeroboam and is the same tactic used in the development of lawlessness. James speaks of this same activity with respect to his audience in James 4:4:

> *You adulterous people! Do you not know that friendship with the world is enmity with God? Therefore whoever wishes to be a friend of the world makes himself an enemy of God.*

Liberal theologians seek to use schools and churches to water down faith in God and teach a new gospel of Christ which is accepted by the lawless of the world. Liberals have taken their cue from groups like the Conspiracy of Equals in France. The Conspiracy of Equals thought to use a gradual system of downgrading and reducing religious activity among the populations in order to eventually purge religion from the minds of men. The strategy for lawlessness and liberal theology is a common one. To be successful, one must disregard the traditional interpretations of God and reframe the image of God to match contemporary events.

During the time between the Old and the New Testament, different religions developed among the Jews. One might argue that they were all different versions of Judaism. However, these religions were so foreign to God that the Son of God could not recognize them. Jesus warned His followers in Luke 12: *"Beware of the leaven of the Pharisees, which is hypocrisy."*

The Pharisees, Sadducees, and other Jewish sects during the era of Jesus were practicing these new religions, which were not recognizable to the Son of God. They were no longer worshipping God in the manner God intended; instead they were worshipping in the manner man intended. The various Jewish sects stood at the foot of the cross, mocking the Son of God while proclaiming their allegiance to God. The liberal church mocks God and Christ when they discard the laws and rules given to the church through the Torah and Jesus' disciples. Lawlessness will not dine with Christ at the table of *"the marriage supper of the Lamb."*

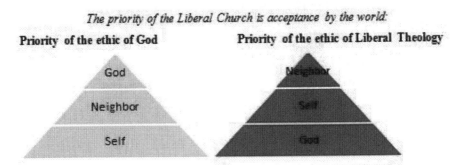

The priority of the Liberal Church is acceptance by the world:

Priority of the ethic of God   **Priority of the ethic of Liberal Theology**

CHAPTER 2

Liberation Theology

§

LATIN AMERICAN CATHOLIC LIBERATION THEOLOGY proposes lending political and military aid to multiple revolutions in Latin America. Certain priests, fed up with their poor communities, used the influence of their official office to encourage their members to join in revolutionary movements against the oppressive regimes of Latin America.

In many case these revolutionary activities have been led by men and women whose goal is to usher in a socialist or communist government. The idea is that people are fed up with the poor getting left overs and the rich living in luxury. The center of socialism/communism is found in the Communist Manifesto:

> *But communism abolishes eternal truths, it abolishes all religion and all morality, instead of constituting them on a new basis; it, therefore, acts in contradiction to all past historical experience*[xxxvii]

Like liberation theology in other areas of the globe, a percentage of Catholics willingly or unknowingly joined with the godless for the express purpose of destroying a common foe. To be fair, the Catholic believer may not even be aware of the issues surrounding the call to arms by certain Catholic theologians.

The militarization of Christianity by Catholic or Protestant theologians compromises Christian doctrine. The Crusades should have served as a lesson for Catholics and Protestants alike.

Priests who espouse liberation theology use Jesus' speech on the poor (Luke 4:18-19) in the synagogue to generate a holy war and exploit believers' actions for revolutionary purposes.

However, Jesus never attacked anyone, nor did He free the poor from economic oppression. In Luke 4:18–19, Jesus read the passage from Isaiah 61:1–3 in the synagogue, singling out the poor for the proclamation of the good news He was bringing to mankind.

> *The Spirit of the Lord is upon me, because he has anointed me to proclaim good news to the poor. He has sent me to proclaim liberty to the captives and recovering of sight to the blind, to set at liberty those who are oppressed.*

The Hebrew sense of the word "poor" carries a meaning far beyond that of being economically poor. For example, one without God or God's Spirit would be considered afflicted, and thus categorized by the Hebrew word translated into English as poor. Any person who finds himself an outcast in a given socioeconomic system would also be referred to by the same Hebrew word, even if the individual was not poor economically. Racial oppression, political oppression, economic oppression, and spiritual oppression are all conveyed by the Hebrew word used in Isaiah 61:1–3 and consequently by Jesus in Luke 4:18–19. Its interpretation is a matter of context. For example, who or what was the word referencing within the context of the given biblical conversation? Furthermore, the interpretation requires the interpreter to place the word or group of words in the historical timeframe in which they were spoken. Whatever oppression is being experienced in the context of the moment of the given biblical conversation, the Hebrew word translated as afflicted/poor carries the meaning of that oppression. For example, a rich man being stripped of his riches by an oppressive government tax system could be referred to as afflicted/poor in the meaning of the Hebrew word used in Isaiah and by Jesus in Luke. The book of Job in the Old Testament is an entire biblical book dedicated to a rich man's affliction and rescue by God. God addressed the poor versus rich scenario in Leviticus 19:15:

You shall not be partial to the poor or defer to the great, but in righteousness shall you judge your neighbor.

A comparison of Jesus' outreach to the poor (Jesus' reading of Isaiah 61:1–3) against the politics of the poor used by lawless philosophies like Marxism and liberation theology is in order. The first thing that comes to mind in contemporary culture when speaking of the poor is the economically poor. How did Jesus reach out to this crowd in the Bible? The answer lies in what Jesus did not demonstrate through miracles as much as what He did demonstrate through miracles. Jesus carried no money. He did not own a home or have excessive clothing. Jesus, in fact, was homeless. Consider Luke 9:58:

Jesus said to him, "Foxes have holes, and birds of the air have nests, but the Son of Man has nowhere to lay his head."

Jesus was the very definition of the contemporary meaning of economically poor. If Jesus were living today, it would be appropriate to say he was impoverished. However, He demonstrated the ability to heal the sick, blind, deaf, leprous, and paralyzed. He also demonstrated that He was superior to any supernatural forces on earth by casting out demons before the people. He could have had whatever He wanted from the people who followed Him, including wealth. Furthermore, He could have led a revolution against the Romans in order to free the oppressed Jews, and the people would gladly have followed Him. However Jesus chose to be poor. The demonstration of poverty on Jesus' part was intentionally done in order to ensure that the least of this world would hear His message of salvation.

Jesus was an itinerant preacher who went from city to city preaching the "good news" to the least (poor) members of society as well as the greatest (rich) of society. Jesus was aware that merely giving lip service to the poor while appearing to be rich would not enable Him to reach them with the message of salvation. Jesus knew if He appeared as a member of the wealthy, the economic poor of His time would only follow Him because of the apparent wealth. They would have followed Him looking to share in the wealth gained from the revolution to overthrow the oppressive Romans. They would be looking for monetary gain. Jesus was offering liberty/salvation to the afflicted/poor. His offer did not include immediate destruction of the Roman oppressors.

Jesus spoke of the importance of humility regarding the least in His kingdom in Luke 9:46–48, where an argument arose among them as to which of them was the greatest.

> *But Jesus, knowing the reasoning of their hearts, took a child and put him by his side and said to them, "Whoever receives this child in My name receives Me, and whoever receives Me receives Him who sent Me. For he who is least among you all is the one who is great."*

Jewish tradition in Jesus' time viewed the child as being the least important member of society. For example, children were not afforded the opportunity to learn in the synagogues until they reached the age of twelve or thirteen. They were not allowed to enter into serious discourse with adults until their time of adulthood. Children, in the Hebrew sense of the word "poor," were poor. Jesus used the child as a demonstration of the least among the people who were in attendance at this discussion. The use of a child to demonstrate who was the greatest among them would have been a radical concept. The implied lesson is that envy of wealth is not what Jesus understood Christianity to be.

Of course, this particular thought process could lead to a follower of Jesus thinking it is necessary to discard all that he/she has to follow Jesus. Christian monasticism was a resulting imbalance in the interpretation of the text. The failure to read and understand the full complement of the teaching of Jesus is in view here. For example, in Matthew 26:6–13, Jesus' disciples were incensed over a poor woman pouring expensive oil over Jesus' head. In verse 10, Jesus responded to the disciples:

Why do you trouble the woman? For she has done a beautiful thing to Me. For you always have the poor with you, but you will not always have Me. In pouring this ointment on My body, she has done it to prepare Me for burial. Truly, I say to you, wherever this gospel is proclaimed in the whole world, what she has done will also be told in memory of her.

What can be taken from these statements of Jesus is that He acknowledged the existence of the economically poor on earth for as long (always) as the age of mankind (with you) exists. Therefore Jesus, among other things, revealed that He did not come to earth to bring economic equality to the inhabitants of earth. In fact, these statements by Jesus imply that an economic inequality is to be expected for as long as the age of mankind survives. When He tells them *"but you will not always have Me,"* He is saying that the kingdom of God is something different than mankind's kingdom. Jesus was expecting to go to another place after His resurrection. In John 14:3, Jesus said that He was going "away" to prepare a place for His disciples. Peter also writes to followers of Christ that they are as exiles in a foreign land:

Beloved, I urge you as sojourners and exiles to abstain from the passions of the flesh, which wage war against your soul (1 Peter 2:11–12).

For Christians, the issue of economy of wealth will only be resolved in God's kingdom, not man's kingdom.

If Latin American Catholic priests who participated in liberation theology-driven rebellions believe Jesus came to free the economic poor from the bonds of oppression, they should be willing to reveal the verses in the New Testament accounts that back up their teaching. They should be able to reveal a Jesus who slays the wicked Romans along with the Sadducees and Pharisees. They should have no problem revealing the passages where

Jesus slaughters the wicked and places His followers in the arbitrator's chair. The fact is, Jesus stated the exact opposite*:*

> *Someone in the crowd said to Him, "Teacher, tell my brother to divide the family inheritance with me." But He said to him, "Man, who appointed Me a judge or arbitrator over you?" Then He said to them, "Beware, and be on your guard against every form of greed; for not even when one has an abundance does his life consist of his possession (Luke 12:14-15)."*

However, what does the New Testament or Jesus have to do with liberation theologians? Liberation theologians follow the lawless tenant of equality among all men.

Of course it is lawlessness which leads a person to ignore the plight of the poor. The book of Amos railed against the rich in the Northern Kingdom because they committed the atrocities. However, to use the poor as an excuse to destroy others or an excuse to take from the rich is also lawlessness according to the Christian God:

> *You shall not be partial to the poor or defer to the great, but in righteousness shall you judge your neighbor (Leviticus 19:15).*

Christians are to have compassion for the needy and help them as they are blessed by God. The objective of God in this helpful hand is to expose the goodness of the Christian God. It has been this way since the time of Moses and the formation of the law given to Moses by God. Consider the commandment in *Leviticus 19:9–10:*

> *When you reap the harvest of your land, you shall not reap your field right up to its edge, neither shall you gather the gleanings after your harvest. And you shall not strip your vineyard bare; neither shall you gather the fallen grapes of your vineyard. You shall leave them for the poor and for the sojourner: I am the Lord your God.*

The goal of this verse is to reveal God through the blessings of God, thereby leading the lost to the knowledge of salvation through Jesus Christ. The lawless component of liberation theology is a discourse which separates God and His commandments from His people by acting out a rebellion against the supposed oppressor and setting up the supposed liberation theologians as saviors of the people. God's goal is to lead people to Him as Savior and a utopian society after death. Liberation theology's goal is a utopian society on earth. One sees God as the answer; the other sees man as the answer. One is heavenly; the other is lawlessness.

CHAPTER 3
Summary

§

THERE ARE OTHER RELIGIOUS ENEMIES of the Judeo-Christian religion such as Islam, paganism and Gnosticism. However, those are old enemies which are common to the church and individual Christians. The old enemy can readily be identified by their stated religious difference or confession. They can easily be identified by the heresy of their confession. The early church was instrumental in exposing religious differences and heresy among the world's religious. The new religious enemies of God are not so easily identified. However, they may be found at Utopia and are exposed by their earthly utopian worldview.

Utopian societies have been the vision of mankind for thousands of years. The famous *City of God* and *Plato's Republic* are two of the most famous works with utopian plots. The *City of God* written by St Augustine represents the Christian utopian ideal, while *Plato's Republic* represents mankind's ideal utopian society. There are those (liberation theologians) who use God to fight for utopian communities on earth, and there are also those (lawless) who fight from a godless perspective for a Platonic society free from religion. The common views on utopia bring cooperation between the two philosophic combatants. They are all convinced that mankind is the answer to the new world utopian society which is emerging. They all have convinced themselves they are the real saviors of the world. Jesus as Savior may be stated by the utopians; however, the acts of the utopians give them away as followers of mankind's ethic.

To better understand the contemporary enemies of Christ, a parody is in order. In the United States (USA), there are those who are affiliated with the ideological group called progressive. Many people view progressives as unpatriotic/not loyal to the United States because the progressive worldview has condemned some of the past actions of the American government. The progressive worldview also would like to remove God from American government and society. One would surely think a progressive in the United States is not loyal to the United States or God. However, the American progressive is loyal to a United States yet to be and he/she yearns for the day when the United States will be a progressive utopian society. The American progressive is a patriot of a United States which is promised by their rebellion against the current United States Republic and its constitution.

The utopian Christian churches view a common utopian society on earth as does the progressive community. The common ground provides opportunities for political allegiances with the lawless progressives, and a pathway to the envisioned utopia on earth opens up.

The pathway to the earthly Utopia has the feel of reality. It appears to have the promise of peace and equality for all. It has the promise to fill all the needs of mankind. It is international in scope and promises to include all. The promised Utopia of mankind has its own gospel driven by the progressive culture. Its members actively recruit and indoctrinate new members in the progressive doctrine. It has many of the promises Christians see in the Bible. However, the promised Utopia depends on mankind for its arrival. After all, Christ has been gone almost two thousand years, and He has yet to return.

There is one question for the utopian Christian churches. If mankind can provide the Utopia spoken of by God and man alike, why does mankind need God or His church? The pathway to this utopian society of mankind is a dead-end street for Christians or any religion. It is the pathway to the death of the church and a life apart from God.

The Christian is also a patriot of a world yet to be. God promises salvation and a world absent of strife and bickering. A perfect utopian society built on God's promises. Symbolically, God promises for His followers (patriots) a return to the utopian Garden of Eden (heaven). The pathway is found within the biblical text. At the end of the path is the door to the utopian society promised by God. His name is Jesus, and He promises a life with God:

> *Truly, Truly, I say to you, I am the door of the sheep . . . I am the door. If anyone enters by me, he will be saved and will go in and out and find pasture (John 10:7, 9).*

The new church ethic seeks to destroy God's ethic from within the ranks of the Christian church, working from inside the faithful to build consensus among men/women to cast out the ethic of God and embrace the ethic of mankind. Agreement with the world while claiming allegiance to God is the calling card of the enemies inside the Christian church.

> *Do you not know that friendship with the world is enmity with God? Therefore whoever wishes to be a friend of the world makes himself an enemy of God (James 4:4).*

The current cycle of God's relationship with mankind may be compared to the earlier cycle which historians call the intertestamental period. The Gentile conquerors demanded the conquered Jews accept the ethic of the conqueror. The Grecian conquerors committed the unforgivable in the temple when they demanded the Jews sacrifice a pig in the most holy place in the temple.

The new enemies of God have placed God and His ethic on the altar inside the Christian church and demand allegiance to mankind's ethic in the current cycle. There are Christians (so-called people of God) who stand with the world demanding allegiance to the new worldview. The Jews called the act in the temple the Abomination of Desolation.

The acts of the rebellious utopians in the current cycle are the Christian version of the Abomination of Desolation. The new conquerors of God's people expect Christians to kneel and worship the new ethic of mankind inside God's church. If the Christian does not kneel before the altar of mankind's ethic, they are punished through a social isolation and name calling. Over the course of generations, Christians will become foreigners (exiled) in their own lands as the Jews were in the intertestamental period. The apostate will set himself/herself up as God in the temple of God, casting out God's ethic and accepting the replacement ethic of mankind.

During the intertestamental period, the impact of the ethical and cultural demands of the conquerors bent Judaism into a religion Christ did not recognize. The followers (Sadducees and Pharisees) of the bent religion did not recognize Christ their God, and Christ did not recognize the Pharisees and Sadducees as His people. Additionally, God will not recognize the ethic of mankind as Christian.

Beware the apostate church

Liberal Theology: These churches synchronize God's ethic with mankind's ethic. Liberal Christian churches and liberal Christians may be identified by their disregard for the Torah (Old Testament), Romans 1-3, Acts 15, and the Pastoral Epistles (New Testament). When a question arises about the ethic of God, liberal Christianity will most always choose the ethic of mankind's culturally driven society and discard God's ethic.

Liberation Theology: These churches seek to use God to gather forces to march on their perceived oppressor. They may be identified by their vocal calls for destroying their perceived enemy in the name of righteousness and God. When ordering the destruction of their perceived enemy, they will almost always quote a verse from the Old Testament judgments of Israel's enemies. One only has to look at the Islamic Liberation movements to find a comparison. They destroy because God would have them destroy is the call.

Beware the friend of the apostate church

Seculars: These seek a society free of the ethic of God. They are called among other names progressive, socialist, communist, and liberals in the West. Seculars have produced the human butchers of the last 150 years. Hitler, Lenin, Stalin and Mao Tse Tung are among the most famous. However, Hitler, Lenin, Stalin and Mao Tse Tung are not alone in the rebellion against the ethic of God and gods.

Many people view the bad men in recent history as anomalies of humanity. They are isolated events, people may say. A surface view of a calm sea is what they see. Most people just believe what they hear without investigation. The surface view of these secular butchers of mankind is that they appeared suddenly and without warning and gripped the crowds that followed them with their speeches and charisma.

Hitler is an example of one of the butchers whom people say mesmerized crowds with his speeches. However, Hitler did not just appear on the scene in post WWI and like a god gather the angels of death. He had a life's journey which prepositioned him and his followers as angels of death. The journey of Hitler was influenced by the culture(s) surrounding him. Hitler became what the cultural environment made him. Hitler lived in a time of great unrest in Europe. He lived at a time when Europe and Russia were embroiled in a rebellion against all things God or gods.

The revolutionary environment of Europe produced the butchers of the World War II and the revolutions of China, Korea, and Viet Nam. Even the revolutions of South America may be traced to the rebellion against the ethic of God which began in Europe. Marxism, Communism, Social Democracies, Bernsteinianism, Owenites, and progressive are names of rebellious movements against the ethic of God. Their history may be found and pursued in the journals of America, Europe and England.

In the Bible there is an end of the current age of mankind. The end chronicles the final battle for primacy over earth. In the epic battle, the Apostle Paul tells of a time of rebellion against God when a man of lawlessness will appear. The man of lawlessness is an apostate who has turned his back on the ethic of God and God or gods.

In Paul's second letter to the Thessalonians, he indicates that the man of lawlessness will precede Christ's return. It is not practical to think that these things will just appear out of the dark. It is practical that the man of lawlessness will appear as a result of his life's journey. Further, it is practical to envision a long drawn out rebellion against the ethic of God. After all, it took four hundred years of silence during the intertestamental period for Christ to appear. After Christ's death, it took until the fourth century AD (Constantine) for God's ethic to find primacy on the European continent. The man of lawlessness is yet to appear. However, the rebellion which is to precede the appearance of the man of lawlessness has not only begun, but it has overtaken much of the world.

The appearance of the man of lawlessness is a sign, according to the Apostle Paul, that the final cycle of God's relationship with man is coming to an end and Jesus will return. In order to find the rebellion, one must venture below the surface. The tracks of the last rebellion are there.

Below the surface one will find the tracks left behind by the men and women of the rebellion against God's ethic. Once the tracks are located, one may move along the path which ends the cyclic relationship with God. By tracking the last rebellion, one may even find God.

Last Rebellion And
The Cycle's End

Let no one deceive you in any way. For that day will not come, unless the rebellion comes first, and the man of lawlessness is revealed, the son of destruction, who opposes and exalts himself against every so-called god or object of worship, so that he takes his seat in the temple of God, proclaiming himself to be God. Do you not remember that when I was still with you I told you these things (2 Thessalonians 2:3-5)?

WHEN SPEAKING OF THIS PARTICULAR biblical text, many if not most theologians concentrate on the man of lawlessness. This biblical figure is also referred to in the books of 1 and 2 John as the antichrist. The antichrist (described in Revelation 13 as the "beast") is the one who will set himself up as God in the house of God. Christians are told to look for him as a sign of the imminent return of Jesus. However, this section will concentrate on the Apostle Paul's reference in the above passage to the rebellion.

The *man of lawlessness* cannot appear until the *rebellion comes first*. Do Christians believe the rebellion of which Paul was speaking will just suddenly appear? Will the presence of the *man of lawlessness* be regarded as some consider Hitler's presence—just a sudden horrible isolated event in history? Will the *man of lawlessness* conjure up this rebellion as a result of his charisma as some say Hitler's presence accomplished? Paul's text says not. The text clearly states the rebellion will come first. Just as the revolutionary environment existed before and even produced Hitler, the *man of lawlessness* will be a product of a rebellion against the ethic of God.

In addition, Paul draws a distinction between the lawlessness being practiced at the time of his letter to the Thessalonians and the rebellion which will come before the *man of lawlessness* is exposed. Paul was stating that a rebellion preceding the second coming of Jesus Christ would come before and set the stage for the *man of lawlessness*, just as the revolutionary activity in Europe set the stage which produced Hitler.

Lawlessness was the setting into which God introduced His ethic through the Thessalonian group to which Paul was writing. In order to make sense out of the rebellion Paul was referencing, one must view the last rebellion in 2 Thessalonians differently from mankind's lawless activity prior to the rebellion of which Paul wrote, which will precede the *man of lawlessness*. One should also acknowledge that this *rebellion* may occur over hundreds, even thousands of years, just as the international initiative of Christ was a rebellion against the ethic of mankind and has been going on for over two thousand years.

There are historical books that chronicle the beginnings of the revolutionary stage which produced Hitler. There are also historical books that chronicle the beginnings of the final rebellion of which Paul speaks in Thessalonians.

What is the *last rebellion*, and where does it come from? **The *last rebellion* is that social system which rejects and rebels against Judeo-Christian law or any law given as a result of religious origins.** According to Paul, the emergence of a *rebellion of lawless* represents the beginning of the **last cycle (rebellion)** away from God's ethic. It represents the last chance of mankind to board the Ark of Jesus. Because the rebellion of lawless of which Paul writes is the last rebellion against God's ethic, it will be referred to as the last rebellion.

Before continuing the journey into the last rebellion, rules of engagement must be explored. In addition, a question arises with respect to assigning last rebellion affiliation to those who wish to conceal their affiliation. Do the stripes on a zebra make a zebra a zebra? The question comes to mind when trying to assess historical affiliation with Paul's last rebellion. Moreover, is it necessary for the template of affiliation to match perfectly, or does consistency in compliance with mankind's ethic form the stripes of the rebellion against God and His ethic? It is true that even a five-year-old can pick out a zebra among horses by identification of its stripes once the child has been instructed. Moreover, the five-year-old can identify the zebra without regard for the different patterns specific to each zebra.

The rules identify the stripes of the last rebellion against God and His ethic. The rules will also reveal the impact of the rebellion against God on the Christian community and reveal a plausible track that leads to the fulfillment of eschatological (end times) prophecy in the Bible. It is not practical to list all the individual rules and teachings regarding the last rebellion. However, the following are rules, passed down by the founders of the last rebellion.

Rules:

- The last rebellion posits mankind as the highest intellectual being on earth.
- The last rebellion recognizes only itself as a source for good and rejects any supernatural being as superstition.
- The last rebellion posits itself as the savior of mankind and the earth through mankind's intellect.
- The last rebellion rejects God as creator.
- The last rebellion proposes an alternative ethic to God's ethic.
- The last rebellion does not recognize any God or gods as moral law giver.
- The last rebellion seeks control over the ethic of mankind through the making of laws in opposition to God's law.
- The last rebellion is a belief in a social foundation which rejects religious faith and worship in society.
- The last rebellion is a developed social system which seeks to replace God's ethic through indoctrination and experience of mankind.
- The last rebellion believes the public domain should be totally free of any religious indoctrination.
- The last rebellion rejects all religion as the basis for a social system.
- The last rebellion recognizes only mankind as title holders to the earth.
- The last rebellion is a worldwide rebellion which seeks to replace all ethics not aligned with its own developed ethic.

There was a time before the last rebellion when social issues revolved around the Judeo-Christian ethical systems. For example, the Holy Roman Empire (Catholic Church) was an ethical system patterned after the Christian way of life. When Protestants broke away from the Catholic Church, they were free to worship as they pleased. Along with freedom of worship came a freedom not to worship at all. Men could not only think of a system without religion; they could now write their thoughts on paper for all to read.

A new social system without religion was created from social philosophers who dreamed of a way of life free of religious influences. Some philosophers who wrote down their thoughts of a social order free of religion are Jean-Jacques Rousseau, Karl Marx, Friedrich Engels, and Eduard Bernstein.

The first factor one should recognize about lawless thought is that it consists of an ensemble of ideas taken from cultures already in existence. For example, lawlessness borrowed from ancient Greek philosophy to begin formulating an ethic without religion. *Plato's Republic* is one of the mythological social ethics from which ideas were borrowed. It involves a utopian society which Socrates and his associates played out in the writings of Plato. *Plato's Republic* is a perfect society where everyone is equal and everything is fair in every way.

It should be noted that *Plato's Republic* mirrors St. Augustine's utopian *City of God*. As is the case with the *City of God*, *Plato's Republic* is nothing but a myth. However, this ancient philosophy has lived in the minds of intellectuals for centuries. For example, in the eighteenth century, the utopian society of *Plato's Republic* resurfaced in the writings of philosopher Jean-Jacques Rousseau. He wrote *The Discourse of the Origin of Inequality and The Social Contract*. Plato's mythological perfect society is one source that contributes to the lawless ensemble of ideas for a utopian social order absent of God's ethic (lawlessness). Greek philosophers Epicurus, Democritus, Aristotle and even Christian ethics contribute to the ensemble ethic of lawlessness.

The second factor one must recognize about the last rebellion is that it has metastasized into different sects or "fronts," based on the means by which the particular lawless faction sought to impose lawlessness on the world.

The imposition of the ethic of the last rebellion on the world may be thought of as a global rebellion against the ethics of gods or God. Wherever the ethic of the last rebellion has taken root, religion has been oppressed and in most cases rendered irrelevant to social discourse. The last rebellion is the mortal enemy of the Christian church, and as in the case of the Christian church, the last rebellion has celebrated leaders who can be considered its "founding fathers."

"Founding Fathers" is a term used to identify the original organizers of a group or movement. The followers imitate the ideas of the original organizers. For example, the founding fathers of the United States are frequently referred to in debates over the direction the country should take on a given issue. Moreover, the Constitution, which was written by the founding fathers, memorializes the thought processes of the original organizers in order to guide those who come after them.

The last rebellion has its own set of founding fathers. Each of the fathers of the last rebellion used their own particular method of imposing it on the world. Their particular methods/denominations have names: communism, socialism, social democracy, or progressivism. In some cases the method was called by the name of the lawless father such as Marxism (Karl Marx), Bernsteinianism (Eduard Bernstein), or Owenite Communities (Robert Owen).

A brief study of the founding fathers of the last rebellion is important to understanding what it is and where it came from. The following is a brief history of the last rebellion and the men who acted on the ensemble ethic of lawless belief and carved out a social system without God.

CHAPTER 1
Babeuf

§

THE FIRST OF THE FOUNDING fathers of the rebellion against God and His ethic were a group called the Conspiracy of Equals in France (1796). The group's leader was a taxman called Francois-Noel Babeuf.

It has been said the blood of a martyr is the beginning of a movement. In the seventh chapter of the Acts of the Apostles, the first Christian martyr is recorded. His name was Stephen, and he was put to death for his religious views. The death of Stephen strengthened the resolve of the small band of people that followed this fledgling movement. This movement was known at that time as **"the Way."** The members of this movement would later be known by the name of **Christian**, a name given to them by the people of Antioch. The persecution of the members of this movement is well documented. The martyrdom of its members is sacrosanct.

The lawless movement parallels the Christian movement in that regard; it too has celebrated martyrs. The first of these is Francois-Noel Babeuf. Scholars estimate that Babeuf was born in the region of Picardy, France, around November 1760. His family lived in the town of Babeuf, in Picardy. The community of Picardy is reported to have been a Protestant refugee site populated by members of Calvinist colonies.[xxxviii]

Babeuf was a taxman in the feudal tax system of the time. When the feudal system was abolished, he was unable to find work as a taxman. He tried to find work in other occupations, but failed. He even tried to become an author. When things did not work out for him, he turned to unethical means for support. He cheated a friend out of an investment by fraudulently presenting a letter of support from a wealthy client. The friend joined what he thought was an investment, but later found out that Babeuf had swindled him out of his money.

During this time, the revolution in France was underway, and Babeuf's future was in doubt. His options were to continue trying to find work in the old system or find a new path to success in the new movement occurring in France. Babeuf chose to join the rebellion and became an activist in his hometown. He railed against the taxes imposed on salt, and the activism earned him several arrests.

Eventually he was arrested and taken to jail in France to answer forgery charges. It was here that Babeuf began a career in journalism, which eventually led to his own publication called the *Tribune of the People*. This journal would serve him and his associates throughout the revolution. Babeuf's revolutionary experience consisted of jumping from one revolutionary group to the next. He held allegiance only as long as he was with the group. Once he changed groups, he lambasted the previous group for their views. He was at one time a follower of Robespierre, Jacobins, and the Thermidorians. He was always a loyal follower and the one who could be counted on—until the next revolutionary came along.

Babeuf's tendency to acquire money through forgery was habit forming, and jail time became a recurring theme in his life. February, 1795, found Babeuf in jail again for forgery. It was during this jail term that the Conspiracy of Equals was hatched. This group, led by Babeuf, was to become the first lawless organization and is the historical marker for the beginning of the last rebellion. Others had written of a lawless Utopia, but this group was the first to attempt to impose it on society. The most notable men, other than Babeuf, in the organization were Sylvain Marechal, an atheist, and Filippo Michele Buonarroti. Marechal wrote a popular work called; *The Atheist's Dictionary* and also composed the *Manifesto of Equals*. Buonarroti's contribution is most understood by his authorship. Years later, he wrote an account of the group.

This group and these men can be called the founding fathers of the last rebellion that has ravaged and terrorized the planet since 1796. The doctrines that they established are memorialized in their manifestos. Moreover, the famed *Communist Manifesto* of Karl Marx and Friedrich Engels reflects many of the doctrinal views found in the Manifesto of Equals. The ideals and doctrines of Babeuf, Marechal, and Buonarroti can also be found in contemporary lawless thought.

Bronterre (1836) chronicles the new social order envisioned by the Conspiracy of Equals when he quotes Buonarroti:

> *In the social order conceived by the committee, the country takes possession of every individual at birth, and never quits him till death. It watches over his first moments, secures him the nourishment and cares of his mother, keeps out of his reach everything that might impair his health or enervate his constitution, guarantees him against the dangers of a false tenderness, and conducts him, by the hand of his parent, to the national seminary, where he is to acquire the virtues and intelligence necessary to make him a good citizen . . . To accomplish this fully, the educators would strive "to render all affections of family and kindred subordinate to "love of country"*[xxxix].

Religion in the Conspiracy of Equals was understood and treated as superstition. Buonarroti wrote of mixing new concepts with old religious traditions. His purpose was to use this watered-down religious teaching to wean citizens eventually from religion and replace their religious fervor with affection for the new order. Bronterre's biography records the Conspiracy's plan:

> *No more domestic education—no more parental sway, but, for the individual authority thus taken from fathers at home, the law would compensate them with authority a hundredfold greater in common.*[xl]

The group Conspiracy of Equals wrote a *Manifesto of Equals* which documents the last rebellion's hatred of God's ethical family structure. The committee that composed the documents was called the "Secret Directory".

They circulated a short version of the manifesto called the *Analysis of the Doctrine of Babeuf.* In addition, the committee drafted a constitution for the new group. The committee's constitutional decrees are in part:

The right of inheritance is abolished.

Every French citizen, without distinction of sex, who shall surrender all his possessions in the country, and who devotes his person and work of which he is capable to the country, is a member of the great national community.

All who have passed their sixteenth year, as well as all who are weak in health, in so far as they are poor, are ipso facto members of the national community.

All private trade with foreign countries is forbidden.

Only persons not belonging to the community are liable to taxation.

This total contribution shall be distributed over all persons liable to taxation, progressively, on an ascending scale, according to the department.

The selected parts of the Conspiracy of Equals' constitution certainly reflect contemporaneous lawless thought. Moreover, the 1796 constitution is similar to American progressivism:

No one may promulgate opinions directly contrary to the sacred principles of equality and of the sovereignty of the people [xli]

Oh! Sorry, that is still Babeuf and the Conspiracy of Equals.

Babeuf and his fellow conspirators were arrested in May of 1796. Babeuf, after a lengthy trial, was delivered to the guillotine. Babeuf and his fellow conspirators are the first martyrs of last rebellion.

The industrial revolution and the elimination of the feudal (tax) system left Babeuf without a job. He responded by taking what he needed through forgery. The French revolution sought to redistribute the wealth of France by taking it from those who had it and passing it around. The revolutionaries, of course, sought to share in that redistributed loot. The fuel for the beginnings of the last rebellion was envy and greed.

Further, the constitution of the group makes it clear that equality refers to conformity. Those who do not conform were not equal. Nonconformists were singled out for punishment by the proposed progressive tax system. Further, equality is defined in economic terms in Babeuf's constitution and it is clear that no one is allowed a religious difference. The religious would not share in the redistributed loot. Free speech was conditional on its conformity to the utopian sacrosanct principles of equality; **equality=conform or die.**

CHAPTER 2
Robert Owen

§

ROBERT OWEN, ANOTHER FOUNDING FATHER of the last rebellion, repre-sents the passive approach for imposing lawlessness on the world. He sin-cerely thought that the world would abandon the Judeo-Christian social system of the day for his lawless social system. His is a story of a successful capitalist, social welfare activist, and social reformer.

Robert Owen was born in Newtown, Wales on May 4, 1771. He lived a traditional existence with his parents. Robert was still a young boy when his father put him on a stagecoach to London with a small amount of money. There he was met by his older brother who provided for him. Robert's father had previously arranged for his employment at a clothing retailer.

Robert Owen was an industrious young man and soon found favor with his employers. Owen worked for several years as an assistant to a clothing retailer. While in this position, he learned the textile trade. Moreover, he was exposed to new and innovative technology for spinning cotton, which revolutionized the industry.

At the age of sixteen, Owen seized on an opportunity to manufacture textile machines with an associate. He soon found a buyer for his share in the manufacturing venture and with the proceeds started his own textile shop. He eventually sold the textile shop to a larger mill owner named Peter Drinkwater. As part of the sale of the small shop, Drinkwater agreed to pay Owen to manage the mill he had sold him.

The amount Owen was to receive was significant for his age. Owen, at a very young age, acquired enough wealth to make him independent. He was a real product of industrialized capitalism of the era.

Owen, the young capitalist, was consumed with the business of the textile industry. He obtained permission from his employer to place his name on the yarn that was shipped out from the mill. This action gave him maximum exposure to industry leaders and financiers. Owen purchased the Dale Mills of New Lanark.

The purchase was to become the source of his lasting fame. New Lanark is where Owen began his experiments with social reform. Up until this point in his life, Owen had been an obsessive capitalist, a man driven to succeed.

The acquisition of Dale Mills and the New Lanark community presented him with a fresh opportunity. For the first time, Owen was in complete control of the lives of the employees of the mill. However, he was unschooled in the role of owner/operator of a nineteenth century mill. His management style would be, understandably, innovative and unorthodox.

The New Lanark mills were not unlike the textile industries of the time. They were places where children between the ages of seven and twelve were given over to the industrialists as indentured servants. The children working in the mills were poor, uneducated, and lived in appalling conditions. Owen himself was not too far removed in age from these circumstances. He was able to identify with the plight of these children through real life observations and experiences. Moreover, the New Lanark mill employed hundreds of these children at the time Owen acquired the mill. In addition to the conditions surrounding the children, Owen observed that the mill employees were idle and that dishonesty was a major concern.

Owen began the work of making things better for the employees. He understood that the new industrialism sweeping across Europe was sweeping away the people and their traditional lives. R. G. Garnett in his book *Cooperation and the Owenite Socialist Communities in Britain* revealed that Owen realized wages were only one factor in the overall well-being of the employees in the mill. Owen connected the social environment of his employees to the economic environment.

When Owen began his efforts in the factories, he devised a plan he called the "silent monitor" to uplift mill employees' spirits. Owen's efforts spilled over into the rest of the mill community. The mill communities of the nineteenth century were not traditional by any means. They were products of industrialization. Entire families formed a good number of the employees, and any newborn infants became residents of the industrial communities. These were a far cry from the orthodox agrarian communities of the previous era.

As a result of the deteriorating conditions among the community, Owen began to deal with the lives of employees outside of the mill and its employment. One of the rules he imposed was a prohibition against drunkenness. In order to curb the activity, he employed watchmen to monitor the streets at night. Moreover, he required the residents to clean up the community. He organized block committees to see to the cleanliness. A significant reform he instituted was the education of children. He contributed considerable financial support for the education of children in his employ, effective until they were twelve years old.

The education of mill employees alone was extreme for the day; to educate a child until he or she was twelve was an unheard-of innovation. As a result, the schools at New Lanark mills became so famous that many prestigious visitors came to observe the communities and schools. The New Lanark experience was a defining moment for Robert Owen.

The obsessive capitalist was replaced with the obsessive social reformer. He never looked back. The rest of his life was spent on experiments in social reform. These experiments would bring him fame in their radical approach to a new world social system. However, the most significant element of his experimental reform at New Lanark and subsequent ventures is not in what he implemented. Rather, it is found in what he left out. **The system was intentional in its absence of the ethics of God**. For the era, it was a most unusual concept. The implied doctrine of this concept became the new religion of Owen and the foundation of his proposed new lawless social order. Religious activity was forbidden. Owen had joined the last rebellion, and his approach would be deadly medicine for the ethic of God.

Owen's ideas and work with the communities were commendable. However, Owen wrongly blamed the social environment created by greedy industrialists on God and the ethic of God. The reality is that the environment which sentenced children to work in factories was never a part of the social system God envisioned for mankind. Owen's response, however, was to eliminate what he perceived was the source of the problem—a social system built around religion.

Owen used the fortune he had accumulated in the capitalist system to fund his vision of lawless communities. He believed these lawless communities would be so well received that there would be no need to impose them through revolution. The world would come to him. All he had to do was to create utopian communities which ascribed to the lawless ethic he had designed.

America with its frontier and independent society presented the opportunity for such a lawless community. In 1825, Owen purchased a commune from a group of Lutherans that had migrated to the United States. The commune was located in Indiana on the Wabash River. Led by George Rapp, it was four thousand acres in size. Furthermore, the Rappites had already developed it. The original residents produced products which they sold in many cities in America. The community presented a near perfect situation for the beginning of the "*New Moral World.*"

Buonarroti, a prominent member of the Conspiracy of Equals, stated from his exile in Brussels,

What the Democrats . . . were unable to execute in France, a generous man has recently assayed, by other means, in practice in . . . America . . . communities founded on the principles of equal distribution of enjoyments and of labors. [xlii]

Babeuf and Buonarroti had not given the movement a name. However, Owen and his followers in Indiana thought better. They named the movement *"socialism"*. They retained the name of the commune the Lutherans had used and called it New Harmony. After the acquisition and population of the new community, Owen went back to England. He left the lawless community in the hands of his son William and other trusted followers. In his absence, however, New Harmony became a community of idlers. A member of the socialist community wrote of the lack of work ethic demonstrated by the members in the community. It appeared that not many in the socialist community were willing to contribute to the social welfare of the group. However, apparently some success was realized when cooperation produced barley for the required beer of the residents.

The people of the lawless community were unable to work together. As a result, the community faltered until by summer of 1827, the project was pronounced a failure. Owen excused the failure and blamed the socially underdeveloped Americans for the debacle. The short life of the community did not illustrate the working power of the envisioned Owenite lawless community. However, it did provide insight into the social order Owen envisioned for the world. When he was criticized for advocating promiscuity among the residents, young and old, of New Harmony, he revealed that he thought marriage to be an unnatural act. He went on to state that he believed men and women could not commit to their future affections and that their feelings could change in regard to future acquaintances or circumstances. When he was criticized for housing boys and girls in the same dormitories, he argued that abstinence was unnatural. He believed nature would take its course in its own time and to interfere would be to commit a crime against the laws of nature. His ethic was lawlessness.

The experience at New Harmony revealed a foundational truth about the coming lawless world; *religion would not be a part of the system*. Owen postulated in his book *New World Order* that every person should join in stamping out religion for all time. He believed religion was a crime against nature.

All, all from the highest to the lowest, from the oldest to the youngest, have the deepest interest—an interest combining their happiness as individuals, the happiness of their offspring, and of all future generations—in striking a deathblow now and at once against this hydra of human ills; in rooting up, without farther delay, this tree of evil, which bears poisonous fruits only, and which produces not a single blossom of good to counteract its ever-increasing evil and destructive effects[xliii].

Owen believed that it was not God's law that should be followed, but nature's law. His decree set the stage for the development of lawlessness as an ethic (way of life) meant to replace God's ethic. For the Jew or Christian, the realization that Owen's system, which was called socialism, represents the lawless in much the same way the traditional Torah (biblical Mosaic Law, Judaism, Hebrew law as given in the first five books of the Bible) is a foundation to Judeo-Christian thought, is profound. For the Jew, socialism proposes to wipe out four thousand years of heritage and with it the foundation of Jewish existence. The Christian is faced with the same issue in regard to heritage and foundation. However, the Christian must feel to some degree vindicated by the arrival of the lawless ethic. The New Testament speaks of the last rebellion in 2 Thessalonians 2:3–4:

Let no one deceive you in any way. For that day will not come, unless the rebellion comes first, and the man of lawlessness is revealed, the son of destruction, who opposes and exalts himself against every so-called god or object of worship, so that he takes his seat in the temple of God, proclaiming himself to be God.

Owen's work to eradicate religion and replace it reveals the truth about the last rebellion. The rebellion will tolerate the ethics of God as long as the people of God retain consensus in a democratic society. When the consensus swings to the last rebellion's side, God's ethic will be marked for extinction.

Robert Owen believed so fervently in the destruction of God's ethic that he devoted vast amounts of time and effort to its demise. He devoted many hours and days writing books about the woes of God's evil ethical system. Consider the following excerpt from Owen's book in 1842:

> *1st. The existing system cannot secure, but is itself an effectual bar to the attainment of "a good organization, physical, mental, and moral, at birth;"*

> *while the proposed system would speedily prepare the way for the human organization at birth to be gradually improved through future generations, in a manner far superior to what man has yet effected in the improvement of any of our domesticated animals.*

> *while under the new [system] all will be so educated, trained, and placed, that all may, advantageously for all, enjoy this highest of all enjoyments . . .*

> *8th. Under the existing system, superstition, supernatural fears, and the fear of death more or less torment the human race;*

> *while under the Rational System they will never be created, and will therefore remain unknown . . .*

> *11th. Under the existing system, a character of ignorance, error, injustice, uncharitableness, and unkindness is forced upon all, even upon those now deemed the best throughout society,*

> *while, under the Rational System, most especial care will be taken, as the first object of society, to insure from birth a character which shall be pervaded with the spirit of universal charity and kindness, and with the most lovely and superior qualities.*

> *12th. Under the existing system, no society can be found upon earth in which its laws, institutions, and arrangements, well organized and well governed, are all in unison with the laws of human nature;*

while under the Rational System every division of society will have its laws, institutions, and arrangements, well organized and well governed, at all times, in perfect unison with the laws of human nature.

Such is the difference between the Irrational System which has hitherto prevailed throughout the world, and the Rational System recommended in The Book for immediate adoption.

For those interested in researching further Owen's teachings, many of his books are free and can be found on the internet in *google Books.*

Evidence of a modern connection to Owen is found in George Lakoff's *Moral Politics, Whose Freedom* and other works of Lakoff. Lakoff's work written in the contemporary setting seeks to accomplish the same comparisons as Owen's *The New Moral World.* For example in *Moral Politics,* Lakoff develops lawless society through a comparison of the biblical family model and the lawless parent model. Like Owen, Lakoff believes that God's ethic should be eradicated. If the last rebellion really believed in tolerance, would its members engage in activities designed to destroy God's ethic and His followers?

The last rebellion had no track record to point to before Owen. He, along with others who dreamed of a lawless ethical system absent of God, had the luxury of touting a system without flaws. However, today the records reveal the destructiveness of the last rebellion. Joshua Muravchik in his work *Heaven on Earth* states that the last rebellion has claimed over one hundred million lives since Owen's day.

In Owen's New World Order, God's people are not regarded as equals. In the lawless ethic, God's people have no right to exist.

The same hatred Owen expressed for God's ethic and capitalism also exist in the writings Karl Marx and Freidrich Engels. The primary difference is the manner in which Owen proposed to impose the lawless ethic on the masses.

CHAPTER 3
Karl Marx

§

KARL MARX IS PROBABLY THE most influential founding father of the rebellion against God and His ethic. The experience-based ethic (sociology of knowledge) spoken of in this work has its roots in Karl Marx's writings, which spawned sociological studies that view daily activities in one's social environment as being critical to ethical development.[xliv] According to this proposed ethic of mankind, mankind's ethic comes from his experience. The proposal is:

1. If one is in a Christian ethical environment, he/she will follow God's ethic.
2. If one is in a lawless environment, he/she will follow an ethic other than God's ethic. The ethic comes from the social interaction with one's particular society.

This thought process of Karl Marx led Marx and his followers to believe mankind could be changed to follow an ethic developed by mankind. All mankind has to do is change the environment in which mankind lives. Karl Marx is as important to the foundation of the last rebellion as Thomas Jefferson was to the development of the U.S. Constitution. For that reason, Christians who follow God's ethic must understand where Marx came from and how he emerged as the most influential leader in the last rebellion.

A family rabbinical heritage and the European tradition of discrimination against Jews is the setting into which Karl Marx was born on May 5,

1818, in the town of Trier, Rhenish, Prussia. Heinrich Marx, Karl Marx's father, rejected the family religious tradition of rabbinical training, wanting something else for himself and his children.[xlv] However, the Prussian government confirmed by decree in 1824 that non-Christians were not eligible for public schools.[xlvi] Henrich Marx's desire led him to become a Lutheran. The conversion to Lutheranism allowed him to pursue an education in law.

Of course, the move by Heinrich Marx was a move to distance himself from the Judeo ethic of God. As a Lutheran he could attend schools that were teaching rebellion against the ethic of God. It was these supposedly orthodox schools which led the rebellion from the vantage point of their platform of mentoring young scholars. The use of scholarship to recruit and mentor members to the last rebellion is a pattern that is ingrained in the movement of the lawless.

Heinrich's experience with his conversion was repeated for his children; they were required to leave Judaism and become Lutherans. His son Karl Marx would make even more radical choices regarding God's ethic. Heinrich traded the ethic of God for success and influenced his children to do likewise. Karl's choice regarding the rejection of God's ethic would influence the world.

Karl Marx was seventeen when he graduated from secondary school and began attending Bonn University in 1835. At first he attended lectures, but after a while he lost interest in the curriculum. He began to get involved in the student extracurricular social activities. The societies he involved himself with were Poetenbund and Landsmannschaft. Poetenbund was a student revolutionary society that made use of poetry as a medium for revolutionary ideas, while Landsmannschaft was a fraternity of student intellectuals. Karl's father did not appreciate Bonn University, and in 1836, Karl was moved to Berlin University.

The faculty and students of Berlin University during that time were engaged in a debate over a book written by D. F. Strauss. The book, *The Life of Jesus*, interpreted the Gospels as myths. David McLellan in his work *Karl Marx, Early Text* reveals that Strauss did not believe Christ was

God incarnate. Strauss, according to McLellan, believed truth could only be found in the *"whole of humanity"*. For Strauss, the view of Christ as both man and God was a myth. Strauss' book followed the philosophical tenets of the famous German philosopher Friedrich Hegel. All things may be traced back to their natural origins.

The students who followed Hegel's philosophy were called Hegelians. For Hegelians, the debate centered on whether one was "conservative" (religious), took a mediated position, or sought to throw out religion based on the criticisms of Strauss. Strauss later used the terms Right, Center, and Left to identify those in the political/religious debate. Young Hegelians became known as the "Left" politically and were the group with which the young Marx became identified.

The definition "left, right and center" of political opponents in the debate over God's ethic is still in use today. Those who desire to keep God's ethic as a social system are called "right". Those who desire to form a new system around the lawless culture are "left". And those who desire to mediate the two positions are "center." The exception is the "left" political ideology which insist nationalists are politically "right" even if they desire a lawless system free of God's ethic. For example, Hitler was the leader of the National Socialist German Workers Party. Because Hitler's party was devoted to Germany, traditional leftists disowned Hitler's national party and labeled them *"far right wing."* Vladimir Putin, of Russia, is labeled *"far right wing"* for the same reason although no one would call Putin religious. Being *"left"* requires a lockstep loyalty to an international utopian society absent of influences of God or man-made borders.

The group evolved into a movement, and some of its most prominent members were Bruno Bauer, Moses Hess, Friedrich Engels, and Karl Marx. McLellan gives a good description of their backgrounds as people of affluent middle-class families. Almost all of the Hegelians had an education and were employed by the university.

The radical views of the group were enough to have them expelled from the university system. The expulsion moved the debate to print media. Over a four-year period, the Young Hegelians wrote forty thousand pages of material regarding their views.

Bruno Bauer led the Young Hegelians. In 1838, he wrote a criticism of the gospels that went well beyond that of Strauss. The work exposed the obsessive critical demeanor the Young Hegelians had for God's ethical system.

Marx was at this stage of his development close to Bauer. Marx wrote his doctoral dissertation with Bauer's help. The dissertation (*On the Differences between the Democritean and Epicurean Philosophy of Nature*) follows a long line of progressive lawlessness in the life of Karl Marx. It is the evidentiary climax of years of training.

Karl and his siblings were baptized into Christianity on August 26, 1824.[xlvii] For Karl Marx, the event preceded a lifelong aversion to religion and religious peoples. Karl Marx as an adult would later express in an article that religion was *"flowers on mankind's chains, the halo above the valley of tears and the opium of the people."*[xlviii] In his early life, it was demonstrated that the way out of poverty was to abandon religion. Success was freedom from religious ties, freedom from God. The experiential impact of the conversion from Judaism to Christianity and Christianity to atheism may very well be the root of the formation of Marx's *"sociology of knowledge"* theories.

Moses Hess, another member of the Young Hegelians and the first German communist, upon reading Marx's dissertation, predicted that Marx would be instrumental in eradicating God's ethic and changing the politics of mankind. Marx's journey to the last rebellion was complete. There was only one question left: how do the lawless manage life in a world which follows the ethic of God?

CHAPTER 4
Friedrich Engels

FRIEDRICH ENGELS PARTNERED WITH KARL Marx to develop an ethic opposed to everything God or gods. He was instrumental in writing the famous *Communist Manifesto*, which called for God and God's ethic to be thrown out of society. His story is one of rejection of God and His ethic. He is also a contradiction to the concept of environment driving ethic. He was raised in a family which followed the ethic of God. If experience dictates which ethic is followed, Engels would have followed the ethic of God. Engels chose the ethic of mankind over God's ethic irrespective of environment. For that reason Christians should understand his history. How did he become lawless?

Friedrich Engels' family was economically prosperous, religiously studious, and well known for their philanthropy toward the employees in their care. The Engels were not typical mill owners of the eighteenth century. They were philanthropic in their approach. Gustav Mayer's biography of Friedrich Engels records the remarks of a friend saying that the Engels were the first to build communities around their factories for their employees. Mayer further reports that another family member, Engels' great-grandfather Johann Caspar, built a school for children in 1796 and during a famine in 1816 led a relief effort for the poor as head of the Corn Union.[xlix]

The Engels demonstrated an extraordinary benevolence for their employees, considering the era. In addition, the family lived a Judeo-Christian lifestyle of eighteenth century Prussia. Friedrich Engels raised his children in a Christian belief system that followed Calvin theology.

The Bible was the center of the family structure and business practices, and those in the devoutly religious Friedrich Engels household were expected to follow both the family religious and business tradition. However, Friedrich Engels Jr. rebelled against his father's expectations.

The rebellion against his father took control of his future and propelled him into a rebellion against the ethic of God.

Friedrich Engels Jr. was born on November 28, 1820, in the township of Barmen in the Rhineland of Westphalia, Prussia. Typical of the area, the family belonged to the Calvinist group of Christians. Calvinists are serious about their faith and are careful to protect their doctrinal views from outside influence. Most especially, the family would have sought to protect themselves from the rebellion against God which had evolved in Europe during the era.

The rebellious lawless movement that migrated from France and German academia presented a challenge to the family, and the family naturally sought to shelter its children from the movement. When Engels' family became aware their son was learning more about Greek ethics and civilization in the university than about God's ethic and Christianity, they removed Engels from school and placed him in the family business.

Engels Jr. was sent to a family business associate for practical training that would indoctrinate him into the business and sever ties to the last rebellion he had developed while in the public school system. However, as one can imagine, the genie was out of the bottle. Engels found the local bookshops to be very good resources for quenching his desire for lawless stimulation. Furthermore, the pamphleteering in the area interested Engels to the degree that he wrote schoolmates back home about them.

The lawless movement so interested Engels that he soon moved from reading and observation to action. At first he began to write poetry, and some of his work was published. The event would serve him and his rebellious lawless cause for the rest of his life.

Engels' journey into lawlessness took him further and further away from his religious roots. At the age of eighteen, he read D.F. Strauss' book, *The Life of Jesus*. He wrote of his experience in reading the work, admitting that the writings of Strauss led him to doubt his faith and the teachings of his father.

The encounter with Strauss led him straight to Hegel and Hegelianism. Hegelianism led to his first contacts with a literary movement called *Young Germany*. This movement promoted the Enlightenment and scorned the old ethic of God. Engels believed these revolutionary ideas could bring freedom from the chains of family, family business, and the obligatory ethic of the God of his father.

The Young Germany movement served to complete his entry into the last rebellion and preceded his affiliation with the Young Hegelians and Karl Marx.

By 1842, Karl Marx had firmly established himself as an atheist *(member of the last rebellion)* and considered himself an extreme liberal democrat who desired to replace the German monarchy with his version of democracy. He was editor of the *Rheinische Zeitung*. This journal was the mouthpiece for the Young Hegelians and other radical journalists. Consequently, it was under close scrutiny from government censors. Marx found himself an umpire in the revolution of radical ideas. In October of 1842, he responded to criticism that the *Rheinische Zeitung* had become a voice for communist ideas. His reply revealed his belief that communism was *"unrealizable"*.

The position he took as editor reveals that Marx was at his core a Hegelian atheist. He was yet to be convinced that communism was the medium which could replace God's ethical system he so vehemently despised.

Engels on the other hand met with Moses Hess in Berlin in October, 1842, during a visit to the *Rheinische Zeitung*. Terrell Carver in his biography of Engels credits this October meeting as the date of Engels' acceptance of communism as a lawless model capable of replacing the old Judeo-Christian model of society.

Engels' conversion to communism was not an abandonment of the last rebellion. According to Carver, Engels' logic was based on the Enlightenment philosophy and revolutionary replacement of the ethical society of God. Communism would have to accept the logic of the last rebellion or compromise the cause. Engels' development of the communist ideology around lawless revolutionary politics was a necessity. He had progressed in his rebellion against God's ethic as far as it would take him logically. Now that the conversion was complete and the rebellion against God was accepted, how does one proceed with rebellion? To say that one does not believe in God is rebellious. However, belief alone does not mount an offensive to take territory.

Lawlessness and communism combined theory with practice, making the new world plausible. Lawlessness sought to rebel against God's ethic. However, lawlessness in and of itself does not provide a means to replace God's ethic in society. Communism was the ethic Marx and Engels agreed upon in order to revolutionize society into a lawless frame. The combination of lawlessness and communism is termed Marxism.

The City of God had failed to materialize under the oppressive structures of Catholicism and European industrialism. Mankind stood in the way with men's lust for power and money, many of whom used the worship of God as an instrument to oppress the population. Communism promised a new beginning for the Promised Land. Communism promised the City of Man, a utopian society where all men and women are equal and the rich and powerful will be no more. Power in the City of Man could be vested in the common people who would all be equal, and the oppressive God and His ethic would not be welcome in the utopian City of Man.

Engels met Marx in Paris on August 28, 1844. The meeting was preceded by Engels' work entitled *Outlines of a Critique of Political Economy*. Engels spent over a week with Marx discussing the politics of religion and economics. The two were in agreement on every issue. Padover in his biography of Marx reveals that the connection was rooted in the last rebellion worldview. Scholars generally accept the Paris rendezvous as the time

Marx accepted communism as a method to replace the God's ethical system in the world. He was a twenty-six-year-old editor of a radical journal and a religiously devout atheist. Communism was an alternate society that promised to replace the existing religious one. Society could be reborn in the image of the lawlessness.

While they might agree on communism as a means to replace the ethic of God, the two communist activists required an organization from which to launch their new society. In that regard, there was a secret revolutionary group founded in France called the League of the Just. Christian Wehelm Weitling, a tailor by trade and utopian Christian in his politics, was founder of the group. Marx and Engels at first ignored the group, forming instead an organization called the Correspondence Committee in Brussels. Weitling attended one of the meetings of the Correspondence Committee. During this meeting, Weitling was attacked by Marx for what Marx concluded was a weak doctrine. Weitling eventually had to give up his post as leader of the League of the Just and retreat to America for safety. The departure of Weitling produced an opening in the League, and Marx and Engels immediately capitalized on it. The name "League of the Just was changed to Communist League in 1847. The event involving Weitling became a model in dealing with wayward thinkers in the Communist Party.

CHAPTER 5

Communist Manifesto

§

MARX AND ENGELS PUBLISHED MANY works. They were, after all, journalists of the last rebellion. The articles and books they wrote served to churn up hate and discontent among labor, mercantile, and government. The purpose of all these writings was to conjure up an army that would usher in the lawless society they envisioned. Furthermore, in their view the issue was not local. They intended to export lawlessness to the world and displace God and gods for all time. To do so required a plan for destabilizing host governments around the world.

The plan would need to be flexible enough to apply to all forms of governments while simultaneously capable of being followed in any international venue. Engels explains the intellectual proposition in the *Communist Manifesto*. They planned to use class struggles wherever they could to destabilize the political environment. The lawless planned to use race, gender, poor, rich, religion, marriage, homosexuals, and children to incite mankind to war with each other for the purpose of establishing lawlessness and its ethic. The *Communist Manifesto* refers to the role of religion in its declarations of the lawless:

> *There are besides, eternal truths such as freedom, justice, etc., that are common to all states of society. But communism abolishes eternal truths, it abolishes all religion and all morality, instead of constituting them on a new basis; it, therefore, acts in contradiction to all past historical experience.[1]*

The proclamation on lawlessness is the center of balance for the new lawless society envisioned by the last rebellion.

It should be noted the *Manifesto* claims that the last rebellion is the champion of the wage-earners of the world. However, Weitling was a champion of the same class of people. He was drummed out of the Communist League for his Christian views. Eduard Bernstein, another member of the last rebellion, would propose using Christian values in the attempt to replace God's ethic.

CHAPTER 6

Eduard Bernstein

§

EDUARD BERNSTEIN MARRIED THE CONCEPT of changing the ethic of mankind to the legislative and judicial processes of the people group targeted for change. In addition, Bernstein believed the target government could be change through a legislative insurgence. Operatives could pose as loyal politicians to get elected to legislative posts. Once elected, the lawless operative would further the ethical change through making of laws.

Bernstein's system of lawlessness provided an alternative to the violent revolutionary overthrow of God's ethic. **He proposed to overthrow God's ethic through a legislative insurgent evolutionary process.** It is crucial Christians understand the political face of the last rebellion. Bernstein and his brand of rebellion is the political face of the lawless rebellion.

Eduard Bernstein was born in Berlin on January 6, 1850. The Bernstein family consisted of fifteen children of which Eduard was the seventh. The family was Jewish; however, they did not practice their faith. Eduard's father was a railway worker, and as one can imagine, he struggled mightily to feed a household consisting of fifteen children. The family's struggle to support its size forced Bernstein to abandon school before he graduated. He took a job as an apprentice bank teller in Berlin. After completion of his three-year apprenticeship program, Bernstein worked in the banking system for nine additional years.[li]

Bernstein lived at a time when radical Marxist ideology was festering among young Germans like a contaminated wound. Marx and Engels had

221

written the *Communist Manifesto* in 1847, and by the time Bernstein had taken to his vocation, the last rebellion was nurturing the seeds of hatred among the classes in Germany. Moreover, the Franco-Prussian war in 1870 magnified the lawless movement. The ruling statesmen persecuted lawless protestors.

Revolutionary romanticism filled the hearts of young men, and Bernstein was not left behind. However, Bernstein's most influential training came from within the family circle. His uncle was an editor for *Volkszeiting (People's Times)*, a German newspaper with rebellious intent and affiliation. It was a logical progression for Bernstein to join the German Social Democratic Party in February, 1872.

The German government struggled to fend off the clandestine rebellion of lawless movement. The lawless made more than one attempt to assassinate Emperor William I. As a result of the struggle, the German government cracked down on the rebellion by passing strict laws regulating its member's activity. The crackdown forced the lawless to scatter into neighboring countries. Bernstein fled to Switzerland where an idealist named Karl Hochberg took Bernstein in. Hochberg, although devoted to the rebellion, disagreed with Marx and Engels on many issues. Bernstein, as Hochberg's secretary, became involved in the disputes, thereby connecting him to Marxism's two patriarchs, Marx and Engels.

As Bernstein's relationship grew with the Marxist patriarchs, so did his own political identity. By 1881, Bernstein was on the staff of a rebellion's newspaper in Zurich called *Sozialdermokrat (Social Democrat)*. The paper flooded the German political arena with the rebellion's propaganda. The German government's response was to use diplomatic efforts to persuade Switzerland to shut down the paper. The Swiss gave into the pressure in 1888 and closed the paper, expelling its members. Bernstein fled to London. While in London, Bernstein developed his Marxist revisionist ideology.

The climate in England was revolutionary in spirit; however, it was nonviolent. The communal experiments of Robert Owens were still fresh in the minds of the English. Furthermore, the Owenites were not alone in carrying the battle of the last rebellion to the people and political climate in London. A group called the Fabians was center stage in the movement. Bernstein's observation revealed that the Owenite and Fabian lawless was every bit lawless in their composition. They believed that God and the social system created by God had to be overturned. Further, they believed the lawless state and its new state ethic—lawlessness—would eventually become the new standard for the world.

However, they disagreed with Marx on the method of imposing their new lawless ethic on the world. Marxist doctrine encourages violent revolutionary overthrow of governments which follow the ethic of God. The English lawless took a more civilized approach. They proposed an "evolutionary" overthrow through the country's own legislature. Their efforts centered on the election process. The same rules that applied to disruption and destruction of the ethic of God could be applied through the electoral process. The whole process, they thought, could be achieved without a bloody revolutionary event.

Bernstein's theory of evolutionary change grew into an ideology and propelled him into a leadership role within the European last rebellion. He wrote several works criticizing the revolutionary approach that were well received by some in the lawless movement. However, other members railed against the assertion that Marx was wrong to say that revolutionary action was the only path to world dominance for the last rebellion. The Marxist purist accused Bernstein of revising Marx's rules of engagement, and floated the term "revisionist" as the label for Bernstein and his followers.

Bernstein's theories were viewed as heresy by leaders in the movement of Karl Marx. From within the lawless organizations, opponents sparred openly in debate over Bernstein's evolutionary theories. Bernstein found himself in a vigorous defense of his views. The debate raged on, and in response to criticism, Bernstein wrote *Evolutionary Socialism* in 1899. *Evolutionary Socialism* was widely read back in the German homeland. There were those who disagreed with Bernstein's methods; however, there were others who accepted his ideas. Lawless rebellious movement leaders who disagreed with him called his followers revisionists, while other lawless leaders who believed in him and his methods called themselves Bernsteinians. Consequently, by the time Bernstein returned to Germany, he had a substantial following. In 1902, he was elected to public office where he served several terms until his retirement in 1928. He died on December 18, 1932. Hitler's *National Socialist German Workers Party (Nationalsozialistische)* seized power just weeks after Bernstein's death. Lawlessness under Adolf Hitler and the *Nationalsozialistische* (Nazi) would eventually be responsible for the deaths of millions during WWII.

Bernstein's work *Evolutionary Socialism* is his masterpiece and should be considered a must-read for friend and foe alike. It defines contemporary movements and methods of the rebellion's fight to remove the ethic of God from the world. Moreover, it reconciles in the mind of the reader the apparent schizophrenic logic paradigms of contemporary lawlessness; therefore, it is invaluable in identifying lawlessness in contemporary settings. For reasons stated, a discussion of the text is appropriate. Bernstein's system of lawlessness (ethic) has no effect on communist/socialist doctrine that requires the overthrow of existing orthodox governments. Bernstein makes this fact clear in the preface of his work.

> *The conquest of political power by working classes, the expropriation of capitalists, are no ends in themselves but only means for the accomplishment of certain aims and endeavors. As such they are demands in the programme of social democracy and are not attacked by me.*[lii]

Bernstein's work simply offered an alternative to the violent overthrow of God's ethic. He strongly believed that all the revolutionary ideas and tactics that had come to be known as Marxism could be applied through the religious government's own governing structure; thereby destroying the government from within.

Bernstein realized that the *Communist Manifesto* was based on the fallacy that capitalism would fail to adjust to the new industrial world. Poverty would rise as a result, and the working class could then be used to organize armies that would overthrow God's ethic. Bernstein wrote, *"Social conditions have not developed to such an acute opposition of things and classes as is depicted in the Manifesto."* Furthermore, it is clear that Bernstein recognized that the goal of Marxism was not to usher in a utopian society that solved all of man's problems. Capitalism had rebounded and was adjusting to the new industrialized world. The number of individuals in the middle class was on the rise, and more people were obtaining property.

If the goal was to help one's fellow man, the rebellion would have sought to work with authorities at this point in history to expand the economic adjustment with all speed. However, the leaders of the new ethic of lawlessness were horrified that the plan had failed.

The last rebellion goal is not goodwill towards man, but rather the overthrow of God's ethic. The promise of goodwill toward man is the lure used to draw the individual away from his/her religious worldview. Lawlessness is like a pedophile that lurks at the playground and uses candy to lure the child into his web. The pedophile has only his desire as his guide, and he will destroy the child's life to satisfy that desire. The first goal of the last rebellion is the desire to eliminate God's ethical foundation of society, and the lawless will use everything at their disposal to satisfy that desire. Bernstein reemphasized the anchor of lawless thought in chapter 1 of his book.

> *No one will deny that the most important element in the foundation of Marxism, the fundamental law so to say which penetrates the whole system, is its specific philosophy of history which bears the name of the* **materialist interpretation** *of history. With it Marxism stands or falls in principle.*

> *To be a materialist means first of all to trace back all phenomena to the necessary movements of matter. These movements of matter are accomplished according to the materialist doctrine from beginning to end as a mechanical process, each individual process being the necessary result of preceding mechanical facts. Mechanical facts determine, in the last resort,*

all occurrences, even those which appear to be caused by ideas. It is, finally, always the movement of matter which determines the form of ideas and the directions of the will; and thus these also (and with them everything that happens in the world of humanity) are inevitable. The materialist is thus a Calvinist without God . . . he does not believe in a predestination ordained by divinity, yet he believes and must believe . . . events are determined beforehand.[liii]

The definition here is a reflection of the Hegelian philosophy adopted by the Young Hegelians. All things can be traced back to their beginning through mechanical means. With respect to species evolution, every step of the evolutionary journey is dependent on its surroundings. The formation of a new species is, therefore, determined by the environmental factors which guide species change. Bernstein applied Darwin's theory of evolution even to ideas. If ideas are controlled by the surrounding environment (education, social discourse, way of life supported by social laws), then destiny is controlled. An individual's life may be predestined to be lawless (free of God) through control of the individual's environment. The Bernstein thesis agrees with the statement in the *Communist Manifesto*:

> *But communism abolishes eternal truths, it abolishes all religion and all morality, instead of constituting them on a new basis; it, therefore, acts in contradiction to all past historical experience.*

The difference is in the means by which the ethic (environment) is changed. Bernstein proposed to insert the lawless ethic into the individual's environment through the legislature of the target country. Marxism proposes to remove the foundation of God's ethic violently through revolutionary destruction of God's ethical system. Marxism would implement the lawless ethic after the destructive revolution.

A contemporary comparison with Marxist strategy could be the Islamic State which has formed in the Middle East. The method for expansion of this Islamic ideology is to conquer territories through violence. After the conquest, residents are given the choice to conform or die. The goal for the Islamist is not necessarily the territory conquered; it is the spread of Islamic theology and ethic. Marxism's goal was the same: take territory through a violent revolution. The residents would then be given the choice to conform or die.

Bernsteinianism requires that ethical change be made through the laws which govern a territory's population. In this way the legislature moves acceptance of the new ethic to the judiciary. The people who follow the ethic of God must choose between being labeled a criminal (accepted by society) or a citizen in good standing. Bernstein's method takes a long time and requires a much greater patience; however, Bernstein's method is every bit as deadly to the removal of God's ethic in a given country.

Marxism's historical attack on capitalism is strategic, but not its end goal.

This proposition which in my opinion is destined to do for history what Darwin's theory has done for biology, we, both of us, had been gradually approaching for years before 1845.[liv]

The evidentiary result is in the reestablishment of capitalism in countries which were violently overthrown by Marxist revolution. China and Russia are two examples of the last rebellion which used evil capitalism as a revolutionary tool in the overthrow of their countries, only to later adopt the capitalist system in order to compete in the arena of international trade. Strategies designed for the overthrow of countries must not be confused with theory of lawlessness.

When in the course of development, class distinctions have disappeared and all production has been concentrated in the hands of a vast association of the whole nation, the public power will lose its political character.

Political power, properly so called, is merely the organized power of one class for oppressing another.[lv]

The definition of theory may be traced back in history beyond Hegel to the Greek philosophers Democritus (460-370 BC) and Epicurus (341-271 BC.). Marx's doctoral dissertation explored the differences between these two Greek philosophers' views on nature. Bernstein's opening statement requiring the materialist to "trace back" is rooted in Democritean and Epicurean thought. Both philosophers believed that the atom was the foundation of all matter. To Democritus and Epicurus, everything in nature was explained in "atomic terms". All things could be traced back to their smallest component, the atom. They rejected the concept of the soul and the existence of matter outside of nature. They also rejected the concept of the Hebrew God. Additionally, they rejected any law proposed by an entity that in their mind could not exist. In the minds of Democritus and Epicurus, Hebrew law—the foundation from which Western society was built—was nothing but a product of man's imagination. The Greek philosophers' religious affiliation may be defined in today's terms as lawless.

Many names have been given to the last rebellion since the time of the Conspiracy of Equals; socialism, communism, and progressivism are a few. Bernstein labeled the people who participate in the last rebellion as "materialist". The contemporary label would be "naturalist". The materialist/naturalist believes in a natural evolution of life on earth as the source of all life. Bernstein's work recognized that all materialists follow the evolutionary belief system.

The effort to understand Bernstein's perspective of the materialist (last rebellion) movement requires recognition of its chronological order.

First: Among the lawless, conversion to atheism came before conversion to communism or the so-called science of socialism. For example, Marx and Engels agreed on their common atheism in 1844.

Second: The *Communist Manifesto* was written in 1847. These two revolutionary atheists worked to create rebellion on the European continent until 1848.

Third: After they failed to achieve revolution, Marx and Engels retreated to the work of forming the science of socialism (*sociology of knowledge*). This science was not completed until after Marx's death (1883).

This chronology indicates that the science of socialism was developed as a strategy for changing God's ethical foundation, which existed during the era in the target countries. Bernstein recognized the flaws in Marx's science and his book *Evolutionary Socialism* is a criticism of the Marxist doctrine.

In his criticism, Bernstein pointed out some major changes that would be required for success. For example, Marx's system and its imposition on society relied on the working class in order to be effective. Marxist doctrine requires the faithful to destroy the rich, and the Marxist doctrine could never stand for rich people among the masses. Bernstein proposed another approach:

> *The social movement of modern times has already survived many a superstition, it will also survive this, that its future depends on the concentration of wealth or, if one will put it thus, on the absorption of surplus value by diminishing group of capitalist mammoths . . . it might cost less surplus labor to keep a few thousand privileged persons in sumptuousness than a half-a-million in wealth . . . and if we had not before us the fact proved empirically by statistics of incomes and trades it could be demonstrated by purely deductive reasoning as the necessary consequence of modern economy.[lvi]*

Bernstein's proposal is amazing. The new lawless model has a "social elite" that is kept, in his words, in "*privileged sumptuousness*" while the workers—the "little people"—support them along with their lawless state. Of course, the elite will see to (their definition of) equality among the little people. What Bernstein is describing is an explanation for what heretofore appeared to be schizophrenic logic paradigms in progressivism. For example, Warren Buffet, a lavishly rich man worth an estimated 47 billion dollars, has stated he wishes for the government to punish the rich and take more taxes from them. This is a case of someone taking full advantage of the capitalist system in the West, but apparently joining with those who fight against capitalism. Buffet appears to fight against his own accomplishments.

One might note Buffet does not need 47 billion dollars to live his life in luxury. In addition, Buffet's fortune should not be passed on to his descendants, according to Bernsteinian doctrine and the lawless political party leadership in the United States. Should not Buffet, then, write a check for, say, 46 billion to the United States Treasury? Mario Cuomo, a rich New York politician, continually insists on the redistribution of wealth. One might say to him, "If you want to redistribute some wealth, write a check containing all the wealth of the Cuomo family, and the wealth will be transferred." However, these two men are not interested in redistributing their own wealth. The aforementioned rich philanthropists and others obviously consider themselves to be the elite to which Bernstein refers. They can be rich as long as they foment the lawless vision of the overthrow of God's ethic in society.

CHAPTER 7
Bernstein's Bridge

THE INCLUSION OF RICH LIBERALS into fighting a class struggle against the rich may be referred to as the ***"Bernstein Bridge"***. It connects liberalism to the last rebellion and its activism. It allows even the lavishly rich to join in class warfare against the lavishly rich in exchange for membership into lawless ideology and activism. The goal is to use the rich to destroy God's ethic in society.

Under the Bernstein plan, contemporary lawless leaders are untouchable. They can even be involved in the death of another and still be considered a member of the elite in good standing. In other words, morality is a matter of God's law, and they are under no obligation to give up their lawless doctrine. As such, liberal social elites are exempt from laws imposed on God's people by God's ethic.

Liberals before Bernstein's era were treated as enemies by the Marxist revolutionaries. They were willing to help the poor in their quest for a better life, but wanted to retain their wealth and social positions. Because they were rich, Marxist treated them as enemies.

For Bernstein, liberals and liberalism were not to be treated as enemies of the lawless cause. Rather, he felt that they were allies in the war against God's society that the lawless were seeking to replace. It should come as no surprise that the aforementioned luxurious elites should be considered the key to the reconciliation of the two doctrines. The philanthropic liberal is absorbed into the lawless rebellion without the loss of his/her luxurious status. Examples of the rich being accepted by those who hate the rich are Jay Rockefeller, John Kerry, George Soros, and Warren Buffet.

If the European social democracies are the model, these luxurious elites will eventually rule the totalitarian lawless state, the end prize for the rich liberal philanthropist.

However, with respect to democracy's use by lawlessness to overthrow religious governments, its weakness lies in its ability to reflect the will of the people.

The goal of lawlessness is not to reflect the will of the people. Democracy has the potential to threaten the New Lawless World if allowed to ramble among the will of the people. For example, Greece has run out of money to pay the unions, and now the unions are burning and looting the cities. In London, the New Lawless World is under attack by those who view the government as the enemy.

To ensure its survival, the New Lawless World must make laws to control such will. For example, wide-reaching legislation such as hate crimes laws and fairness in media laws will be instrumental in silencing any free will that raises its head in the New Lawless World. The media will need to be controlled in order to control the will of the people.

The European lawless governments today are falling into bankruptcy because they failed to seal the deal. Democracy was left in place, and the rebellion of the working class seeks to rebel against the lawless ruling class. While Bernstein was right about his nonviolent approach to destroying God's society, Marx was right about democracy being only a tool to overthrow religion. After the overthrow is complete, the workers must then hand over the spoils of war to the new lawless totalitarian state. Otherwise the rebellion never ends. The will of the people may end up spoiling the lawless dream.

There can be no doubt lawlessness is manufacturing the destruction of God's ethic in the West. As for liberal theology and liberation theology, they are standing with the lawless in the same way the Hellenized Jews stood with the Greeks when the Jewish Abomination of Desolation was committed in the Jewish Temple during the intertestamental period. It is an amazing historical turn of events which places the Greek civilization and its philosophers Democritus and Epicurus in the proverbial temple with the lawless and modern day Hellenized Jews (liberal and liberation rheology), demanding God's people conform or die.

Ethics Of The Rebellion Of Lawlessness

THE LAST REBELLION HAS COME a long way since Babeuf in 1796. It has developed through experience a new ethic for mankind to follow. The ethic is confusing for most Christians. It can appear as Christian in some cases. For example, God's ethic and the new ethic of mankind help the poor. The common ground of these ethics makes it difficult to recognize. For that reason it is important for the Christian to recognize the lawless ethic of mankind.

The last rebellion follows a hybrid ethic. It is a mixture of Christianity without God (Engels) and Greek philosophy (Marx). It was Eduard Bernstein who put the ethical system together. In 1899, Eduard Bernstein said in his book *Evolutionary Socialism:*

> *To be a materialist (secular) means first of all to trace back all phenomena to the necessary movements of matter. These movements of matter are accomplished according to the materialist (secular) doctrine from beginning to end as a mechanical process . . . Mechanical facts determine, in the last resort, all occurrences, even those which appear to be ideas . . . the movement of matter which determines the form of ideas and directions of the will; and thus these also (and with them everything that happens in the world of humanity) are inevitable. The materialist (secular) is thus a Calvinist without God.*[lvii]

John Calvin, a 16th century Theologian, thought that mankind was predestined before birth to either live with God or with Satan for eternity. In Geneva, where Calvin's community lived, Calvin set up an environment for the people predestined to live with God for eternity. The Calvinist community was required to live free of the sins of the outside world. For example, the people in the community were compelled to obey (*nanny state*) all the commandments of God identified in the Bible. If they did not, they were punished for it.

This type of religious community is called a theocracy. Calvin's theocracy followed his interpretations of the Bible. All the schools for children in his theocracy were taught from the interpretive well of *Calvin's*

Institutes. Calvin's Institutes are an in-depth commentary on the Bible authored by John Calvin.

Theocracy deprives mankind of the freedom necessary to choose God's path freely. It enslaves the people with religious compulsion. People follow because they are instructed, educated, and indoctrinated into theocratic predestination. Theocracy produces no other alternatives. Choices are made based on education and the experience of culture. Its members are the elect and must follow the path of the elect. They have no other choice, members of a theocracy are taught, since they are predestined by God to follow the path they are on.

Calvin, of course, was Christian. How does a Christian theocrat relate to modern lawlessness as explained in Bernstein's *Evolutionary Socialism*? One might refer to Darwin's Theory of Evolution as a comparison. In fact, Bernstein's book title *Evolutionary Socialism* is a takeoff of the meaning of Darwin's evolutionary theory. The idea runs parallel to Calvin's idea. The secular state attempts to set up an environment for people predestined to live their lives in a lawless community without God.

If it were not so, seculars would not demand public education be free of God, and exclude all learning about God. The evidence is in the punishment of those who would attempt to present God in any form in public school. Further evidence may be found every year during the so called "war on Christmas" or war on religious symbols in the public environment.

Why do people follow the lawless ethical rebellion? People follow the lawless ethic because they have been indoctrinated into lawlessness in the public forum, not because there is or is not a God.

The rebellion's control over the public environment deprives mankind of the freedom necessary to choose freely anything other than the lawless path. It enslaves the people with lawless compulsion. People follow because they are instructed, educated, and indoctrinated into a godless predestination. Lawlessness produces no other alternatives. The lawless make choices based on education and the experience of culture. They are the elect and must follow the path of the elect. They have no other choice;

they are predestined by public education and indoctrination to follow the path of lawlessness.

Lawlessness achieves the parallel ethic through the development of a resistance to God while embracing components of Christianity. For example, Eduard Bernstein stated in *Evolutionary Socialism*, a materialist (lawless) was a Calvinist (Christian) without God. Calvin believed predestination was from God. Bernstein believed in predestination, but at the mercy of one's environmental surroundings. God was not a component of Bernstein's predestination.

Bernstein's view is that destiny may be changed if one's environment is changed. A new destiny can be developed for mankind through education. His view was developed in part by Marx in *Das Capital*, where Marx wrote on man's ability to learn a different ethic through experience. What was needed then to change destiny was to replace God and ideas or morality attributed to God in society while maintaining the familiar social justice components of the Bible.

Bernstein's statement agrees with the replacement of religion as a foundation of society except for one thing. Marx and Engels in the *Communist Manifesto* of 1847 requires the whole of religion be thrown out:

> *"But communism abolishes eternal truths, it abolishes all religion and all morality, instead of constituting them on a new basis; it, therefore, acts in contradiction to all past historical experience* "[lviii]

The doctrine of the *Communist Manifesto* required casting immediately out the old religious ethic upon which European society was built. As a result, communist doctrine clashed openly with long standing religious ethics because people were indoctrinated into the religious ethic. Communists believed that this confrontation would bring revolution and change. But the communists never contemplated losing their manufactured revolution.

Bernstein realized that the generation communists were facing in the 19th century would fight for their faith and their way of life. The Bernstein doctrine called for patience to build, through a legislative and judicial insurgence into the governing body of the existing ethic, a system of education and indoctrination in society which mirrors a theocracy's compulsion to follow lawlessness (i.e.: "the materialist is a Calvinist without God").

For example, if an individual grows up in poverty, his/her decisions will be based on the impoverished surroundings in which the individual finds himself/herself. The impoverished surroundings, Bernstein would say, guides the individual's destiny. Taking Bernstein's logic further, the nature and reason developed from one's surroundings decides a person's destiny. Marx and Engels are in agreement:

> *Instead of constituting them on a new basis; it, therefore, acts in contradiction to all past historical experience.*

Religion only plays a part in destiny, Bernstein asserts, when it takes a deciding factor with respect to one's surroundings. The Bible has common ground with Bernstein. For instance, Proverbs 22:6 states, *"Train up a child in the way he should go; even when he is old he will not depart from it."* Likewise, Deuteronomy 4:1 instructs, *"Listen to the statutes and the rules that I am teaching you, and do them, that you may live."*

The issue is not whether mankind has a predestined path. It is rather who or what guides mankind's destiny. Christians believe that God and His Word form the destiny of man. Babeuf, Owen, Marx, Engels, Bernstein and other lawless believe in predestination, but without God's sovereign guidance. Mankind can decide his own destiny, the lawless would say. Mankind only has to change the surroundings that lead the decision-making paradigm of mankind to a worship of God into surroundings that would lead mankind to choose the frame of lawlessness. The change would reflect a control over men and women (a "nanny state") in the same way a theocracy controls men and women who live under theocratic laws and judiciary.

Bernstein compares his ethic to Christianity without God in his book *Evolutionary Socialism*. Consider Bernstein's statement:

It has repeatedly happened to me (and certainly also to others) in former years that at the conclusion of a propagandist meeting, labourers and workmen who had heard a socialist speech for the first time would come to me and declare that what I had said was already to be found in the Bible; they could show men the passages, sentence for sentence.[lix]

Bernstein is referring to Acts 4:32–37:

Now the full number of those who believed were of one heart and soul, and no one said that any of the things that belonged to him was his own, but they had everything in common. And with great power the apostles were giving their testimony to the resurrection of the Lord Jesus, and great grace was upon them all. There was not a needy person among them, for as many as were owners of lands or houses sold them and brought the proceeds of what was sold and laid it at the apostles' feet, and it was distributed to each as any had need. Thus Joseph, who was also called by the apostles Barnabas (which means son of encouragement), a Levite, a native of Cyprus, sold a field that belonged to him and brought the money and laid it at the apostles' feet.

The Acts 4:32–37 passage may be troublesome for Christians. It would appear to be the source of lawless thought on communal living. One might argue Marx and Engels were referring to historical communal societies of man. However, Bernstein would have believed Engels' version of communism reflected his early childhood indoctrination into Calvinism. What Bernstein is admitting in his book is that the communal caring nature of Engel's familial tradition and their religious roots is the source of the communal system in communist philosophy. How could one who believed that destiny was controlled by mankind's instruction, education, and indoctrination think otherwise? Engels simply removed God and eternal truths of God from the text. Examine, for example, the Acts text without God.

> *Now the full number of those who believed in mankind was of one heart and soul, and no one said that any of the things that belonged to him was his own, but they had everything in common. There was not a needy person among them, for as many as were owners of lands or houses sold them and brought the proceeds of what was sold and laid it at the communities feet, and it was distributed to each as any had need.*

The biblical text reflects the combining of all things in common and re-distribution of the combined wealth of the community; Note verse 34 states, *"there was not a needy person among them . . . and it was distributed to each as any had need."* Punishment for those who did not follow the communal order was death. In the Bible, the center of focus in the community described by Luke is God. In the lawless communal system, man replaces God.

> *But communism abolishes eternal truths; it abolishes all religion and morality,*

The Bernsteinian lawless formula does not seek to replace the proverbial wheel; it merely seeks to replace the hub. Simply remove God and religion, and replace it with man. The lawless ethic is formed around social components of the Bible such as love of your neighbor, the Christian communal society in Acts 4:32-5:11, and the Greek philosophy requiring man to trace his existence back to the beginning of time. God and all things that require worship of God are removed.

It should be noted at this point that the Christian community in Acts is probably not the architect of the monastic-style community. It is most likely a replica of the Essene community revealed by scholars during the study of the Dead Sea Scrolls. According to those scholars, the *Manual of Discipline* found among the Dead Sea Scrolls indicates a Jewish community, probably Essene according to scholars studying the Dead Sea Scrolls, which followed the communal distributive order.[lx] If that is true, the lawless doctrine of equality-driven redistribution was borrowed from the root of Judeo-Christian beginnings. It could even be called a form of plagiarism since lawlessness posits the system as its own.

Early lawless who embraced Marxist philosophy to replace God in the public arena attempted to force Marxism on the public through violent revolutionary means. An example of this would be in China where Mao Tse-Tung killed millions of Chinese who disagreed with lawlessness over the best ethic to follow. In these revolutionary experiences, the lawless attacked the economy of society. To be specific, they attacked capitalist societies with the promise of a communal system which was borrowed from the Acts community. They sought to impose fairness and equality on society violently, leaving out God's internal truths. Metaphorically speaking, **lawlessness seeks to throw God out of the Garden of Eden**.

One image in particular stands out in the mind. The *Black Book of Communism* chronicled an event where communists executed a supervisor. The image depicted a man on his knees with his hands tied behind him. The rifleman behind him was in the act of executing the supervisor. The image reveals the contempt lawless have for the capitalist system. The man in the image was a supervisor of agricultural workers. In the lawless mind, the supervisor, by making more wages than the workers, had exploited the peasantry and broken the sacred redistribution rules of the lawless system.

Bernsteinian lawless doctrine is much more subtle than the early lawless doctrine of Marxism. Bernsteinianism united the lawless need to destroy the enemy with the Owenite lawless desire to impose the system humanely and with the monies and power of the philanthropic liberal community. The political structure which Bernstein proposed to unite Owenite lawless, hardline lawless, and liberalism has been termed the *Bernstein Bridge* by this author.[lxi]

The Bernstein Bridge seeks to insert like-minded legislators and adjudicators into the ranks of the host government it is trying to destroy. The result is law and a judiciary that moves the host government, through its own governmental systems, ever closer to total lawlessness and a lawless state. Using the example of the executed supervisor, a comparison of the two means of imposition may be made. Laws have been passed in many U.S. states allowing the employee to sue a supervisor for as much as $25,000 for misconduct. The image is much less offensive, but has the same result. The supervisor will be rendered ineffective and the lawless ideal is advanced.

The idea of replacing the supervisor is to remove the authority of the supervisor and replace it with a court system favorable to the lawless system. In this way the company's production and policies will conform to policies set forth by the emerging ethic of mankind. In the ethic of mankind government will control every aspect of life. In the scenario of the removed supervisor, mankind exchanges one tyrant for another.

The Bernstein Bridge has been effective in many areas of public discourse in the West, particularly in removing God from the public schools. Judeo-Christian symbols are being attacked in European countries and in the Americas. For example, the phrase "In God We Trust" on U.S. currency is one symbol the lawless seek to remove. The term "Merry Christmas" is under attack year after year. The opposition's goal is to replace the religious celebration with a totally secular holiday. Another example is the repeated attacks on public displays of the Ten Commandments. The pledge of allegiance to the U.S. flag is also under attack for the words "one nation under God". Since World War II, those who follow the lawless movement's ethic insist on the removal of any reference to God from an unsuspecting populace. The end goal is to destroy any orthodox religious affiliation in the world.

Another arena where the Bernstein Bridge has seen success in removing God from the field of ideas is the fabulously rich entertainment industry. The center of the world entertainment community is Hollywood. It has become its own domain, known in North America and throughout the world as simply "Hollywood". It is a place where fiction and fantasy become visual reality, where heroes are memorialized and demons are slain. The question viewers should ask themselves when viewing Hollywood's epic films is "What is a hero?" The answer to the question may be found in the history of man.

In order to understand the hero and his journey, the work of Joseph Campbell is critical. Campbell defined the essence of Western heroism in his book *The Hero with a Thousand Faces*.

The hero's journey, which Campbell revealed, did not follow a specific religious sect. In fact, Campbell found the hero and his journey in Buddha, Christ, Muhammad, the Navajo Indian deity, and all other religions. He called this common story of the hero the *"monomyth"*. Campbell's book developed a 17 step model for the hero. Those who use it to tell the hero's story have reduced the steps to twelve.

1.   The story begins with the hero in his/her normal world.
2.   The hero is faced with a problem or challenge and feels a call to duty.
3.   The hero refuses the call.
4.   The hero meets a guide for his journey.
5.   The hero advances into a different setting/world.
6.   The hero's journey is filled with trials. He meets allies and confronts evils.
7.   The hero falls on hard times.
8.   The hero faces a life-or-death crisis.
9.   The hero survives the life-or-death test.
10. The hero returns to the normal world.
11. The hero faces death.
12. The hero is resurrected with the "elixir" for the world.

Campbell discovered that religious mythological heroes around the world shared a common cyclic structure. For example, Jesus' life journey on the earth is one of the cyclic stories Campbell alludes to in his book. This particular story is important for historically Christian societies because the steps of the hero's journey emulate the journey of Jesus Christ. The "hero" in the mind of Christian society closely follows with Christian religious symbols. Campbell's discovery was not lost on Hollywood. Blockbuster hits evolved using the steps Campbell had discovered. Star Wars and the Matrix are among the most noted movies which follow Campbell's steps for the hero's journey.

This discovery by Campbell was not new to Western society. For example, J. H. Wellhausen in the 1880s wrote a critique of the Torah, the first 5 books of the Bible, which revealed cyclic structures in biblical stories. Other theologians also recognized a cyclic structure in the books of Judges and Kings. The stories in the book of Judges in particular bear a resemblance to Campbell's cycle. Consider the following cyclic structure:

1. Israel does evil in the eyes of Yahweh.
2. Yahweh gives/sells them into the hands of the oppressor.
3. Israel serves the oppressor for X number of years.
4. Israel cries out to Yahweh.
5. Yahweh rises up a deliverer.
6. The Spirit of Yahweh is upon the deliverer.
7. The oppressor is subdued.
8. The land has "rest" for years.

Campbell's "monomyth", the common cyclic structure, is identified in religious stories around the world. Stories such as the ones chronicled in the Bible are the foundation of contemporary societies that are built on religious orthodox history.

Recognition of the importance of religious symbols in moviemaking as a model for making movies has been a large part of Hollywood's success. With the historical relevance of religious symbols in mind, any change in the making of movies or telling of stories, imagined or real, would be extremely significant with respect to a specific culture.

Hollywood in recent history has begun shifting from the use of traditional religious symbols to using lawless symbols as a structure to make movies. God is no longer the hero; He is the villain in these epic adventures.

An animated movie called *Happy Feet* reflects the shift in Hollywood's approach to moviemaking. There are many other examples; however, this particular movie has two qualities that clearly identify it as an example. First, it is a cartoon and appeals to young and old alike. Second, the penguins are cute and adorable. Who would not want to save the penguins?

The film is an example of the passive approach of Bernsteinianism. The message of *Happy Feet* follows the elements of Bernstein's lawless doctrine. Consider the following chart which identifies five elements of the Bernstein Bridge and the corresponding applications from the film:

BERNSTEIN BRIDGE

BERNSTEIN LAWLESS ELEMENT	HAPPY FEET CORRELATION
Individuals are elected based on their knowledge and the knowledge of the elect.	Mumbles, the animated hero of the movie, must attain knowledge of the aliens (mankind) in order to save the penguin society from starvation.
Only the elect have the benefits of the elect. Liberals are included in the elect. All non-elect are required to support the elect secular state.	The old order is based on religion, and Mumbles convinces the elders of the penguin society to reject the old religious symbols in favor of the new saviors.
Man can achieve salvation without God.	Salvation for the penguin society is achieved without God.
Man empowers himself to overcome any obstacles through his own free will.	Once Mumbles makes contact with man, man empowers himself to over-come all obstacles to save the penguin society.
An elect can fall away from his elect status.	Once the elect status is achieved, survival depends on conformity to the elect.[lxii]

It is unlikely that the makers of this movie studied Bernstein's principles set forth in 1899 in his book *Evolutionary Socialism*. The filmmakers probably did not have a guide other than their own ideological traditions. For that reason, it is important to use history, as Campbell has done, to connect ideological traditions through time. For this task, theological criticism may be used to determine ideological affiliation. Internal evidence found in the text or framework of the subject material may be used to identify contemporary ideological trends with their source. Ideology can be assigned through documented ideological thought over the course of time, even centuries. In other words, internal evidence in historical documents may be used to trace ideology to its source. In the case of *Happy Feet*, the movie clearly illustrates Bernstein's definition of the materialist (lawless) that was written by Bernstein in 1899.

The model for telling stories is a further example of what Bernstein wanted the lawless to accomplish. He wanted to use the existing religious orthodox structures which indoctrinate the people into religion to indoctrinate the people into lawlessness instead of obedience to God. In the case of *Happy Feet*, God is evil and mankind is good, taking God's place as savior of the world. The leaders of the community in *Happy Feet* were portrayed as religious zealots following old religious doctrine handed down in the community. The religious figures in *Happy Feet* are portrayed as ignorant leaders and the hero, mankind, is portrayed as the god of salvation.

CHAPTER 1

Lawlessness Revealed

§

THE LAWLESS SYSTEM WHICH EVOLVED in the shadows of Europe is a rebellion against all things religious. The rebellion spread through Europe. It philosophically transformed itself into a denominational correctness among national and sectarian targets. For example, England presented itself as a passive target to rebellion, and a legislative insurgence sufficed to deliver victory. In Russia and China, the rebellious movement was characterized by violent and murderous insurgent warfare. In Germany a heretical national socialism (NAZI) murdered 6 million Jews in its quest to rule the world.

Whatever the means of imposition, the movement sought to overthrow the influence of religion in each of the nations targeted for transformation. The transformation is sealed with legislative and judicial discourse designed to eliminate all past historical experience of religious influence ruling mankind.

The rebellion vehemently rejects the laws of God as a basis for society and places the contradiction to God's moral law as the law of the land.

The viral rebellion against the ethics of God moved west and may be found in American politics and politicians. The recent decisions in America to allow same sex marriage are a case in point. Whether one is for or against the laws that were approved is not germane to the observed philosophical and moral shift to lawless policy. For example, the move allowing same sex marriages in New York and in the Supreme Court decision there serves to abolish all God's moral influence in the public arena of homosexual activity. The governing bodies in the U.S. must now move to protect the newly established norm among the residents. Oppression of people who follow God's ethic will eventually follow the decisions. America will be required to make laws that protect the new lawless ethic and prohibit and abolish God's ethic (biblical eternal truths). Freedom to follow openly the ethic of God will be outlawed.

Cyclic comparisons may be drawn with the Constantine era. Before Constantine, paganism and sexual immorality was accepted and even encouraged by government authorities. It took another eighty years or so to outlaw paganism and accept the Christian ethic as the law of the Roman Empire, but it eventually occurred. While the overthrow of the Judeo-Christian ethic in Europe has already occurred, one may see clear examples of the last rebellion gaining primacy over the ethic of God in America. According to Governor Cuomo of New York, Christians and Christian ethics are not welcome in New York. The world has only to look at the leaders of the movement to replace God's ethic given in the Bible in order to find the leaders of the last rebellion.

The cyclic shift to lawlessness as an ethic in America reaches all the way to the White House as President Obama threw his political capital behind the move to throw out past historical practice and reconstitute law on a new basis. President Obama moved from God's ethic which opposes sexual immorality to the lawless ethic to embrace sexual immorality, and what was once unacceptable is now acceptable.

President Obama has reversed in America what Constantine accomplished in Rome. The cycles of the initiative of Christ may be evidenced by the movements of the last rebellion (Obama) and Constantine.

The cycle of the last rebellion sets itself up as an alternative to religious morality and reveals its purpose to replace God with man as the center of worship in the world. The Apostle Paul warned Christians to watch for events such as the global lawless rebellion as a sign of the time when the Lord Jesus Christ will gather His faithful. In 2 Thessalonians 2:3–4 we read:

Let no one deceive you in any way. For that day will not come, unless the rebellion comes first, and the man of lawlessness is revealed, the son of destruction, who opposes and exalts himself against every so-called god or object of worship, so that he takes his seat in the temple of God, proclaiming himself to be God.

The Apostle Paul wrote these words to Christians in Thessalonica to assure them that the day of the Lord had not yet come.

In assuring the Thessalonians they had not missed the second coming of the Lord Jesus, Paul gave all Christians a peek into the future. Christians may look for a rebellion that seeks to replace the ethics of all so-called God or gods or objects of worship as a sign that the current age is coming to a close.

Paul's discourse could not have been something he just pulled out of the air to make his case. How could the Thessalonians understand what he was saying unless there was a foundational basis in their minds as to what he was referencing?

Paul's conversation was obviously in reference to current events or recent historical events of the era. There was a close parallel of man attempting to place himself in the temple of God in Jerusalem. In AD 40, a Roman emperor named Gaius attempted to have a statue of himself placed in the temple in Jerusalem. Although the actual placement of the statue was never accomplished, the attempt alone would have been memorable to all Jews, especially those who had rabbinical ties to Jerusalem as Paul did. In addition, considering the writing of 2 Thessalonians to be around nine or ten years after this event and the Jewish disdain for such imposition into their theological sensibilities, Paul's comments may have been referring to Gaius' attempt to set himself up as God in the temple of God.

Paul's reference could also have been a cyclic parody which coupled the recent events of Gaius with the Greek incident during the intertestamental period. Additionally, it would have been a normal event for kings and emperors to declare themselves a god in the era of the epistles to the Thessalonians. For centuries temples had been erected to Roman emperors and Greek conquerors who had declared themselves to be a god. Examples are Roman emperors and Alexander the Great.

Residents of the Greek city of Thessalonica would have been aware of the philosophies of Democritus and Epicurus. Epicurean followers were very active during the era. Paul, having grown up in Tarsus, Greece, would have had a unique perspective with Jewish and Grecian historical worldviews of the era based on real life experiences.

Thessalonian understanding would have drawn on previous conversations Paul had with the Thessalonian Christians. The Thessalonians would have known at least two things about the man of lawlessness that were not true during the time in which they lived. First, the man of lawlessness would be a product of a rebellion of lawlessness. If the discussion were about rebelling against the laws of God, which it is, God's structure of laws would have to be foundational with respect to the makeup of the government being rebelled against.

Of course, a good part of the epistles to the Thessalonian Christians is dedicated to the troubles they were experiencing as a result of their minority status among the residents of the city. Their struggles were associated with the hostility of ruling authorities and citizens toward the Thessalonian Christians. This little group would have been categorized as rebellious by the citizens and authorities of Thessalonica. In fact, Acts 17:6 chronicles this very attitude among the Jewish residents in Thessalonica:

And when they could not find them, they dragged Jason and some of the brothers before the city authorities, shouting, "These men who have turned the world upside down have come here also, and Jason has received them, and they are all acting against the decrees of Caesar, saying that there is another king, Jesus."

Lawlessness was rampant in Thessalonian culture. The Thessalonian Christians would have understood they were attempting to bring about a day when God's law reigned. How could a rebellion occur against a godly ruling establishment that did not yet exist? The second thing they would have known is that no rebellion or sect had set itself against the other so-called gods and objects of worship in Thessalonica. Alexander the Great was thought of as a god at the time. Zeus, Dionysus, Apollo, Aphrodite, and a plethora of gods from Rome to Egypt were accepted in the arena of polytheist Thessalonica. The Thessalonian Christians would have understood that no rebellion against all the so-called gods and objects of worship was currently underway. They would have understood their place in the relationship cycles of God. Their concerns over possibly having missed the coming of the Day of the Lord would have been answered.

However, the lawless movement is a rebellion with respect to an established Judeo-Christian society in Western civilization. Eduard Bernstein immortalized the lawless position when he stated that lawless (materialism) believe that human existence can be traced back to the smallest of causes and thus discover creation through evolutionary science. The lawless do not believe in God or gods at all. The goal of the lawless is to replace the influence that God or gods have on society with a totally godless perspective. The lawless may be recognized by this lawless trait and one's cycle position realized.

Leon Trotsky, a famous lawless leader and disciple of Stalin, once claimed that man, without the myth of God holding him back, could cause himself to evolve to unimaginable heights. The whole point of lawlessness is to rebel against all religious experience and establish a society that places emphasis on man as the preeminent ruler on earth.

Without religion influencing the society of man, one man may end up becoming the most powerful creature on earth. He would need a political power structure to propel him to the top of mankind and maintain his status. A political coalition of nations could deliver such power of life and death over the whole earth.

The reference to the temple is more difficult to understand. The temple was destroyed in 70 AD. Obviously Paul's referral to the temple was to the one in Jerusalem. The temple at the time Paul spoke in 2 Thessalonians (approximately 52 CE to 56 CE) was still in use and well maintained by the Jews.[lxiii]

While Gaius' attempt to set an image of himself in the Jewish temple failed, it would have brought back painful memories of Antiochus Epiphanies IV's attempt to sacrifice a pig on the sacred altar. In the Jewish/Greek episode, the temple was the object of the Jewish Abomination of Desolation during the time between the Testaments.

In order to understand the temple reference, one must view the phrase, *"set himself up as God in the Temple of God"* as a reference to a time yet to come when the Abomination of Desolation reoccurs. Paul is referring to an event which involves replacing God with man as if man is God, and the phrase is a parody of when to expect the second coming of the Lord. The parody refers to a time when rebellion against God's commandments (lawlessness as it relates to God's ethic, way of life) is underway. The rebellion's purpose is to replace religious ethic with an absence of God/gods and His/their commandments. Lawlessness is the belief in a social foundation which rejects religious faith and worship as a foundation for society. The idea is to remove God or gods, and in its place lawlessness would rule over all mankind without competing religious utopian worldviews. The Greek "god", of course, involved in the "Abomination of Desolation" event was a man—Antiochus Epiphanies IV. The lawless god is also a man—the man of lawlessness.

The rebellion of lawlessness is happening around the world. One estimate that is the rebellion has consumed over 100 million lives.[lxiv] Lawless rebellions and infighting among the lawless for control of the rebellion have caused major wars over the last one hundred and fifty years. Hitler's National Socialist German Workers Party, Lenin's Marxist internationalism and Mao se Tung all violently imposed their will and lawless ethic on the world. In recent history, Vladimir Putin, the Russian president, invaded Ukraine. Putin was labeled as a "nationalist" (Adolf Hitler) by "internationalist Marxist" (Eastern Europe). However, Putin is a devout Marxist in the ideological lineage of Lenin and Stalin. It appears more a feud between the generals of lawlessness as to who will lead the last rebellion.

It is not clear as to where the man of lawlessness, who will emerge as the leader of the lawless rebellion, will come from. However, it is probable that the man of lawlessness could come from within the ranks of the global community that is called Christian, the offspring of the Holy Roman Empire.

According to Paul in 2 Thessalonians, there is something restraining the lawless one from appearing.

And you know what is restraining him now so that he may be revealed in his time. For the mystery of lawlessness is already at work. Only he who now restrains it will do so until he is out of the way. And then the lawless one will be revealed.

The Spirit of God restrains the force. One might ask if God's Spirit is physically restraining lawlessness. Yes, it is.

Spirit is consciousness of what cannot be seen as in one's personality or spiritual presence. The knowledge of a movement as in the lawless movement may be referred to as a spiritual movement based in an idea. The idea of lawlessness clashes with the idea of God. One could state this sentence another way, the spirit of lawlessness clashes with the Spirit of God. One may not see the actual movement, but can feel an ideological spirit of the movement through a real emotional attachment or rejection. One may even be controlled by the idea or spirit of lawlessness. The recent flap over religious legislation in Indiana is an example. People who fight against God's ethic and His people openly challenge any law which asserts the rights of Christians. Of course, the rallying call for the lawless is their rights are being cast aside.

In the same way, people of religion feel an emotional attachment to the conscious belief in God. God's Spirit working upon the people of the earth creates resistance to the rebellion and man of lawlessness. **Thus lawlessness is restrained through the influence of God's Spirit on the people groups in the world.**

Religious people of the earth believe there is a higher power which influences the daily activity of mankind. Many of the people on earth are Christian; many of the people on earth are of different religions. While Christianity has worked to educate the world as to the true God, there can be no doubt many who believe in higher power worship other gods.

> *For what can be known about God is plain to them, because God has shown it to them. For His invisible attributes, namely, His eternal power and divine nature have been clearly perceived, ever since the creation of the world in the things that have been made. So they are without excuse (Romans 1:19-20)*

Christians call the phenomena *"general revelation"* and see the worship of other gods as an error. However, these other worshippers do exist, and their awareness of a higher power contributes to restraint of the man of lawlessness.

For example, Islam, misguided and offensive as they are, believe in a higher power. A physical global guerilla war has broken out between the last rebellion in the West and Islamic radicals who see the lawless rebellion and wish to destroy it. It may very well propel the world into World War III.

One might refer to the Old Testament for clarity in this balance of power in the modern world restraining the lawless. God used unbelieving nation such as Assyrians, Persians and Egyptians to bring about His will in the Near Eastern Old Testament world. It should come as no surprise the method of restraint in the modern world would be to use current antagonists in the modern world to restrain the man of lawlessness until God is ready to remove His restraining influence.

More evidence the last rebellion of which Paul wrote is the modern day rebellion can be seen in the connection between lawlessness and Greek philosophy as documented in Karl Marx's doctoral dissertation *On the Differences between the Democritean and Epicurean Philosophy of Nature.*

A famous argument against God or gods from the well-known philosophy introduced by Epicurus is the Problem of Evil. The logical paradigm argues:

* If God exists, then evil does not exist.
* Evil exists in the world.
* Therefore God does not exist.

This logic paradigm is argued today by scholars around the world. Epicurean followers were active during the time period of Paul's missionary trips to Thessalonica, Greece and his writing of the two epistles to the Thessalonians. Epicureanism would have been a competing worldview, and *the mystery of lawlessness is* (was) *already at work.*

Greek philosophy is the well from which lawlessness was drawn. Paul was referring to the mystery of the Greek philosophy which requires man's destiny to be free of God (lawlessness).

An example of a spiritual war turning physical is the Egyptian crisis. In 2011, the Egyptians overthrew their government and ousted the sitting president. In the aftermath, the world watched a democratic election unfold. Religion won the day, and a member of the Muslim Brotherhood was elected to office. The new Egyptian president began a campaign to transform Egypt into an Islamic theocracy. The lawless were hoping for a secular government to evolve out of the Egyptian rebellion, and were horrified when the government became Islamic. European lawless threw their support behind the Egyptian military in Egypt, resulting in a military coup which displaced the Moslem president and labeled him a terrorist.

Islamic theocracies have displayed a brutal side of mankind. One may think the secular coup in Egypt was to prevent the brutality of Islam from taking place again. However, what followed was a brutal attack on Islamic people in Europe by the secular government which forced its way into leadership.

*For that day will not come, unless the rebellion comes first, and the man of lawlessness is revealed, the son of destruction, **who opposes and exalts himself against every so-called god or object of worship**, so that he takes his seat in the temple of God, proclaiming himself to be God.*

Paul's statement reveals a movement which will set itself against *"every so-called god or object of worship"*. If the lawless rebellion were interested in democracy reflecting the will of the people, would there have been the murder of civilians who protested the secular takeover? Regardless of what one thinks of Islam or Islamic theocracies, one should recognize the movement which sets itself against any *"so-called"* governing authority of people groups as the revelation of the last rebellion.

It appears the Egyptian people exchanged one tyrant for another, Islamic theocracy for lawlessness, one supposed City of God for a City of Man. It is a clear indication Utopia and heaven are not of this earth. Christ is the only pathway to a utopian society.

As stated in the *Communist Manifesto*, the last rebellion uses democracy as a tool for destabilizing religious governments in the world. If democracy fails to deliver a Godless/godless government, the rebellion will resort to violence to attain their goals. While Christians may agree with the rebellion on the brutality of Islamic theocracies, Christians must refrain from joining the last rebellion in destruction of others. Christ sacrificed Himself; He did not sacrifice others.

The battle between the last rebellion and other religions will intensify. The methods used will be on display for all to see. For example, Islam will sacrifice others to make its point of superiority. The last rebellion will insert their ideology into the Islamic world in an effort to train Islamic children in the ethic of mankind. Desperate to stop the insurgence, the Islamic communities will increase their brutality.

Simply stated, the battlefield and methods of combat on display in the world are not Christian. Salvation is through Jesus and the Ark He has built for His followers.

In the United States, initiatives of the last rebellion take a more subtle approach. For example, democratic discourse has been discarded in favor of an authoritarian style of governing. If the president cannot get what he wants out of Congress to change America, he simply writes an executive order to accomplish his lawless goals. The Senate or judges appointed through judicial politicking block any interference from the will of the people, and it all has the appearance of democracy. George Lakoff in his work *Whose Freedom* revealed the lawless strategy in his discussions regarding the freedom to insert lawlessness into the American ethic.[lxv]

The Spirit of God in the world opposes the initiatives of the last rebellion. Even one, who is lawless, believing in no god, must recognize the war between the lawless and religious peoples of the world. While Christians may cheer the godless on as the godless destroy religious enemies around the world, Christians must remember man is not the savior and the *City of Man* is not the Promised Land (Heaven).

If one recognizes the war between religion and lawlessness, then this must lead to recognition of the ideology (spirit) of each as they move through time. It is the Spirit of God (*general revelation*) which restrains the Antichrist (*man of lawlessness*). When the Spirit is removed, earth will be overrun by the last rebellion.

Revelation 17 speaks of a time to come when a coalition of nations that "*are of one mind*" hand over their authority to one individual. It is the "one mind" that is important when looking for a clue to the formation of the end-time coalition spoken of in Revelation. Throughout its history, the United States has been the main force opposing secularism around the world, a nation that has called itself "*one nation under God*". The United States has been a major force in the world with respect to the Spirit of God and the mobilization of forces to combat lawlessness around the world.

However, America is now moving toward lawless control. When a majority of Americans embrace lawlessness, a significant influence of God's ethic will be lost.

There are other areas of Christian growth around the world. However, they are surrounded by elements of the last rebellion. For example, South Korea is a growing Christian community. However, to the north is North Korea and to the west China, both of which are firmly governed by godless authorities. In addition, Vietnam to the south fell to communism in 1975. South Korea was formed and survives only because America and some of its WWII allies led efforts to stop the spread of communism in the region.

With America's decline comes a change of allegiance. America no longer expresses a desire to battle the movements of the last rebellion. It is not a stretch of one's imagination to think of a time in the future in which there would only be Korea. With the predominate culture around South Korea being godless, it is almost assured a newly united Korea would march to a godless society and begin to purge Christianity and other religions from Korean soil.

Africa is another area of Christian growth in the world. In Africa Christians not only compete among the godless rebellion, but must confront the deadly Islamic fighters. With the call to follow Christ's example of sacrifice, many Christians are martyred. How long will God's people have to endure? How long before Jesus vindicates His followers?

The cyclic decline of God's ethic in America and the world is significant. Biblically speaking, in past eras God has intervened on behalf of His ethical presence on earth. The godly intervention has always been preceded by prophesy of what is to come. For example, Christ was expected because the Old Testament prophets told of a time when Christ would appear. In this ethical decline, there is no cyclic renewal of God's ethic foretold in the biblical text. There is only a foretelling of the end of the cycles. America's turn to lawlessness is truly a significant turn in the cycle.

Let no one deceive you in any way. For that day will not come, unless the rebellion comes first, and the man of lawlessness is revealed, the son of destruction, who opposes and exalts himself against every so-called god or object of worship, so that he takes his seat in the temple of God, proclaiming himself to be God. Do you not remember that when I was still with you I told you these things?

With the loss of America as a place which follows the ethic of God, a major obstacle to a coalition of like-minded lawless governments will be removed. Lawless governments, which will include the United States, will need something to draw them together. The infighting for leadership of the global lawless movement has in the past been a stumbling block for unity among the lawless divisions. The coalition will need a common goal that is so urgent in their minds it transcends any border arguments or competition among nations or groups for leadership.

What could be so pressing as to make men forget their battles for supremacy? When climate change and overpopulation are perceived as being so out of control that it threatens mankind with extinction, it could create a situation where the lawless rally around a united coalition of governments designed to save mankind as a species.

In the minds of the lawless leaders, the salvation of mankind could trump any infighting for supremacy. It is in this context that like-minded lawless could come together and form a coalition of the lawless. Jeffrey R. Grant in his 2011 book *The Global-Warming Deception* reveals a sinister plot by the "global-warming elite" to use the issue to enable the workings of a one-world government. Grant also connects the global warming movement to the global lawless movement. However, Grant is not alone in his assessment of the global-warming movement. Consider what the former science advisor to British Prime Minister Margaret Thatcher had to say in *WND*, the largest independent news source on the Internet. Lord Christopher Monckton told the world the purpose for the climate change conference in 2009 was to use the global warming hype as a pretext for laying the foundation for a one-world government.

To be effective, a coalition must have an executive committee that is representative of the nations involved. The executive committee must elect one to guide the lawless in their efforts to save the world. A man supported by a political super-coalition produced by the last rebellion could be a product of such an agreement among leaders in a lawless coalition.

Scientists have revealed that the population is growing at an alarming rate. For example, in AD 1400, the world population was about 250 million. By the nineteenth century, it was nearly one billion. By 1950 the population increased to 2.5 billion, and in 1990 the population was 5 billion. Currently, depending on the source, the global population is estimated to be somewhere between 7 to 7.2 billion people. Most sources are predicting there will be approximately 10 billion people living on earth by mid-century. The numbers here are approximate and derived from a cross-section of material found in the data published by U.S. census bureau, United Nation data materials, or one's local library.

Abortion issues in the West are related to the overpopulation issue. The common cry of political candidates advocating a woman's right to choose is noble, but it is a red herring. The root issue is overpopulation of the earth. But what part of the population would buy into a major political movement on reducing population size to such an extent that they would act out their conviction at the polls? A reframing of the issue into a privacy concern for individuals turns the trick. However, the battle rages on over whether the child in the womb is a person. For those who believe the population must be trimmed to save the world from extinction, the child's life is irrelevant. Thus the frustration of the pro-life lobby is that it is dealing with the results of the red herring and not the root issue.

The science of climate change is also connected to the overpopulation issue. A majority of environmental scientists believe that overpopulation of the earth is causing the earth's climate to heat up. Polar ice caps are in danger, say the climate change scientists. The result for humans if these conditions remain constant is a hostile environment causing mass death or even extinction of human life. In fact, scientists such as Frank Fenner of Australian Nation University have predicted that the human race will be extinct within a hundred years because of the population explosion. Al Gore, the former Vice President of the United States, is in agreement with climate change science and can be seen on various media outlets encouraging women to find ways to remain childless. Mr. Gore believes that the world's future is held in the wombs of women.

The issue for the lawless is not whether an embryo is a living human being, but whether more life should exist where there is too much life. It also should be stated that the homosexual issues in the West present a favorable alternative to populating the earth. Same-sex marriages do not produce life, and for the climate change lawless who have rejected God as the moral lawgiver and savior, the alternative is practical. The push to normalize same-sex marriages is tied to the population explosion. It is at least one explanation for the political movement's fast pace to normalization of same-sex marriage in the United States.

There has been a lengthy discussion in recent times as to whether the science of climate change is accurate. The charge that climate change scientists have displayed a political agenda or manipulated the data in order to make their case is being vehemently discussed across the world.

The issue of climate change has died down recently. However, climate change supporters have not retreated. World leaders have opened an initiative on climate change which includes a war on coal. At a time when the people of North America are in danger of freezing, heating oil for their homes may be cut off. Prince Charles of England called deniers of climate change "headless chickens". Al Gore compares disbelievers to people who thought the earth was flat during the time of Columbus. No matter what is experienced or what the data shows, climate change supporters will not be discouraged.

Religious people of the world believe God or gods are in control of climate change, and hence no action is required. The prophecies of the Bible speak of a time on earth when the climate will become hostile to mankind.

Religious groups passionately fight against population controls imposed on them by the lawless. However, the climate change initiative will become more aggressive with time. Further, it is unlikely that attrition through abortion and birth control will meet the demands for reduction of the world's population. The lawless are increasingly hostile towards people who disagree with the science, and the pressure by the lawless will increase exponentially.

Religion will increasingly be required to conform to the new lawless world. An example of lawless ideology imposing its will on religion can be seen in a recent UN attack on the Catholic Church. The United Nations issued a report demanding Catholicism abolish its traditional views on underage sex among children, homosexuality and abortion in favor of the lawless worldview.

John Podesta, an advisor to President Clinton and President Obama, has worked with the United Nations to develop an approach to advance the teaching of global behavior change for the express purpose of supporting a global effort to combat climate change (*Fox News George Russell editor-at-large, 2/12/2014*). The assault on religion and God's claim to the earth is already a global movement which finds energy from world leaders.

It is only a matter of time before Christians will be deemed a threat to national security and mankind's existence on the globe because of their refusal to accept climate change initiatives. The Christian church which follows the rules of the original church in the book of Acts will be marked for extinction. Salvation of the authentic Christian church is only realizable through supernatural intervention. It is only realizable through the second coming of Jesus Christ.

Summary

IT IS IMPORTANT FOR CHRISTIANS to understand where they are in the biblical cycles. The Manifest Destiny initiative of the United States in the 19th century may be used as an analogy to explain the drive of lawlessness to control the earth. In the development of the United States, Manifest Destiny was a term used to define American's destiny of continental expansion and control of western territories. The idea was that American culture was superior to the Native American Indian cultures. Americans further thought the west should be remade in the image of their own special character and culture; it was after all, the new American culture's destiny to rule the continent. Manifest Destiny sought to consume the old world of the Indian tribes and remake it in its own image.

Lawlessness is an international version of Manifest Destiny. The lawless view their godless system of the New World Order as being destined to replace the old religious order throughout the world. In order to achieve their destiny, the lawless will lie, cheat, steal or even kill. The old world must be replaced in order to save the species.

Native Americans can testify to the abuse meted out by those who believed their culture was superior to others. Treaties using fanciful words such as the words below were employed to move Indians off their land.

"As long as water flows, or grass grows upon the earth, or the sun rises to show your pathway, or you kindle your camp fires, so long shall you be protected from your present habitations."—President James Monroe, 1817

Of course as soon as Manifest Destiny required the land, the superior culture of the Americans pushed the Native American Indian off the Promised Land. Indian nations all across the continental United States who resisted were slaughtered. Similarly, the lawless have slaughtered over 100 million people while imposing their version of global Manifest Destiny on what they believe to be inferior cultures.

The founding fathers of the last rebellion (Marxism and socialism) made it clear the movement was to be an international affair. It is why the last rebellion faithful distance themselves from any national socialist or national communist movement. Thus Hitler's national socialists were labeled "far right wingers."

Vladimir Ulyanov (Lenin) is the communist voice from the past which states the international goals of the last rebellion. Lenin is the communist leader who overthrew the Russian czar in 1917. He revealed the rebellious international doctrine as:

The Lenin doctrine allowed for war only in the advancement of international Marxism. International Marxists are not loyal to any one country, not even their own. Any war fought in order to preserve a non-Marxist country works against the aims and goals of international Marxism. Furthermore, the Lenin doctrine demands that Marxists wage an internal war against their own country while the country is preoccupied with an external threat. For example, Lenin could not be said to have opposed war. He, in fact, planned for a revolution in Russia. The plan came to fruition in 1917, when he and his Marxists seized power in Russia. The Lenin doctrine on waging war is clear: The only war supported by Marxism is social revolution. Lenin's doctrine, then, requires Marxists to do all in their power to impede or stop the host country from waging war when that war preserves the non-Marxist state of the country. Any war that is not waged for Marxism is to be opposed.[lxvi]

Internationalism is the cry from the last rebellion which proposes a worldview absent of God or gods. Nothing short of total authority over the earth's population will be tolerated. Internationalism is the term which best defines the lawless initiative to destroy national borders in the world. Internationalism is Manifest Destiny on a global scale and the goal of the last rebellion. The last rebellious culture views all cultures outside mainstream lawlessness as inferior to lawlessness and unworthy of a place at the governing council of mankind in the City of Man. God and people of God or gods are not invited to the banquet table of the lawless City of Man.

Nationalism is a position which wishes to honor current borders. Nationalism is treated with an evil contempt by members of the last rebellion. Nationalists are perceived as evil and accused of racism and haters of cultural diversity. Nationalists are demonized and vilified in the lawless journals across the lawless cultural spectrum. The idea is to shame and ridicule patriotism of any national brand in favor of patriotism for the rebellious international City of Man, which is yet to come to fruition.

Even lawless who are nationalist are perceived to be traitors to the international last rebellion and are grouped together with the evil religious ones as far right wing nationalist. Vladimir Putin of Russia is the latest lawless traitor who seeks to make Russia and its national borders the focus of the last rebellion. His actions are viewed with contempt by lawless internationalism on the political left wing.

Of the old religious free world, the United States is the last major outpost of nations under the Christian God. The rebellion is ravaging the United States. The Christian outpost is crumbling. No treaty was honored with the American natives until total domination of the continent was realized. American natives signed many treaties, and most of them were broken by the U.S. government in order to facilitate the next wave of settlers. Native Americans found no compromise until most of their lands were settled by Europeans. The last rebellion will move using the same method across the American continent. Only total annihilation of what was once known as a Christian nation will suffice. The required international identity of the last rebellion will destroy the national borders of the United States at all costs. Global Manifest Destiny of the last rebellion demands the sacrifice of national borders.

One may say the movements of the United States government were and are at times godless themselves. That is true. It is true of all governing bodies of mankind. Displacing the American Natives was wrong if not criminal. Taking property which is not yours is at least morally wrong. However, is not the last rebellion repeating the criminal behavior when it takes possession of the same land from those who acquired it from the Native Americans?

It would appear the first Europeans who settled America and members of the last rebellion have the same noble goal—to create a superior society as compared with the past society. Europeans fled to America to build the City of God, and the rebellion seeks to build the City of Man. Both cities would be led by mankind, and the end is predictable from the past experiences of mankind. If there is no superior being, there can be no superior society. God is the only answer.

However, the United States is not special with respect to the Manifest Destiny component of the last rebellion. She is just another in a long line of conquered peoples. China, Russia, Europe, North Korea, Canada, Mexico, numerous countries in South America and others have all fallen to the last rebellion and the promised City of Man.

Some of the lawless countries such as China have maintained their national borders. Completion of the Manifest Destiny component of the last rebellion will provide opportunity for unity, and total world domination can be seen on the horizon. With unity of the rebellious, the "man of lawlessness" may be revealed as stated in 2 Thessalonians 2:

> *Let no one deceive you in any way. For that day will not come, unless the rebellion comes first, and the man of lawlessness is revealed, the son of destruction, who opposes and exalts himself against every so-called god or object of worship, so that he takes his seat in the temple of God, proclaiming himself to be God.*

Since the time of the Garden of Eden and the fall of man, a war has been waged between good and evil, between the godless and God. The war is really a legal battle over ownership of the earth. Consider the claim of Satan in Luke 4:6:

> *[Satan] said to Him [Jesus], "To you I will give all this authority and their glory, for it has been delivered to me, and I give it to whom I will."*

Listen to Jesus as He speaks of two fathers with respect to mankind:

Jesus said to them, "If God were your Father, you would love Me, for I came from God and I am here. I came not of My own accord, but He sent Me. Why do you not understand what I say? It is because you cannot bear to hear My word. You are of your father the devil, and your will is to do your father's desires. He was a murderer from the beginning, and has nothing to do with the truth, because there is no truth in him. When he lies, he speaks out of his own character, for he is a liar and the father of lies. But because I tell the truth, you do not believe Me (John 8:42–45)."

The legal battle over who owns the earth is moving forward to a climactic end. Revelation reveals that Jesus will open the deed to the earth to show God's legal claim to the earth. He will reach for the scroll with seven seals which have held the deed closed for millennia.

Then I saw in the right hand of Him who was seated on the throne a scroll written within and on the back, sealed with seven seals. And I saw a strong angel proclaiming with a loud voice, "Who is worthy to open the scroll and break its seals (Revelation 5:1–2)?"

The seven seals may be compared to the seal on an envelope. Only the one designated by the addressee is authorized to break the seal. As each seal is broken, corresponding events occur. The opening of the fourth seal is a preview of the coming battle over legal claim of the earth. The Bible states in Revelation 6:8:

And they were given authority over a fourth of the earth, to kill, with sword and with famine and with pestilence, and by wild beast of the earth.

A question arises as to the motive of those people who would destroy 25% of the earth during the events recorded in the fourth seal. One answer is climate change fanaticism. For example, Hillary Clinton before the senate confirmation hearings stated that wars would be fought over climate change issues. The largest issue for the fanatical climate change community is population reduction and control. In their thinking, the forces that pit themselves against all religions and objects of worship could be ridding the earth of those who refuse to accept population controls on earth. Control of the human herd in their view is salvation.

The lawless believe Jesus is a myth, therefore the belief that Jesus saves is also a myth. The population of the earth must be reduced to acceptable levels in the mind of the lawless. The religious, having refused to cooperate, have made themselves targets for eradication. Lawless forces in the confrontation will seek to erase religion from the earth as Hitler once tried to erase the Jewish race and religion from existence. Once religion is destroyed, global Manifest Destiny could be completed. The earth and all that is in it would belong to man.

Cyclic parody may be drawn from Exodus chapters 1 through 14, which tell the story of an afflicted/poor Israel. The Hebrew people were enslaved in Egypt and toiled under Pharaoh Ramses. The Hebrew people were blessed with an abundance of offspring, and Ramses became worried over the overpopulation of the Hebrew people. They might become too numerous to handle, and he feared they might take over Egypt. In order to control their population, Ramses issued orders to kill every male child. Moses was one of the male children who were marked for death. His mother placed him in a basket in the Nile near where the Pharaoh's daughter went to bathe, and subsequently the Pharaoh's daughter discovered Moses. Pharaoh's daughter raised Moses, and he eventually led the exodus of the Hebrew people from Egypt. The biblical account of Moses documents the trigger (i.e., the Egyptian attempt at population control) that released the succession of events that ultimately brought about the first exodus of God's people. The modern battle overpopulation could be ta similar trigger for the last exodus.

Will what is left of the Christian church be taken out before the great Battle? An excellent case revealing God's provisions and protection from His wrath is found in Jeremiah 24:3:

And the Lord said to me, "What do you see, Jeremiah?" I said, "Figs, the good figs very good, and the bad figs very bad, so bad that they cannot be eaten."

The Lord then explains that the good figs are those to whom He will give

"a heart to know that I am the Lord, and they shall be My people and I will be their God."

The text may be favorably compared to Hebrews 8:8 and 10:16. The point God is making to Jeremiah is that the people He has chosen to save have already been removed from Jerusalem and what is left in Jerusalem (the bad figs) He *"will make them a horror to all the kingdoms of the earth* (Jeremiah 24:9)." In the era of the Ark of Jesus, all have to be boarded and the door closed, awaiting the judgment of God.

It should be noted the residents left in Jerusalem called themselves by God's name and believed in God. However, they did not follow His voice:

Now therefore, if you will indeed obey My voice and keep My covenant, you shall be My treasured possession among all peoples, for all the earth is Mine; (Exodus 19:5).

The same pattern exists today with respect to a people who call themselves Christian but refuse to obey God's commandments. There will be people who call themselves Christian left outside the Ark of Jesus:

Jesus said, "Not everyone who says to Me, 'Lord, Lord,' will enter the kingdom of heaven, but the one who does the will of My Father who is in heaven. On that day many will say to Me, 'Lord, Lord, did we not prophesy in Your name, and cast out demons in Your name, and do many mighty works in Your name?' And then will I declare to them, 'I never knew you; depart from Me, you workers of lawlessness (Matthew 7: 21-23)."

With respect to 2 Thessalonians 2:6–8, the divine precedent in Jeremiah and Matthew reveals a God that moved to protect His chosen by removing them from the battlefield of His wrath. It is most likely that whatever is left of the Christian church will be removed during the last battles of the last rebellion and before the revelation of the "man of lawlessness" and the opening of the fourth seal.

A warning is in order for those counters of days. No one knows the timetable of God's plan. According to Matthew 24:36, not even Jesus knew the time of His own return:

> *But concerning that day and hour no one knows, not even the angels of heaven, nor the Son, but the Father only.*

However, He gave the signs of the end times to His people. **The last rebellion (falling away/apostasy) has been underway since the Reformation.** The reformation opened the door, so to speak. Reformation of the church gave people the right to worship as they pleased and gave people the right to challenge interpretation. It was a glorious time for God's people. However, the new freedom of expression spawned something new. From the well of ideas came a challenge to God altogether.

A democratized people emerged from the oppressive Catholicism of Europe. Many began to choose godless journeys for their lives. Evolution and man's ability to save himself eventually framed the vision of the City of Man scenario of Karl Marx. In the City of Man, mankind is the savior of mankind. The problem with being a savior is the accomplishment of salvation. Mankind, the savior, struggles to find a salvific formula for its citizens.

Climate change (global warming) fanatics will continue to propel a lawless vision of control over the earth because the lawless believe power over the earth's climate will save the earth and mankind from extinction. The facts are in: the majority of governments on earth have embraced the real or supposed climate change crisis, and climate change is the fuel of global Manifest Destiny. Even if science in the future disagrees with the movement, the perspective is set, and the movement will continue to gain momentum. There is just too much of the last rebellion's capital invested in the movement for the lawless to allow it to fail. Those who disagree with the lawless will have to be silenced. God, according to the last rebellion, will have to relinquish control of the earth.

Mankind and the earth are headed for the end of the book called the Bible. The Bible is mankind's guide. Preachers stand in front of believers every week and point to the cycle of time. Do believers understand the cyclic nature of the text, or are they focused on the moment? Do believers realize their place in the cycles of the Bible? Do they understand a godless rebellion is underway to destroy all religions?

Eduard Bernstein would say that religion is entangled in the destiny of mankind due to its influence in the development of mankind's destiny over thousands of years. He would argue that the current cycle (destiny of mankind) is at this time a combination of theology and lawless thought imposed on the whole of mankind. However, that does not change the facts. Mankind lives on a planet that prominent scientists believe is running out of air and resources. Mankind has nowhere to go. The vacuum of space offers no answer for mankind's salvation. The only answer mankind can offer for his dilemma is the killing of billions in order to reduce the earth's population to an acceptable level. The lawless doctrine begs the question; who should die so others may live? Lawlessness promises equality, and those found not equal will die.

Christianity increasingly views lawless approval as being necessary for Christian survival. Approval is maintained through lockstep agreement with lawless sacred rules of equality. Religious tolerance is the cry for equality among lawless churches. Liberal theology and liberation theology have already surrendered their Christian cross to the lawless and have joined the enemy in the assault against the orthodox Christian Church.

Presentation Of The Bride Of Christ

ACCORDING TO THE BOOK OF Ephesians, the Bride of Christ, which is the Christian church, will be presented to Christ without blemish. What is considered a blemish on Christ's Bride? Ephesians 2:26 states:

> *That He might sanctify her, having cleansed her by the washing of water with the Word, so that He might present the church to Himself in splendor, without spot or wrinkle or any such thing, that she might be holy and without blemish.*

The Christian church was formed by the Word of God and maintains its purity and identity through the Word of God. When a denomination or church chooses to ignore or disobey the Word of God, that particular denomination or church disqualifies itself as the Bride of Christ or as being followers of Christ because it has been soiled by the world.

Jesus is solely responsible for the presentation of the church and the individual to His Kingdom. Man may not impose his own presentation of the Bride on Christ. Christ is the Word of God, as stated in John 1:1-2:

> *In the beginning was the Word, and the Word was with God. He [Jesus] was in the beginning with God.*

Religious experiences which do not meet the criteria in the Word of God have to be regarded as having blemishes and cannot retain an identity as the Bride of Christ.

What then is the Christian who follows the Word of God (Christ) to do in a world which demands a presentation of an unholy bride? The answer is in the footsteps of Jesus. The followers of Christ must maintain purity as Christ maintained His purity. Christ did not change His message to fit into the lawless environment of the era as liberal theology does today. He did not attempt to use God to gather forces to destroy the Jews who attempted to oppress His message of salvation. He did not save the Jews from the oppression of the Romans. He did not preach a sermon meant to incite the Jews to destroy the Romans. He did not call on people to riot in His name as the liberation theologian of today does. Christ maintained until the end that He is the Word of God, He is *"the Way, the Truth and the Life (John 14:6)"* of His followers.

Jesus was scorned and beaten with a scourge. He was crucified by the world at the request of His own people, yet He found life in His resurrection. Christ suffered at the hands of God's people in His day of crucifixion, and His Bride must join Him in enduring crucifixion by people who are called by Christ's name.

The Bride of Christ will maintain her purity in the footsteps of Christ that lead to Golgotha. She will maintain her purity by maintaining the Word in the midst of mocking and hateful scorn of unbelievers on her path. She will maintain purity by maintaining the Word when impostors and false prophets accuse her of cultural crimes. The purity of the Bride of Christ will be measured in the scars of persecution as she maintains the voice and commandments of God. As the evidence of Christ's divinity was in His life, crucifixion and resurrection, it will also be for the Bride of Christ. The footsteps of Jesus will lead her to her husband at the cross.

Consider what Jesus said of persecution against His followers in Matthew 5:11, 12:

> *Blessed are you when others revile you and persecute you and utter all kinds of evil against you falsely on My account. Rejoice and be glad, for your reward is great in heaven, for so they persecuted the prophets who were before you.*

Could there be more honors bestowed on the faithful than to be crucified with Christ? Could there be a more perfect bride than to experience the cross with Christ?

It is increasingly clear Christians must embrace the second coming of Christ as the life of the church. Christ will save His Bride from total destruction. Christians must understand that God knew of the global last rebellion insurgence before it began. God's servant, the Apostle Paul, foretold of the event in 2 Thessalonians. God was in control then, and He is in control now.

Stand and be counted for Christ in these last days of the Bride of Christ. Join together in Christ as "one" in all things.

Christian, where will you be when Jesus comes to collect His bride? Will you deny Christ as Peter denied Christ?

Jesus said to him (Peter), "Truly, I tell you, this very night, before the rooster crows, you will deny Me three times." Peter said to Him, "Even if I must die with You, I will not deny You!" And all the disciples said the same (Matthew 26:34- 35).

Peter later states: "*I do not know the man* (Matthew 26:74)."

At the end of the Bible's story, where will you be? At the end of the last cyclic act and during the presentation of the Bride of Christ, will you be hiding among the lawless and false prophets at the foot of her cross, or will you be on your cross beside Christ?

Then Jesus said to His disciples, if anyone would come after Me, let him deny himself and take up his cross and follow Me. For whoever would save his life will lose it, but whoever loses his life for My sake will find it **(Matthew 16: 24- 25)."**

The presentation of the bride of Christ is symbolic of the end of the Christian church age. There will be no more Sunday service or evangelical initiatives for true followers of Christ after the presentation of the bride of Christ. It marks the beginning of the eternal journey with Christ.

The Ark of Jesus filled with those who believe will journey to and disembark in a new world. It is a place where Christ went to prepare for His followers.

And if I go and prepare a place for you, I will come again and will take you to Myself, that where I am you may be also (John 14:3).

The place Christ went to prepare for His followers is called heaven by Christians. When Christians enter the place Christ has prepared, there will be a great banquet celebrating Christ's victory over the enemies of God. There will be peace as was in the Garden of Eden.

In reality the Bible story ends where it began. It ends in a place God prepared for His creation.

For the followers of Christ the story continues at the place mankind always knew existed and always strove to acquire. It is a place where all mankind are equal. There are no deceitful political motives to deal with. There are no crimes to punish. There is no death. God is the center of focus and worship. Mankind in this new place God has prepared will be at peace. Where does this story continue? The story continues in the celestial City of God.

The end of the biblical cycles is nearing to a close. The chains that draw the doors of the Ark of Jesus closed are beginning to draw tight. Soon the door will be lifted to its closed position. As in the Noah story in Genesis, once the doors are closed, no one else may enter the Ark.

Will you choose to live eternity in the City of Man or in the City of God? If it is the City of God, accept Christ as your Savior and board the Ark of Jesus.

The righteousness of God through faith in Jesus Christ for all who believe; For there is no distinction: for all have sinned and fall short of the glory of God, and are justified by His grace as a gift, through the redemption that is in Christ Jesus (Romans 3:22-24).

Jesus is the way, the truth and the life of the Christian eternal hope. Amen!

BIBLIOGRAPHY

Alinsky, Saul D. Rules for Radicals A Practical Primer for Realistic Radicals. New York: Vintage books, 1989.

Augustine, Saint. City of God. New York: Doubleday, 1958.

Bawer, Bruce. While Europe Slept, How Radical Islam Is Destroying The West From Within. New York: Doubleday, 2006.

Bax, Ernest Belfort. "Gracchus Babeuf/1." Marxist.org, 3/15/04, 2004. http:// www.marxist.org/archive/bax/1911/babeuf/ch01.htm. (accessed 6/6/07).

Bax, Ernest Belfort. The Last Episode of the French Revolution. London: Grant Richards LTD, 1911.

Berchall, Ian H. The Spectre of Babeuf. New York: St. Martin's Press, INC, 1997.

Bernstein, Eduard, Translated by Edith C. Harvey. Evolutionary Socialism. New York: Shocken Books, 1899 reprint 1961.

BostonGlobe.http://www.boston.com/news/globe/magazine/ articles/2005/10/02/to_be_frank/.http://www.boston.com/news/ globe/ magazine/articles/2005/10/02/to_be_frank// (; accessed Aug. 18, 2007).

Briefwechsel, edited by E. Siberner. Moses Hess.

Bronterre. Babeuf's Conspiracy for Equality. London: H. Hetherington, 1836.

Brzezinski, Zbigniew K, Friedrich, Cal J. Totalitarian, Dictatorship, and Autocracy. New York: Friedrich A. Praeger, 1961.

Buonarroti, Phillippe, Translated by Bronterre O'Brien. Babeuf's Conspiracy of Equals. London: H. Hetherington, 1836.

Busky F., Donald. Communism in History and Theory. Westport, CT: Praeger Publishers, 2002.

By his relatives. Reminiscences of Lenin. Moscow: Foreign Languages Publishing House, 1956.

Campbell, Joseph, The Hero With A Thousand Faces, Princeton University Press, New York, 1949, reprint 1973.

Carver, Terrell. Friedrich Engels, His life and thought. New York: St. Martin's Press, 1990.

Corsi, Jerome R. "Http://www.wnd.com/?pageid=113219#ixzz1a11r3qtx." World Net Daily, October 17, 2009. http://www.wnd.com/ (accessed October 7, 2011).

Delaney, James J. "Jean-jacques Rousseau (1712–1778)." The Internet Encyclopedia, Jan, 2006. http://www.utm.edu/research/iep/r/rousseau.htm. (accessed June 5, 2007).

Democritus [Internet Encyclopedia of Philosophy]. http.www.iep.utm.edu/d/ democrit.htm. http.www.iep.utm.edu/d/democrit.htm (Essay on Democritus; accessed August 17, 2007).

Eisenman, Robert. The Dead Sea Scrolls and the First Christians. Edison, NJ: Castle Books, 2006.

Engels, Friedrich, Marx, Karl Marx, Edited by Robert Manard. Great Books of the Western World, Capital, Manifesto of the Marxism Party. All quotes from this source Reprinted from Great Books of the Western World, © 1952, 1990 Encyclopædia Britannica, Inc.

Fallaci, Oriana, The Force of Reason Rizzoli International Publications, Inc, 300 Park Avenue South, New York 10010, 2004

Friedrich, Carl J., Reprinted by permission of the publisher from TOTALITARIAN DICTATORSHIP AND AUTO CRACY: REVISED EDITION by Carl J. Friedrich and Zbigniew K. Brzezinski, pp. 290, 299,302, Cambridge, Mass.: Harvard University Press, copyright © 1956, 1965, by President and Fellows of Harvard College, Copyright© renewed 1984 by Carl J. Friedrich

Fruchtenbaum, Arnold G., TH.M., PH.D, Ariel's Bible Commentary, The Messianic Jewish Episles, Ariel Ministries, P.O. Box 792507, San Antonio, TX, 78279-2507.

Gale, Thomson. Eduard Bernstein. Online: Contemporary Authors Online, 2006.

Garnett, R. G. Cooperation and the Owenite communities in Britain. Manchester: University Press, 1972.

Grant, Jeffrey R. The Global Warming Deception, How a Secret Elite Plans to Bankrupt America and Steal Your Freedom. Colorado Springs: Waterbrook Press.

Green, Gene L The Pillar New Testament Commentary. Grand Rapids: William Eerdmans, 2002.

Grenz, Stanley J., The Moral Quest, Foundations of Christian Ethics, InterVarsity Press, P.O. Box 1400, Downers Grove, IL, 60515-1426, 1997

Gregor, James A. Young Mussolini and the Intellectual origins of Fascism. London: University of California Press, 1979.

Hamburger, Philip, Separation of Church and State, Harvard University Press, Cambridge Massachusetts, 2002.

Henry, C. F. H. God, revelation and Authority. : Crossway Books.

Hess, Moses, The Holy History of Mankind and Other Writings, Cambridge University Press,, The Edinburgh Building, Cambridge, 40 West 2oth street New York, NY 1oo11, 2004.

Hitchcock, William I. The Struggle for Europe. New York: Doubleday, Random House Inc, 2003.

190

Hitler, Adolf. Mein Kampf.

http://www. Quotes From Democrats on Weapons of Mass Destruction – Break The Chain_org.htm/(accessed May 27, 2007).

Internetencyclopedia.http://www.iep.utm.edu/e/epicur.htm.http://www. iep.utm.edu/e/epicur.htm (Essay on Epicurus; accessed August, 17 2007).

Jones, Robert C., Between the Testaments, Pharisees, Sadducees an Essenes, Zondervan Publishing House,1973

Lakoff, George, Moral Politics. London: The University Press of Chicago Press, 1996/2002.

Lakoff, George. "Politics 1." Huff post, Feb 24, 2009. http://www.huffngtonpost. com/george-lakoff /the-obama-code_b_169580. html. (accessed August 12, 2011).

Lakoff, George. don't think of an elephant. White River Junction, VT: Chelsea Green Publishing Co, 2004.

Lakoff, George. Moral Politics, How Liberals and Conservatives Think. Chicago and London: The University of Chicago Press, 2002.

Lakoff, George. Whose Freedom?. New York: Farrar, Straus and Giroux, 2006.

Lange, Peter, Vannicelli, Maurizio, The Communist Parties of Italy, France, and Spain; Postwar Change and Continuity; A casebook. London: George Allen & Unwin, 1981.

Literature and Revolution. New York: International Publishers, 1925 reprinted 2005.

Lucas, Fred. "Republicans Believe Illegal Immigration 'should Be A Crime.'" Cnsnews.org, May 31, May 31, 2011. http://www.cnsnews.com/news/article/new-dnc-chair-faults-gop-wanting-illegal/ (accessed August 16, 2011).

Marx, K., and Engels, F. Collected Works, Marx and Engels. London: Lawrence & Wishart, 1975.

Marx, K., Engels, F. Selected Works. Moscow: Moscow, 1969.

Mayer, Gustav, Translated by Gilbert and Helen Highet, ed. R.H.S. Crossman. Friedrich Engels. New York: Howard Fertig, 1969.

McLellan, David. Karl Marx, Early Text. New York: Barnes & Noble, 1971.

Muravchik, Joshua. Heaven on Earth, The rise and fall of Socialism. San Francisco: Encounter Books, 2002.

Mussolini, Di Benito. Operaomnia. Florence, 1951.

New York AP. "Liberals Attack Fox News." Cantonrep.com, July 28, 2007, 2007. http://www.cantonrep.com/index.php?ID=367417/ (accessed July 31, 2007).

Owen, Robert Dale. Threading My Way. New York: Robert M. Kelly, 1967.

Owen, Robert, Selected Works of Robert Owen, Edited by Gregory Claeys. London: Pickering & Chatto Ltd, 1993.

Owen, Robert. The Book of the New Moral World. New York: Augustus M. Kelly, 1842, reprinted in 1970.

Padover, Saul K. Karl Marx. San Francisco: Encounter Books, 1978.

Paul, The Apostle of Jesus. Holy Bible, English Standard Version, 2 Thessalonians. Wheaton, Illinois: Crossway Bibles, 2002.

Pears, Thomas and Sarah, ed. by Thomas Clifton Pears jr. New Harmony, An Adventure in Happiness. Clifton, New Jersey: Augustus M. Kelly, 1973.

Pipes, Richard. Communism. New York: Modern Library Edition/ Random House, 2001.

Service, Robert, Lenin. City: Harvard University Press, 2000,

Smith, Dennis Mack. Mussolini a Biography. New York: Vintage Books, 1983.

Subrata Mukherjee, Susila Ramaswamy. A History of Socialist Thought From the Precursors to the Present. London: Sage Publications, 2000.

Toland, John. Adolf Hitler. Hertfordshire: Cumberland House, 1976, re-printed 1997, 1998.

Trotsky, Leon, Edited by William Keach, Compilation 2005, Translated by Rose Strunsky.

Tucker, Robert C. The Marx and Engels Reader. London: W.W. Norton & Company, 1972 reprint 1978.

Tudor, H., Tudor, J.M., editor and translators, Introduction by H. Tudor. Marxism and Social Democracy. New York: Cambridge University Press, 1988.

Wellhausen, Julius, The Pharisees and Sadducees, An examination of Internal Jewish History, Translated by Mark E. Biddle, Mercer University Press, 2001, Macon GA.

ENDNOTES

i   Peter L. Berger and Thomas Luckman, The Social Construction of Reality, A Treatise in the Sociology of Knowledge, Open Road, integrated Media New York, (Garden City: Doubleday, 1966

ii   Peter L. Berger and Thomas Luckman, The Social Construction of Reality, A Treatise in the Sociology of Knowledge, Open Road, integrated Media New York, (Garden City: Doubleday, 1966

iii   Peter L. Berger and Thomas Luckman, The Social Construction of Reality, A Treatise in the Sociology of Knowledge, Open Road, integrated Media New York, (Garden City: Doubleday, 1966

iv   Author, *L&D & Hasel Understanding the Book of Amos* (EX: New York: Publisher, 1999), 420.

v   Longman III, Temper and Dillard, Raymond B., *An Introduction to the Old Testament*, Zonervan 1994, 2006, 423.

vi   Longman and Dillard,427.

vii   Abid., 425.

viii   Abid., 427

ix   Abid., 427

x   Longman and Dillard, 431.

xi   Abid., 431.

xii   Longman and Dillard, 433

xiii   Abid., 433

xiv   Abid., 434

xv   Ralph L. Smith, *Word Biblical Commentary, volume 32 Micah-Malachi* (Waco: Word book publishers, 1984), 63.

xvi   Ibid., 63

xvii   Alfred J. Horeth, *Archaeology and the Old Testament* (Grand Rapids: Baker Books, 1998), 356.

xviii   Alfred J. Horeth, *Archaeology and the Old Testament* (Grand Rapids: Baker Books, 1998), 352.

xix   Tremper III Longman, Dillard Raymond B, 458.

xx   Ibid., 458

xxi   Ibid., 458

xxii   Tremper, III Longman, Dillard Raymond B, 458.   Alfred J. Horeth, 352

xxiii   Walter A. Maier, *the Book of Nahum, A commentary* (Saint Louis: Concordia Publishing House, 1959), 212.

xxiv   Everett Furguson, Church History, Volume 1, From Christ to Pre-Reformation, 2005, Zondervan, Grand Rapids, Michigan 49530

xxv   IBID, 71

xxvi   Hamburger, Philip, Separation of Church and State, Harvard University Press, Cambridge Massachusetts, 2002

xxvii   Everett Furguson, Church History

xxviii Ibid

xxix   Ibid

xxx   Ibid

xxxi   Ibid

xxxii   Ibid

xxxiii Ibid

xxxiv   Augustine, Saint. City of God. New York: Doubleday, 1958, 333

xxxv   Bronterre, Babeuf's Conspiracy for Equality, London: H. Hetherington, 1836

xxxvi   Lakoff, George, Moral Politics, How Liberals and Conservatives Think, The University of Chicago Press, The University of Chicago Press Ltd., LOndon2002

xxxvii Friedrich Engels, Marx, Karl Marx, Edited by Robert Manard, Great Books of the Western World, Capital, Manifesto of the Marxism Party (: ,), 416

xxxviii Ernest Belfort Bax, "Gracchus Babeuf/1," Marxist.org, 3/15/04, 2004, http://www.marxist.org/archive/bax/1911/babeuf/ch01. htm. (accessed 6/6/07).

xxxix   *Bronterre, Babeuf's Conspiracy for Equality, London: H. Hetherington, 1836*

xl   Ibid, 32

xli   Book was accessed as public domain on Google books. Ernest Belfort Bax, The Last Episode of the French RevolutiOwen, Robert Selected Works of Robert Owen, ed by Gregory Claeys(London, William Pickering, 1993)on (London: Grant Richards LTD, 1911)

    R. G. Garnett, 54. Co-operation and the Owenite communities in Britain (Manchester: University Press, 1972)

    Robert Dale Owen, Th reading My Way (New York: Robert M. Kelly, 1967)

xlii   Phillippe Buonarroti, Translated by Bronterre O'Brien, 61. Babeuf's Conspiracy of Equals (London: H. Hetherington, 1836, 213

xliii   Robert Owen, The Book of the New Moral World Convictions are independent of the will (New York: Augustus M. Kelly, 1842), 41.

xliv   Berger, Peter L., Luckman, Thomas, The Social Construction of Reality, A treatise in the Sociology of Knowledge, Open Road, Integrated Media, New York (1967)

xlv   Saul K. Padover, Karl Marx (San Francisco: Encounter Books, 1978)

    David McLellan, Karl Marx, Early Text (New York: Barnes & Noble, 1971)

xlvi   Padover, Saul K. Karl Marx. San Francisco: Encounter Books, 1978

xlvii   Ibid

xlviii   Ibid

xlix   R.H.S. Crossman, Friedrich Engels (New York: Howard Fertig, 1969)
          Susila Ramaswamy Subrata Mukherjee, 109. A History of Socialist Th ought From the Precursors to the Present (London: Sage Publications, 2000)
          Terrell Carver, Friedrich Engels, His life and thought (New York: St. Martin's Press, 1990)
          Marx and Engels, 116. Collected Works, (vol. 2)Marx and Engels (London: Lawrence &Wishart, 1975)

l   Friedrich Engels, Marx, Karl Marx, Edited by Robert Manard, Great Books of the Western World, Capital, Manifesto of the Marxism Party (: ,), 416

li   Eduard Bernstein (Online: Contemporary Authors Online, 2006)
          H. Tudor, Tudor, J.M., editor and translators, Introduction by H. Tudor, Marxism and Social Democracy (New York: Cambridge University Press, 1988)
          Eduard Bernstein, Translated by Edith C. Harvey, Evolutionary Socialism (New York: Shocken Books, 1899 reprint 1961)

lii   Eduard Bernstein, Translated by Edith C. Harvey, Evolutionary Socialism (New York: Shocken Books, 1899 reprint 1961), 296.

liii   Ibid., 7

liv   Friedrich Engels, Marx, Karl Marx, Edited by Robert Manard, Great Books of the Western World, Capital, Manifesto of the Marxism Party, 416

lv   Ibid., 429

lvi   Ibid., 48, 49

lvii   Ibid., 7

lviii   Friedrich Engels, Marx, Karl Marx, Edited by Robert Manard, Great Books of the Western World, Capital, Manifesto of the Marxism Party (: ,), 416

lix   Bernstein, Evolutionary Socialism, 166

lx   Jones, Robert C., Between the Testaments, Pharisees, Sadducees an Essenes, Zondervan Publishing House,1973 81-97

lxi   The term "Bernstein Bridge" is a term developed by the author of this book as a metaphor that labels the Bernsteinian philosophic shift to include the rich philanthropic liberal into the socialist/communist movement in exchange for membership in the socialist/communist movement without loss of wealth.

lxii   This table was developed by the author of this book to illustrate Bernstein Bridge elements. It is a comparison of Calvin and Arminian five points of doctrine developed at the Synod of Dort in the 17th century and the secular doctrine of Bernstein.

lxiii   Most biblical scholar's place the letters to the Thessalonians in the mid 50's CE of the first century before the destruction of the temple in 7 CE. A discussion on date may be found in many commentaries about the Thessalonian epistles.

lxiv   Muravchik, Joshua. Heaven on Earth, The rise and fall of Socialism. San Francisco: Encounter Books, 2002.

lxv   Lakoff, Whose Freedom (New York: Farrar, Straus and Giroux, 2006), Discussion on activist judges.

lxvi   Lord, William G., Battle for America, Crossbooks, 2012, discussion on Lenin

Made in the USA
Middletown, DE
19 August 2021